MARATHON

MARATHON

THE ULTIMATE TRAINING GUIDE

BY HAL HIGDON

Senior Writer, **RUNNER'S** *WORLD.* magazine,
and author of *Hal Higdon's Smart Running*

RODALE

© 1999 by Hal Higdon
Cover photograph © 1998 by Jeffrey Aaronson/Network Aspen

All rights reserved. No part of this publication may be reproduced or transmitted in any form or by any means, electronic or mechanical, including photocopying, recording, or any other information storage and retrieval system, without the written permission of the publisher.

Runner's World is a registered trademark of Rodale Inc.

Printed in the United States of America
Rodale Inc. makes every effort to use acid-free ∞, recycled paper ♻

"High-Carbohydrate Foods" on page 132 was adapted from *Nancy Clark's Sports Nutrition Guidebook* by Nancy Clark with permission from the author.

"Oxygen Power Table" on pages 146–47 was adapted from *Oxygen Power* by Jack Tupper Daniels and Jimmy Rhett Gilbert with permission from the authors.

"Myers Performance Prediction Table" on page 149 and "Myers Pace Table for 3:00 Marathon" on page 153 were reprinted with permission from the author.

Book Designer: Christina Gaugler
Cover Photographer: Jeffrey Aaronson

Library of Congress Cataloging-in-Publication Data
Higdon, Hal.
    Marathon : the ultimate training guide / by Hal Higdon.
        p.   cm.
    Includes index.
    ISBN 1–57954–171–2 paperback
    1. Marathon running—Training. I. Title.
    GV1065.17.T73H55   1999
    796.42'52—dc21   99–35214

Distributed to the book trade by St. Martin's Press

    6 8 10 9 7 5   paperback

Visit us on the Web at www.runnersworldbooks.com, or call us toll-free at (800) 848-4735.

WE **INSPIRE** AND **ENABLE** PEOPLE TO IMPROVE
THEIR LIVES AND THE WORLD AROUND THEM

For Bill Fitzgerald and Brian Piper

*Thanks for your support
in the Chicago Marathon training class*

ACKNOWLEDGMENTS

The following coaches contributed information based on their experience as runners and with runners. The author thanks each and every one.

Dan Ashimine (Gardena, California)

Wayne E. Baldwin, Jr. (Kirkwood, Missouri)

Roy Benson (Atlanta)

Jay Birmingham (Alamosa, Colorado)

Mark S. Bredenbaugh (West Columbia, South Carolina)

Clark Campbell (Lawrence, Kansas)

Joe Catalano (East Walpole, Massachusetts)

Mike Caton (El Paso, Texas)

Happy Chapman (Honolulu)

David Cowein (Morrilton, Arkansas)

Daniel Deyo (Saline, Mississippi)

Greg A. Domantay (Lake Forest, Illinois)

Sue Ellis (Holland, Michigan)

Robert Eslick (Nashville)

Lee Fidler (Stone Mountain, Georgia)

Dan French (Iowa City)

Joe Friel (Fort Collins, Colorado)

Jeff Galloway (Atlanta)

John Joseph Garvey (Oklahoma City)

Ted Giampietro (Bitburg, Germany)

Paul Goss (Foster City, California)

Tom Grogon (Cincinnati)

Nobuya Hashizume (Minnetonka, Minnesota)

Fritz Ingram (Roseburg, Oregon)

Brad Jaeger (Baltimore)

Teri Jordan (State College, Pennsylvania)

Susan Kinsey (La Mesa, California)

Henry Laskau (Coconut Creek, Florida)

Steve Linsenbardt (Springfield, Missouri)

Frank X. Mari (Toms River, New Jersey)

Ken Martin (Sante Fe, New Mexico)

Ben Adams Moore, Jr. (Annapolis, Maryland)

Alfred F. Morris (Washington, D.C.)

Tim Nicholls (Pembroke Pines, Florida)

Gary O'Daniels (Creston, Iowa)

Diane Palmason (Englewood, Colorado)

Danny Perez (Norwalk, California)

Gaylord E. Quigley (St. Louis)

James Redfield (Salt Lake City)

Doug Renner (Westminster, Maryland)

Dennis J. D. Robinson (Dayton, Ohio)

Craig B. Sanders (Simi Valley, California)

Rich Sands (Longmont, Colorado)

Patrick Joseph Savage (Oak Park, Illinois)

Will Shaw (Beverly, West Virginia)

Daryl J. Smith (Newburgh, New York)

Sherwin Sosnovsky (Pomona, California)

Jim Spivey (Glen Ellyn, Illinois)

Roy Stevenson (Bothell, Washington)

Drew Sutcliffe (Eugene, Oregon)

Laszlo Tabori (Culver City, California)

Judy Tillapaugh (Fort Wayne, Indiana)

John E. Tolbert (New Haven, Connecticut)

Gary Tuttle (Dover, New Hampshire)

Joy Upshaw-Margerum (Kamuela, Hawaii)

Robert H. Vaughan (Dallas)

David W. Virtue (Westwood Hills, Kansas)

Robert Wallace (Dallas)

William Wenmark (Deephaven, Minnesota)

Danny White (Marion, South Carolina)

Bob Williams (Portland, Oregon)

Keith Woodard (Portland, Oregon)

CONTENTS

Chapter 1

The Mystique of the
MARATHON

I heard the comment in passing, approximately eight miles into the Twin Cities Marathon. "To think," said a woman spectator, "they paid to do this." Her comment floated out of the crowd, but by the time I turned to look, my stride had carried me past where she stood beside the course.

I understood what she meant. Twenty-six miles *is* a long way. Even thinking about running that far takes a certain amount of endurance. Yet somehow those of us who call ourselves marathoners do it again, and again, and again.

Yet the woman's comment didn't disturb me. First of all, I thought there was some truth to it. Second, I was too busy running as fast as I could to worry about what the spectators were thinking.

Only later would her remark return to haunt me. It was obvious that she failed to comprehend the mystique of the marathon. Yet how do you fully explain to spectators the joy and pain that go into running 26 miles and 385 yards? The woman certainly would have found ludicrous the personal quest on which I had just embarked. As a sixtieth birthday challenge, I had decided to run six marathons on six successive weekends. The Twin Cities Marathon, which links Minneapolis and St. Paul, was the first of the six. The effort almost destroyed me, and I came close to dropping out of several of the races. Reporters asked if my six-in-six stunt was a world record for successive marathons. I smiled, because obviously they had never heard of Sy Mah, who in his lifetime finished 524 marathons (more about him later).

1

Sy Mah would have understood my obsession with running marathons. He knew that it's not merely the race itself but also the preparation that goes into the race: the steady buildup of miles, the long runs on Sundays, the inevitable taper, the ceremonial aspects of the total experience. Two positive aspects of marathoning are that it provides focus for your training and offers a recognizable goal.

The woman watching at Twin Cities probably would shake her head in disbelief if any of the 5,076 finishers that day told her that they had enjoyed the experience, that it had been fun. *Fun* isn't a word that occurs to most nonmarathoners when they consider the marathon.

Doug Kurtis, however, understands. Kurtis serves as director of the Detroit (formerly Motor City) Marathon, but during his competitive career he ran 190 marathons in 25 countries, winning 39 of them overall and running faster than 2:20 on 76 separate occasions. Typically, Kurtis ran a dozen marathons a year. One year at the Barcelona Marathon, he went out too hard on a hot day and faded to eighth. The Danish race winner asked him afterward, "Was that one fun?".

Kurtis had to admit that it wasn't, but he said he wouldn't run a dozen marathons a year if he didn't think they were fun. "Often, the enjoyment is the training before and the memory after," he says.

Like Kurtis, I believe the actual running of the marathon is secondary to the training leading up to the event. If you love to run, then you appreciate the motivation the marathon provides for those long Sunday runs and those fast midweek track workouts. Marathon training focuses the mind, and that may be the best excuse for racing this distance.

"I go out for my daily workouts because I enjoy running," claims Kurtis. "At noon, I pick scenic routes through surrounding streets near my office. In the evening, I often run from home along a parkway. I like to find pleasant places to run and see the sights. I enjoy being out there day after day. Races are just a by-product."

MARATHON IMMUNITY

Marathon running also has the potential to increase your life span and to improve the quality of your life. Again, it's not so much the running of the race that affects your health but the lifestyle changes that often accompany the commitment to run a marathon. To become a successful runner/marathoner, you need to: (1) follow a proper diet, (2) eliminate extra body fat, (3) refrain from smoking and avoid heavy drinking, (4) get adequate sleep, and (5) exercise regularly. Epidemiologists such as Ralph E. Paffenbarger, M.D., who analyzed the data of Harvard University alumni, have determined that these five lifestyle changes have the potential to add several years to our lives. The marathon lifestyle is definitely a healthy lifestyle.

We have known this at least since the mid-1970s, when the first running boom got under way. One of the first individuals responsible for promoting marathon running as a healthy activity—or at least not a *dangerous* activity—was Thomas J. Bassler, M.D., a pathologist at Centinella Valley Community Hospital in California, and one of the founders of the American Medical Joggers Association. Dr. Bassler proposed the theory that if you could train for and complete a marathon, you would become immune to death by heart attack for at least six months. He later extended that immunity to a year—then beyond a year.

Dr. Bassler's marathon immunity theory ignited an instant controversy. Many people, including members of the medical establishment, considered his theory not only unfounded but outrageous. A few considered it dangerous because they thought it would lure ill-prepared people to the starting line.

The criticism centered on Dr. Bassler's lack of evidence. He had not done a controlled study. All he had done was propose a theory and ask medical experts to prove him wrong—that was not how serious medical research was conducted.

Over a period of years, eminent cardiologists attempted to dispute Dr. Bassler's theory. They would cite evidence of a runner who died of a heart attack, and Dr. Bassler would point out that the runner didn't run marathons. They would cite a marathoner who had collapsed in the last mile, and Dr. Bassler would note that the runner didn't finish the race. Dr. Bassler refused to accept anecdotal evidence of coronary deaths, demanding to see x-rays. In several apparent marathon coronary deaths, he identified the culprit as dehydration or a cardiac arrhythmia rather than the standard heart attack caused by blocked arteries. On several occasions, when seemingly pinned into a corner with his theory disproved, Dr. Bassler would modify the theory just enough to maintain the controversy.

On numerous occasions over the years, I interviewed Dr. Bassler for books and articles and found him almost pixielike. His face was serious, but his eyes twinkled. Although he always professed to be 100 percent committed to his theory of marathon immunity, I was never quite certain whether he was serious or merely putting us on.

But he certainly succeeded in convincing the general public that running distances of 26 miles and 385 yards was not fraught with danger, that marathoners were not routinely collapsing, clutching their hearts, that marathon running should not be banned from city streets as a matter of public safety. By digging deep to uncover examples of supposed marathon deaths, each critic of Dr. Bassler was inadvertently proving what I consider to be the doctor's main message: that marathon running is a relatively safe sport, and a benign activity as long as you train intelligently, behave rationally, and take proper precautions (such as drinking plenty of liquids on hot and humid days).

I'm not sure if cardiologists ever succeeded in disproving the Bassler theory of marathon immunity. More likely, everybody simply lost interest as marathons became a fixture of twentieth-century civilization. By the mid-1980s, a decade after the start of the running boom, enough marathons had been run and enough runners had survived marathons that an occasional cardiac death in a race was considered no more or less alarming than someone dying while attending a symphony concert (which I once saw occur). Dr. Bassler faded into the backwaters of marathon celebrity, but his immunity theories certainly should be credited for helping create the marathon mystique.

BIGGER AND BETTER

There definitely is a mystique about running a marathon—no doubt about it. You can run 5-K races until your dresser drawers overflow with T-shirts, but it's not quite the same as going to the starting line of a marathon. "For many runners, it is their personal measuring post and the one distance they want to conquer," says Robert Eslick, a coach from Nashville.

Marathons, on average, seem to be bigger events than 5-K or 10-K races, even when those shorter-distance events attract larger fields.

Arrive several days in advance of a marathon and you *know* you're at a Big Event, regardless of how many people are entered.

Maybe the excitement is partly anticipation among those who have entered. Each runner has committed so many miles in training for this one event that the race takes on a level of importance above and beyond the ordinary, regardless of the size of the field. One year I visited Toledo, Ohio, to lecture the night before the Glass City Marathon, which attracted about 500 runners. Compared to marathons in New York or Honolulu or London with their fields of 30,000 runners, that's pretty small potatoes. Yet despite Glass City's relatively small field, the same premarathon excitement was present. I could feel it around me as I spoke. People often talk about there being a "glow" around pregnant women. That's certainly true, but there's a similar glow around expectant marathoners. Many of them have devoted nine months of preparation for their big event. All the people in my audience at Toledo had worked hard to get ready for the race. Looking at their faces, I envied them.

After my talk, I climbed into my car and drove home to Long Beach, Indiana. The trip took me three or four hours and wasn't much fun. But the marathon my audience would run the next morning—which would also take three or four hours—*would* be fun. Meanwhile, I had to wait eight more weeks before I would run the marathon I was training for.

What is it about the marathon? Is it the race's history? Its traditions? The many fine runners who have run it? The marathon is all of that, but there's also a mystique about the distance itself. Would the race have the same appeal if it were a more logical 25 miles? Or 40 kilometers?

FOOTSTEPS OF PHEIDIPPIDES

The establishment of the marathon at the unquestionably odd distance of 26 miles and 385 yards (or 42.2 kilometers) certainly adds to the mystique. The first event to be called a marathon was held in 1896 at the first modern Olympic Games in Athens, Greece. This long-distance footrace was staged at the end of those games to re-create and commemorate the legendary run of Pheidippides in 490 B.C.

In that year, the Persians invaded Greece, landing near the plains of Marathon on Greece's eastern coast. According to the legend, an Athenian general dispatched Pheidippides, a *hemerodromo*, or runner-messenger, to Sparta (150 miles away) to seek help. It reportedly took Pheidippides two days to reach Sparta. The Spartans never did arrive in time to help, but the Athenians eventually overwhelmed their enemy, killing 6,400 Persian troops while losing only 192 of their own men. Or so it was recorded by Greek historians of the time.

Some historians dispute those numbers, suspecting they are the typically exaggerated claims of the victors. Then there is the question of whether the messenger dispatched to Athens with news of the victory was the same Pheidippides who ran to and from Sparta.

Regardless, a *hemerodromo* apparently did run a route that took him south along the coast and up and across a series of coastal foothills before descending into Athens, a distance of about 25 miles from the plains of Marathon. According to legend, Pheidippides announced, "Rejoice. We conquer!" as he arrived in Athens—then he fell dead.

Ah, legends. Latter-day historians doubt the total accuracy of the legend. That includes the late Jim Fixx, who traced Pheidippides's journey for a *Sports Illustrated* article that became part of *Jim Fixx's Second Book of Running.* If there were a *hemerodromo*, claimed Fixx, he may not have been the same one known to have relayed the request for troops to Sparta. There may or may not have been a *hemerodromo* by the name of Pheidippides who died following a postbattle run to Athens. Fixx and others noted that Herodotus, who first described the Battle of Marathon, failed to mention a *hemerodromo*; the story appeared four centuries later when the history of the battle was retold by Plutarch.

Nevertheless, the legend took on the imprint of historical fact and was certainly no less worthy of respect than legends involving mythical Greek gods such as Hermes or Aphrodite. It seemed perfectly suitable at the 1896 Olympic Games to run a race in Pheidippides's honor from the plains of Marathon to the Olympic stadium in downtown Athens. It was particularly fitting that a Greek shepherd named Spiridon Loues won that event, the only gold medal in track and field won by the Greeks on their home turf. Among the

American clubs represented at those first Games was the Boston Athletic Association (BAA), whose team manager was John Graham. So impressed was Graham with this race that he decided to sponsor a similar event in his hometown the following year. Races of approximately 25 miles (40 kilometers) had been held before in Europe, including one held in France before the Olympics. But nobody had attached the name *marathon* to these races, and there wasn't yet a marathon mystique.

Fifteen runners lined up at the start of the first Boston Athletic Association Marathon in 1897 to race from suburban Hopkinton into downtown Boston, and a new legend was born. (A previous American marathon was run in the fall of 1896 from Stamford, Connecticut, to Columbus Circle, near the finish line of the current New York City Marathon, but it failed to survive.) The Boston Marathon remains the oldest continuously held marathon. It continues to retain its status and prestige, and it attracted a record 38,000 runners in 1996, its 100th running.

DETERMINING THE DISTANCE

For a dozen years, the official marathon distance was approximately 25 miles. That was the distance run in the 1900 Olympic Games in Paris and the 1904 Games in St. Louis. Then in 1908, in London, the British designed a marathon course that started at Windsor Castle and finished at the Olympic stadium. This was long before course certification experts measured race distances to an accuracy of plus or minus a few feet. Nobody challenged the British course design, which reportedly was laid out so that the royal family could see the start of the race. The distance from start to finish for that marathon was precisely 26 miles and 385 yards. For whatever reason, that distance became the standard for future marathons.

Frank Shorter tells the story of running the marathon trials for the 1971 Pan American Games. At 21 miles, he was lockstep with Kenny Moore, a 1968 Olympian. "Why couldn't Pheidippides have died here?" Shorter groaned to Moore. In that case, it was Shorter who "died" and Moore who went on to win the race.

The running event that is so popular today might not be the same if the plains of Marathon had been closer to Athens. Exercise physiologists tell us that it is only after about two hours of running—or about 20 miles for an accomplished runner—that the body begins to fully deplete its stores of glycogen, the energy source that fuels the muscles. Once glycogen is depleted, the body must rely more on fat, a less efficient fuel source. This is one of the reasons runners hit the wall at 20 miles, and successfully getting past that obstacle is what makes a marathon such a special event.

Many of us who consider ourselves accomplished runners—and who are well trained—run 20-milers as part of our marathon buildup without excessive pain and with little fanfare. It is only when we stretch beyond that point that people sit up and take notice. Would a million people line the roads along the Boston and New York City marathon routes if the distance were only 20 miles and if there were no wall to conquer? No, they want to see us tempt the fate of Pheidippides. They come to see us suffer, although inevitably both spectator and runner leave fulfilled only if we demonstrate through our successful crashing through the wall and crossing of the finish line that we are victorious.

CHANGING YOUR LIFE

For many runners, completing one marathon is enough. This is particularly true for many first timers today. It changes their lives forever. Professional photographers who take pictures of runners crossing the finish line find that two or three times as many people order prints of their marathon finishes, compared to runners who finish shorter races. It's the same reason that people order more pictures at weddings. A marathon is an extra-special event. It's like tacking a Ph.D. at the end of your name, getting married, having a baby. You're special, whether anyone else knows it or not. *You* certainly do. Your life will never again be quite the same, and regardless of what the future brings, you can look back and say, "I finished a marathon." Others consider running marathons to be a continuing challenge of numbers: personal records (or PRs), which exist to be bettered at each race. Even when aging brings the inevitable decline in performance, new challenges arise as the lifetime marathoner moves from one five-year bracket to another.

It is also possible to run marathons recreationally, not caring about time or finishing position, but participating merely for the joy of attending a Great Event with all its accompanying pleasures. I have run many marathons in this manner, running within myself and finishing far back from where I might have had I pushed the pace harder. One year at the Honolulu Marathon, I started in the back row and made a game out of passing as many people as possible—but doing it at a pace barely faster than theirs so as not to call attention to my speed, so it didn't seem that I was trying to show them up. Beginning with the 1995 St. George (Utah) Marathon, *Runner's World* began to organize pacing teams led by editors running slower than usual while shepherding others. I've led pacing teams on several occasions. It's fun, and it's rewarding to help others meet their goals.

I've also run marathons in which I stopped at planned dropout points, using the race as a workout to prepare for later marathons. At the World Veterans Championships in Rome in 1985, I ran the marathon at the end of a week's track competition mainly so I could enjoy the sights and sounds of the Eternal City. In the last miles of the race, as I entered a piazza with a panoramic view of St. Peter's Cathedral across the Tiber River, I paused for several minutes to absorb that view, then continued toward the stadium used for the 1960 Olympic Games. How fast I ran, or how well I placed, were the last things on my mind. Crossing the finish line, more refreshed than fatigued, I was approached by an Australian runner, who announced, "This is the first time I ever beat you."

I felt obliged to correct him: "You didn't beat me. You merely finished in front of me."

The Australian stammered an apology, but he had missed what I believe to be the point of the marathon. Or at least he was not aware of the way I had chosen to run the marathon that particular day. In a marathon, you don't beat others, as you might in a mile or a 100-meter dash. Instead, you achieve a personal victory. If others finish in front of or behind you, it is only that their personal victories are more or less than yours. A person finishing behind you with less talent, or of a different age or sex, or various other limiting factors, may have achieved a far greater victory. At the 1992 Boston Marathon, John A. Kelley, age 84, finished in a time of 5:58:32. The officials stopped timing at five hours, at which point 8,120 runners had crossed the line (not counting those running unofficially without numbers). It was the 61st and final time "Old John," a two-time winner of the race, would run Boston. None of the thousands finishing in front of Kelley could be said to have beaten him. He is a legend—like Pheidippides.

One beauty of the marathon is that there are many more winners than those who finish first overall or in their age groups. "Everyone's a winner" is a dreadful cliché, but it happens to be true when the race involved is 26 miles and 385 yards long.

A LIFETIME OF MARATHONS

Reporters sometimes ask how many marathons I have run. Until recently, I would respond, "About a hundred."

This amazed them: "You've run 100 marathons?"

I had to correct them, because I didn't want to read in the newspaper the next morning that I had just run marathon number 101. "No," I would say. "I don't know how many marathons I've run. But it must be about a hundred."

Then in the spring of 1995, a year before the 100th Boston Marathon, I got curious about the exact number. (I now keep a daily training diary, but there were periods of my career when I did not.) Using the library at the Boston Athletic Association, I searched through old running magazines and newsletters for old marathon results. I was able to identify several races that I had little memory of running, including one in which I had finished first! But the actual total number of marathons I had run was less than what I had been telling reporters for years: it was only 90.

That was the bad news, but the good news was that with a little effort over the next twelve months, I would be able to run my 100th marathon at the 100th Boston. Thus running a marathon a month became my goal for a year. Fittingly, I ran my 99th at the Trail's End Marathon in Seaside, Oregon, one month before Boston. Since that historic event, I've once more lost track. Ask me the correct number again before the 200th Boston.

I'm far from being the record holder when it comes to the number of marathons run. Sy Mah, the Toledo, Ohio, runner who often ran two and sometimes three marathons on a weekend, finished 524 races that were longer than 26 miles before his death from cancer at age 62 in 1988. Adding to the total was the focal point of Mah's running, so it was important that he keep precise records for each of his races. He was another legend. Mah usually finished in the high three-hour range. I once told him that if he focused his attention for six months on a single race—training specifically for it, resisting the temptation to run other marathons so that he could taper and peak—he could probably improve his time by half an hour, and maybe even break three hours, putting him near the top for his age group. Smiling, he conceded my point, but we both knew that was not what he was about. His joy was running as many marathons as possible and adding to his impressive string of numbers, which earned him an enviable spot in *The Guinness Book of World Records*. (In 1994, Norm Frank of Rochester, New York, broke Mah's record. Frank, who runs approximately 40 marathons a year, had pushed his record number to a devilishly difficult 666 by the end of 1998.)

In comparison, my own achievement of running 10 marathons in a year so I could run my 100th at the 100th Boston was trivial, almost inconsequential. My lifetime total of "over a hundred" is merely a blip on the chart compared to the hundreds of marathons finished by Mah and Frank.

The marathon never ceases to be a race of joy, a race of wonder. Even when disaster strikes, when bad weather overwhelms you, when an intemperate pace results in a staggering finish, when nerves and anxiety stand in the way of giving your maximum effort, when your number one rival soundly thrashes you, when nine months of training appear to have gone down the drain with little more than an ugly slurping sound, there remains something memorable about each marathon run.

I would have a hard time explaining that to the woman standing beside the course at the Twin Cities Marathon, who considered it odd that we had actually paid to "abuse" our bodies. But anyone who has crossed the finish line of a 26-mile, 385-yard race would understand. Sy Mah knew. It's all part of the mystique of the marathon.

Chapter 2

A Word to the
BEGINNING RUNNER

People need not be taught how to run. Children learn to run almost as soon as they learn to walk. Visit any elementary school playground, and you'll see kids sprinting all over the place. All children are born sprinters.

Children modify their behavior as they get older. Running starts to become a discipline rather than a natural form of exercise. An athlete who goes out for any sport in high school—football, basketball, tennis, or whatever—runs as part of the conditioning for that sport. High schoolers run either because their coach tells them to, or because they know that getting in shape will help them make the team. Usually, young athletes run middle distance: a few laps on a track, then off to the main activity. It is only as adults that people forget to run and sometimes have to be retaught.

Let's talk about being a beginning runner. If you're an experienced runner who trains regularly and competes in 5-K races, you may be tempted to skip this chapter. With one or two exceptions, it probably won't teach you anything you don't already know. But hold on: In training runners for the LaSalle Banks Chicago Marathon, I often find I learn as much from novices as they learn from me. I enjoy talking to beginners and revisiting paths that I once may have tread. Maybe you'd like to look over my shoulder as I talk to beginning runners and get them started on their first journeys.

Before you can hope to run long distances, you must start by running short distances—and running slowly. Some beginners (particularly if they're overweight) need to walk first, beginning with half an hour, three or four days a week. Then they start to jog a short distance until they get slightly out of breath, walk to recover, jog some more. Jog, walk. Jog, walk. Jog, walk. After a while, they will be able to run a mile without stopping.

Before we move forward, there are some important kernels of information hidden in what I have just said. Even experienced runners can learn from it.

The pattern is: Jog, *walk*. Jog, *walk*. Jog, *walk*. Expressed another way: Hard, *easy*. Hard, *easy*. Hard, *easy*. The most effective training programs—even at the basic level—mix bursts of difficult training with rest. Train, *rest*. Train, *rest*. Train, *rest*.

Rest. That may be the single most important word you will read in this book. (You'll encounter it again and again.) In a questionnaire I sent to coaches to gather information for this book, one of the questions was "How important is rest in the training equation?"

The very first coach to return a completed questionnaire was Paul Goss of Foster City, California. His response was simple and direct: "More important than most runners know."

None of the other coaches who eventually responded improved on what Goss had to say.

LEARNING TO RUN

With beginners the problem is not to get them to rest but to get them to *stop* resting. They have to get off the couch and away from the TV. They need to learn to become participants in sport, rather than spectators of sport. To those of us who accept running as a natural activity, that's not as easy as it might seem.

Beginners need motivation to begin—and to keep at it once they have begun. "The key factor in any beginner's training program is motivation," suggests Jack Daniels, Ph.D., exercise physiologist and coach at the State University of New York at Cortland. "If you're genetically gifted but not interested in training, you'll never develop."

Barring some medical problem, most people can run, but they aren't motivated to do so. Even if they want to start running, it takes courage to put on running shoes and step out on a sidewalk for the first time in front of friends and neighbors. A lot of potential runners never get moving out of fear of looking foolish. They lack self-confidence. They fear failure.

It sometimes helps to join a class. Many running clubs offer classes for beginning runners. One advantage of a class situation is the group support you get from others of equal ability or lack of ability. The most important information any coach can offer beginners is not how to hold their arms, or how far to jog without stopping, but simply, "You're looking good. You're doing great. Keep it up." Basic motivation. Once you start, natural running instincts, overlooked but not forgotten from childhood, will take over.

Joining a class can provide you with support, information and good training routes, but in particular it can give you motivation as you train with others. If you are looking for a running class in your area, check with local health clubs, running clubs, sporting goods stores, or the organizers of major races. One good source of information is the Road Runners Club of America (RRCA, 1150 South Washington Street, Suite 250, Alexandria, VA 22314; (703) 836-0558; www.rrca.org). The RRCA has 635 member clubs with 180,000 members. The organization's Web site lists clubs and contact information. The RRCA can point you in the right direction if you're looking to connect with other runners and runner support groups.

Many books have been written on beginning running as well. *Jim Fixx's The Complete Book of Running*, which sold nearly a million copies in the United States alone, got many people started running. I wrote a *Beginning Runner's Guide* for *Runner's World On-line* (www.runnersworld.com), and it is also available in booklet form. Most books and classes for beginners provide similar advice: Begin at an easy level; don't try to do too much too soon; don't get discouraged when your muscles ache.

How soon should you begin to consider a marathon? When I asked coaches this question at the time I was writing the first edition of this book, most preached caution. "Too many runners attempt the marathon far too early in their careers and then become ex-runners," noted Robert Eslick, a coach from Nashville. When asked how long it should take a beginning runner to train to be able to complete a marathon, the coaches I surveyed concurred that most people could do so in just over a year.

But in the half dozen years since the publication of the first edition of this book, I've begun to think differently. Contact with the current breed of marathon runner—young, eager, goal oriented—causes me to reconsider this cautious approach. Many of today's new runners take up the sport solely to finish a marathon. This is particularly true with individuals who join the Leukemia Society of America's Team in Training. Members of Generation X want their gratification *now* and don't want to dally over their training for a year or more just because some running expert from an older generation claims that's the sensible approach. Since motivation is the single most important reason that people succeed in the marathon, I'm inclined to shrug and say, "Go for it!"

Nevertheless, before beginning to think about running a marathon, you first need to think about beginning running.

CHECKING OUT THE SYSTEM

People older than 35 who want to start exercising should consider having a medical examination, including an exercise stress test. The American College of Sports Medicine recommends testing at age 40 for men and age 50 for women—if you're apparently healthy. But if you have any risk factor for coronary artery disease (high blood pressure, high cholesterol, smoking, diabetes or a family history of heart problems), you should be tested prior to vigorous exercise, at *any* age.

"This is particularly important if your family has a history of heart disease," states Jack Scaff Jr., M.D., one of the founders of the Honolulu Marathon. "If you have been overweight or recently were a smoker, your risks also are high." Running is a relatively safe activity, but why take a chance?

The cardiology departments of many major medical centers provide exercise stress tests for around $250, often covered by health insurance. The best type of test is "symptom-limited," in which you exercise until you attain your maximum heart rate, unless symptoms develop. A cardiologist uses an electrocardiograph (EKG) to monitor your heartbeat while you walk or jog on a treadmill. Or they may test you as you pedal an ergometer (exercise bicycle). The cardiologist will also record blood pressure. If your coronary arteries are even partially blocked, it should become apparent during stress. Changes in your heartbeat will appear on the EKG screen, and you will be asked to stop. This does not mean you cannot run, but you will need to begin under careful medical supervision. Doctors regularly prescribe exercise, including running, for patients who have suffered heart attacks. It is not uncommon for heart attack victims, even those who have had quadruple bypass operations, to finish marathons.

If no symptoms develop during your exam—and assuming there are no other medical problems—you will be cleared to start running.

Just because you pass an exercise stress test once, however, is no guarantee you will never suffer a heart attack, either while running or while engaged in other activities. Physicians now recommend that you have a physical every two to three years, more often as you get older or if your cardiologist determines you're in a high-risk category. Also, learn the heart attack symptoms. The classic symptoms include chest pain, but symptoms can include *any* generalized pain between the eyeballs and the belly button, even a toothache. "It's a myth that tingling occurs only in the left arm," says Dr. Scaff. "It can appear in the right arm, too." If such symptoms develop during a run, stop running immediately and seek medical advice. Even if the symptoms seem to diminish as you continue to run, that doesn't mean that you're safe.

How to Begin

If you've never run before, focus your attention on time rather than distance or pace. Put on a pair of comfortable shoes. Although you will eventually need running shoes, for your first couple of short outings, you can start with whatever you have.

Start to jog gently, on a smooth or soft surface if possible. Jog until you're somewhat out of breath, then begin to walk. Resume jogging when you feel comfortable, walking again if necessary. "Most people overestimate what they can do," says Stan James, M.D., an orthopedist from Eugene, Oregon. When your tired muscles won't let you jog any farther, finish by walking. Set as your goal 15 minutes of combined jogging and walking.

Record your time in a diary or simply on your calendar. Don't worry about distance and pace this early in your training.

Take the next day off. On the third day, repeat the first day's workout, but again, don't worry about distance. If you go much farther or faster than the first day, you may be progressing too rapidly. Take the fourth day off.

On the fifth day, again repeat the basic workout, then rest the sixth and seventh days. Your training has followed the classic hard/easy pattern used by former University of Oregon track coach Bill Bowerman and countless other top coaches in training world-class runners. The pattern is the same; only the degree of difficulty is different.

The second week, simply repeat the workouts you did during the first week. You may feel that you can run farther or go faster, but hold back. When Bowerman developed his championship athletes at the University of Oregon, he always felt it was better that they be somewhat *undertrained* rather than *overtrained*. Even though there was a chance the Oregon athletes might perform slightly below their potential while undertrained, their chances for injury were greatly reduced. If that conservative approach made sense for his highly talented athletes, why shouldn't it also work for you?

The second week is critical in any beginning running program. You may have been able to run through week one just from sheer beginner's enthusiasm. Even if your muscles were sore, running seemed harder than you expected, and you failed to see any improvement, you probably were able to keep going from the momentum generated by your decision to begin.

But now you're into your second week. Maybe your muscles are still sore, you're getting bored with the same every-other-day routine, and it's dawned on you that you probably will never win an Olympic gold medal. You haven't yet experienced that "runner's high" one of your friends promised you. And it may feel as if running will never get any better.

Hang in there. It will.

When to Run

Run at a time that is convenient for you. Here are the advantages and disadvantages of running at different times of the day.

Morning. Many runners run in the morning, before they eat breakfast. It's a good way to begin the day. Running can both wake you up and refresh you. If you run in the dark (particularly in winter), wear a reflective vest so cars can see you. The one downside of training at this hour is that morning runners seem to get injured more often than afternoon runners do. That's probably because they're stiff after just getting out of bed. To combat this problem, start your morning run by walking or running very slowly, then stop to do some brief stretching exercises before continuing.

Midday. If you have an hour or more for lunch, you may be able to squeeze in a workout at this time. Some offices have health clubs with showers and encourage workers to exercise at midday. Learn to manage your time. Plan your lunch in advance so you can grab a quick cup of yogurt or bowl of soup before returning to work. Noon is a good time to run during the winter when temperatures can be warmer, but for that same reason it's a bad time during the dog days of summer.

Evening. Stop for a workout on your way home from work. Or go for a quick run after returning home and before dinner. This may not work if *you* are the one who is expected to put food on the table, or if there are kids waiting to be fed. If this is the case, negotiate days when you and your spouse can alternate training and homemaking. Late evening after the kids go to bed is another option, but this probably means running in the dark. You should always run in a safe area. There are some places where you do not want to run alone even in the daytime.

Weekend. On Saturdays and Sundays, most runners have more time for training. That being the case, you may want to plan your workout week so that you do most of your mileage on the weekends. Most runners (particularly those training for a marathon) do their long runs on the weekend.

Anytime. Who says that you need to run at the same time every day? There's a virtue in regularity, but you can also get caught in a rut. Once running becomes a regular part of your lifestyle, feel free to experiment with different training patterns.

CONTINUING TO RUN

Beginning with week three, and continuing through weeks four, five, and six, add three minutes to your workout each seven days. During a six-week beginner's training period, your daily and weekly (based on three workout days per week) training mileage should look like this:

Week	Time per Day (min.)	Time per Week (min.)
1	15	45
2	15	45
3	18	54
4	21	63
5	24	72
6	27	81

How fast should you be running? It doesn't matter. You should be worrying about time, not distance or pace. You can record distance and pace, but if you try to increase either, you're more likely to get injured. Better to go too slow in the beginning than too fast.

At the end of this initial six-week training period, treat yourself to a half-hour run. When finished, consider what you have accomplished. In a period of six weeks, you have *doubled* your initial workout load. As you continue to run, there will be few times when you will be able to improve at this rate: 100 percent improvement in only six weeks! Improvement comes easily and suddenly when you're a beginner. It's more difficult for more experienced runners and *incredibly* difficult for those at the top of the performance charts. But you should be able to continue to improve as a runner for many months, and perhaps years to come, as long as you follow a sensible training program.

MOVING UP THE TRAINING LADDER

Almost all training designed to improve runners is based on moving from level to level. You work harder and improve, moving from a low level to a higher level. This is your body's progressive adaptation to increasing stress. The 18-week program I use with my marathon training class in Chicago features increases of approximately one mile a week for the weekend long runs. Over that time period, weekly mileage doubles. The changes in numbers are small; the changes in fitness and the body's capacity to adapt to stress are great.

Naturally there are limits to how hard you can train and how much you can improve. Not everybody can move from the first level in training programs through the second and then to the third. Moving to the second level may provide all the challenge you need. But even genetically gifted athletes need time to move from level to level to level. If you overtrain, you're likely to crash. Even if you don't injure yourself, you may discover that your competitive efforts deteriorate. You begin to run slower instead of faster. Sooner or later, this happens to almost all top athletes. According to Dick Brown, the former Athletics West coach from Eugene, Oregon, "Most of the time, athletes need to be held back rather than pushed."

Top athletes are constantly pushing the envelope, trying to measure the limits of human performance. "There are two ways to learn about training," states Dr. James, the orthopedist from Oregon. "One is by having access to a very knowledgeable coach. The other is by trial and error." With a knowledgeable coach, you make errors less frequently.

If you are an athlete working without a coach, you may have difficulty recognizing how much and how fast to run. "Most people misestimate what they do," says Dr. James. "There is a difference between what the body perceives and what the mind perceives."

THE 5 PERCENT SOLUTION

How can you maximize your performance? How much can you improve?

When asked how much improvement runners might expect following a year's hard training, Dr. Daniels initially suggests 5 percent as an upper limit. But it's a tough question. "There is no physiological basis for saying how much you can increase your workload," he finally admits. Runners differ *enormously* in both their capability and their capacity, he says. "Some people with little training background have tremendous potential for improvement.

Others who have been running for many years may have improved as much as they can."

A new runner capable of running a 5-K in 30:00 may find it relatively easy to improve by 5 percent, which would mean cutting 1½ minutes to run a 28:30. A similar 5 percent improvement for a runner capable of running a 5-K in 15:00 would be somewhat less: 45 seconds, or a final time of 14:15. But few athletes improve that much at that level of performance without many years of increased training—and they may not improve even then.

So if you can improve by 5 percent, you can be said to have outperformed the world's elite. That should be sufficient motivation to get you moving. Most reasonably talented runners, however, would settle for a 1 percent improvement, which would mean that runners who do a 5-K in 20:00 could get their time down to 19:48.

KEY PERFORMANCE FACTORS

Anyone can improve with practice, summarizes Dr. Daniels. "Where you start, and whether or not you are genetically gifted, dictates where you finish—provided you optimize what you have," he says. "Optimizing what you have is the tricky part."

Dr. Daniels suggests four areas in which runners can improve in ability.

1. Oxygen delivery. When the heart muscle becomes stronger, your oxygen delivery system becomes more efficient.
2. Oxygen absorption. Training also results in increased blood flow through the muscle fibers and improvement of the fibers themselves—all of which improves your ability to use oxygen.
3. Economy. You can learn to run faster while expending the same amount of energy by improving technique and form.
4. Endurance. This means increasing how fast you can run before you hit your pain threshold. Basically, stronger muscles contract more effectively.

To improve to the highest level requires talent. But even those of average talent can rise above their abilities and achieve extremely high levels of success as runners. In perhaps no event is this more true than in the marathon.

Chapter 3

Your
FIRST
MARATHON

W hen I wrote a profile of Gale Williams for the August 1991 issue of *Runner's World*, it was more because of her celebrity status as a horn player with the Chicago Symphony Orchestra (CSO) than because of her ability as a runner. Williams ran mainly for fitness. Three or four days a week she jogged the several miles from her Evanston, Illinois, home to the lake and back. When the CSO played at Ravinia during the summers, she biked 11 miles to rehearsals. Williams told me at that time that someday she'd like to run a marathon.

Half a dozen years later, she still hadn't run one.

Then Williams learned that the daughter of one of the CSO bass players had leukemia. Williams had recently received a mailing from the Leukemia Society of America about its Team in Training program, in which marathon runners raise money to help cure leukemia.

"That provided the push I needed," said Williams. She finished the 1997 Chicago Marathon in 4:41:46 and enjoyed the experience so much she made almost immediate plans to run the race again the following year, which she did.

People decide to run a marathon for different reasons. The

training class I teach in Chicago offers workout runs in different locations, one of them being the Prairie Path west of the city. The Prairie Path provides a great place to run long because of its forgiving, gravel surface, and overhead trees that shade runners from the sun. During one of my visits several years ago, a runner in his fifties fell into step with me. He said that in addition to playing tennis, he had been running for nearly 30 years. Yet here he was training for his first marathon!

I asked him why it had taken him so long to get around to running a marathon. He shrugged and smiled as though to suggest there was no answer: "It seemed like the right time." The following year I encountered him again training with my class for his *third* marathon. Between the two runs in Chicago, he had sandwiched in Grandma's Marathon in Duluth, Minnesota.

Olympic gold medalist Kerri Strug ran her first marathon in 1999. Strug didn't win her Olympic medal as a runner. She won it as a gymnast. Is there anybody who watched the telecast of the 1996 Olympic Games from Atlanta who missed the image of Strug's coach, Bela Karolyi, carrying the gymnast off the floor after she injured her ankle in the vault?

Yet here was this Olympic champion finishing the 1999 Houston Marathon in 4:12:06. That's a time countless recreational runners better each year. That's a time you could match with a bit of training. Retired as a competitive gymnast, and at age 21 a student at Stanford University, Strug decided she wanted to run a marathon in her hometown. I loved her explanation, which was quoted in an article in the *Houston Chronicle*.

"I spent my entire life focused on only one thing: gymnastics. All I wanted was to compete and win. Everything I did, every moment of my life, was dedicated to only one goal. And I wouldn't change anything about that part of my life.

"But I've learned there are different phases in a person's life. Now I know there are a lot of things out there, and I want to experience as many of them as I can. I'm sick of doing serious stuff. I want to do cool stuff. I want to accomplish neat things, personal things. The greatest thing in my life was winning the gold medal, but I realize I don't have to win to be happy."

DIFFERING GOALS

There are three goals in marathon running: to finish, to improve, and to win. Which goal you strive for depends on what level of running you're at.

To finish is important to the beginning or novice marathoner. More and more runners are running their first marathons these days. For them, covering 26 miles and 385 yards equals victory. Regardless of time, regardless of place, the prime goal is to get to the finish line standing up and in reasonably good shape. And to enjoy the experience, like Kerri Strug did. Regardless of how fast or slow you run—unless you set your goals too high—you will look on that first completed marathon as a significant experience, a portentous point in your life.

Whether or not you enjoy the experience as a first-time marathoner enough to become a next-time marathoner may be irrelevant. For most beginners, to finish is to win. And for many, once is enough.

To improve is the goal of the seasoned runner. Seasoned could describe anybody who has been for running several years, has finished a first marathon—or two or three—and wants to run faster. For these runners, improving from six hours to five, from five hours to four, from four hours to three, or various gradients within those hour blocks is akin to victory. Setting personal records is the name of the game for many of us. It doesn't matter if the PR is for your career, your current age group, the year, or the month of June. Take your victories where you can find them.

Improvement doesn't come easily. You have to work at it. If you finished your first marathon by training 35 miles a week, you may need to increase your mileage to 45 or 55, or more, to improve in future marathons. You may need to add speedwork and other means of fine-tuning your skills (or compensating for lack of skills). You may need to add supplemental exercises, lift weights, and learn to stretch properly to get better. You also may need to pay attention to diet. Prerace diet is particularly important for endurance events lasting over two hours, as is fluid intake, but your day-by-day diet is equally important, maybe more so.

If you run many marathons, at some point in your life it becomes increasingly difficult to snip seconds off your PR. And inevitably, if you stay in marathoning long enough, improvement may become impossible—at least as measured on the clock.

Nevertheless, each move to a new (five-year) age group provides an opportunity for improvement within that age group. And because as an aging runner's career passes peaks and valleys, it is possible to allow yourself to sink to new lows (by backing off training) so that you can establish new highs (by increasing that training). For some runners, every marathon is like their first, each one is a new adventure. Even after 100 marathons, I certainly feel that way, and I don't consider myself unique. Depending on how you view the sport, you can continue to improve as a marathoner forever.

To win is the goal of the elite runner, but winning is a goal only a small percentage of runners will ever achieve. In my long career I've won four marathons overall: Windy City in Chicago in 1964; the Cayuga Marathon in Indiana in 1966; Heart of America in Columbus, Missouri, in 1968; and Longest Day in Brookings, South Dakota, in 1972. I've won my age group on numerous occasions, including a TAC (The Athletics Congress) national championship. I also won my age group (45 to 49) and a gold medal at the 1981 World Veterans Championships, although I was beaten by runners in the younger age group.

My early wins came relatively easily. Decades ago in the United States, the typical road race attracted at best a few dozen runners. If you were a reasonably competent runner, the odds were decent that you might cross the finish line in first place sometime if you trained properly and chose the right race. My four victories were with times slower than 2:30, pedestrian by today's standards.

In today's marathon scene, with race fields as large as 30,000 and first-place cash prizes of $100,000 or more, the odds of crossing the line first have diminished considerably. Fewer than 1 percent of those running—many fewer—have a chance of crossing a finish line first. A slightly larger percentage might earn an award for finishing high in their age group. Most people return from a completed marathon with no more than a race T-shirt and a medal or certificate that is given to all finishers.

Nevertheless, the training secrets that work for the running elite—the athletes whose pictures appear on the cover of *Runner's World*, if not *Rolling Stone*—can help the less gifted to improve and maximize their potential. And this in itself may be a more significant victory than merely crossing the finish line first.

BOSTON: A FAVORITE GOAL

One standard of achievement is running fast enough to qualify for the Boston Athletic Association Marathon, the granddaddy of American marathons. When I first ran Boston in 1959, anyone could enter—and there wasn't even an entry fee! Fewer than 200 of us appeared that Patriots' Day. Within the decade, however, the Boston race had become so popular that organizers imposed a qualifying time of four hours to limit the field.

That requirement merely spurred runners to train harder. Boston became *the* standard for marathon excellence. By qualifying for the Boston Marathon, runners achieved status among their peers. It earned you bragging rights to be able to say nonchalantly that you had "qualified for Boston." Boston's numbers continued to increase, because once a runner qualified, it seemed almost obligatory to go to Boston to run. So the organizers of the marathon lowered the standard from 4:00 to 3:30 to 3:00, until by the mid-1980s if you were a male under 40, you had to run 2:50 to qualify.

That standard was too tough. Four hours is a reasonable time for a runner of average ability who is willing to train hard, but to run the course more than an hour faster requires a certain natural ability. To get into the Boston Marthon, you needed to combine talent and training.

Eventually, Boston relaxed its standards to 3:10 for the fastest age group with a sliding scale of slower times in other categories depending on age and sex. In recent years, to qualify you had to run that time on a certified course if you were a male younger than 35. If you were older, the standard relaxed five minutes for every five years: 3:15 for age 35, 3:20 for age 40, and so forth. The base standard for females is 3:40 with a similar upward-sliding scale.

Actually, most studies on aging suggest that sedentary people lose fitness at the rate of about 1 percent a year, which is 10 percent a decade. Most runners who maintain their training probably decline at a lesser rate, perhaps 0.5 percent a year, 5 percent a decade. So as runners continue in the sport, theoretically it becomes easier for them to qualify for the Boston Marathon, at least up to a point. A time of 3:30 for a man aged 50, or a time of 4:00 for a woman the same age is within reach of many readers of this book—if they're willing to devote a decade of their lives to attaining it. For that reason, a majority of the field at Boston is made up of masters, runners over age 40.

What to Aim For

The first rule for anyone starting his or her first marathon, unless you are already among the running elite, is to make your goal merely finishing the race. Select a pace and shoot for a time much slower than you think possible, just to get a finish under your belt. After achieving the "victory" of a finish, then—and only then— should you contemplate training harder to finish with faster times.

Almost anyone can finish a marathon. The distance of 26 miles and 385 yards is not that far when you think about it. By walking at a comfortable pace of three miles an hour, you could cover the distance in about nine hours. Not many people would be waiting around to greet you, but you could finish. More and more people, particularly those in the Leukemia Society of America's Team in Training program, choose to walk rather than run the marathon. Lately, marathons have begun to provide early starting times for walkers and slower runners. The Trail's End Marathon in Seaside, Oregon, offers an early start one hour before the main start; the Bermuda Marathon offers slow runners a two-hour lead. Many other marathons allow walkers out on the course early without publicizing it.

Starting early offers mixed blessings. One problem is that there may be few volunteers on the course to assist you. If you want fluids, you will need to provide your own. While trying to do enough races so I could run my 100th marathon at the 100th Boston, I chose early starts at both Bermuda and Trail's End as a way to conserve energy. Despite a gentle beginning, I found myself "leading" the race in Bermuda after a half-dozen miles, several other runners tucked in behind me.

Unfortunately, there was no lead vehicle to guide the early starters. Although I had visited Bermuda before and thought I knew the course, I took a wrong turn. I realized my mistake a half mile or so later, but didn't want to make a U-turn to get back to the course, since that would have meant running 27 or 28 miles that day. We weren't in a race for prizes, so I told those accompanying me that they could either turn back or continue to follow, since I thought I knew a shortcut back to the course. Some turned back; some followed. After twisting through the interior of the island, I finally found my way back onto the main route.

I might have been tempted to congratulate myself for my navigating skills, but after several more minutes of running I came to a mile marker and realized I was now running the course backward! I eventually got myself turned around and finished. I have no idea how far I actually ran that day, but I still count Bermuda as one of the 99 marathons run en route to the 100th Boston.

Slow runners are accommodated better today than they were when I ran my first marathon at Boston in 1959. The last finishers in the Honolulu Marathon, one of the few races in which the officials wait for everybody, usually come in at around eight or nine hours. That's a walking pace. By jogging as well as walking, you should be able to move at a speed of four miles an hour. That pace will get you to the finish line in under seven hours.

In 1983, my wife, Rose, took a year's sabbatical from her work as a teacher to research her family history. I was leading a tour of runners to the Honolulu Marathon and said that I'd take her, but only if she ran the race. She said okay, trained a bit in addition to her usual exercise of tennis, biking, and other activities, and finished the marathon in 6½ hours, walking a good portion of the second half of the course. I bought her a special plaque commemorating what she still considers a special achievement—although she has no plans to run another marathon.

Several years later, our daughter Laura trained hard enough to knock an hour off the family female time at the Chicago Marathon. I ran with Laura, who walked a lot in the closing stages and finished in better shape than I did. Slow running is not necessarily easier than fast running. Four-time Boston and New York City Marathon champion Bill Rodgers once said respectfully about those in the back of the pack, "I can't even imagine what it's like to run for five or six hours."

With a little more conditioning and determination, you can run at a pace of 12-minutes-per-mile, or 5 miles per hour. At this rate you could complete the marathon distance in close to five hours, which is a reasonable goal for a "fitness jogger" who only wants to finish. In taking its pacing teams to different marathons, *Runner's World* offers five hours as its slowest pace group. In 1998 I led the five-hour group at Chicago, and had a lot of fun doing so, interacting with the several hundred people following me. Chicago now offers its own pacing teams.

In Chicago, at least I didn't get anybody lost, but I had help from two other leaders: Mary Burke and Fred Hoehn. Mary kept us relaxed by leading group chants: "Who are we?" *"Five hours!"* "What are we?" *"Best looking!"* Midway through the run, another runner turned to me and said, "I've run 11 marathons and never had this much fun before." In most of the big marathons today, many people cross the line at around five hours, smiling proudly, looking and feeling better than many of those who preceded them in half that time.

Moving into the four-hour or three-hour bracket requires more training, and getting into the two-hour bracket requires both training and talent. The world record for men is currently 2:06:05, the time Ronaldo da Costa of Brazil ran to win the 1998 Berlin Marathon. We may be years away from seeing a runner break two hours and move into the one-hour bracket. Some pundits believe we will *never* see that day—although I can remember when the world record was in the mid 2:20s. Great Britain's Jim Peters, once described as the greatest marathoner ever, improved the world record from 2:26:07 to 2:17:39 between 1952 and 1954.

In that era, less than a half century ago, many considered a sub-2:20 marathon nearly impossible, but we have been required to revise our thinking about the limits of human achievement. As I write this book, the women's marathon record is 2:20:47, run by Tegla Loroupe of Kenya at the 1998 Rotterdam Marathon. Records improve rapidly. It is quite possible that by the time you read these words, some woman will have run faster than 2:20. Yet at one point, female runners were restricted to races of a few miles, because male officials believed women were incapable of going much farther.

Impossible goals sometimes prove possible. Most people, of course, never come close to achieving the times of the running elite. At the 1998 Chicago Marathon, the median time for male finishers was 4:04:20, meaning that half the men ran faster, half ran slower. The median time at Chicago for females was 4:31:13. But that same year at the Los Angeles Marathon (hillier course, warmer weather), male and female finishers had median times of 4:50:07 and 5:30:20. The Boston Marathon, which attracts a faster field because of its qualification standards, had median times of 3:18:24 and 3:41:28 in 1991. The Chicago data is probably typical for most marathons, according to Basil Honikman of the USA Track and Field Road Running Information Center. That means that if you want to rise above average, the goal for a man should be 4:00 and for a woman, 4:30.

At the bottom of the scale, some finishers at the New York City, Los Angeles, and Honolulu marathons that same year finished slower than 10 hours. The slowest marathon may have come at Honolulu one year where one man took more than 29 hours! (He fell, was injured, went to the hospital, and returned the following day to finish.)

Although statisticians find it convenient to talk about median or average times, I like to believe that there are no average runners. I consider us all *above* average—at least as individuals. When you even begin to consider the possibility of finishing your first marathon, you move well beyond anything that might be described as "average."

Time as a goal becomes irrelevant for someone attempting a marathon. The only goal worth considering for first-time marathoners is the finish line.

CHOOSING YOUR FIRST MARATHON

Selecting your first marathon may be a critical decision. Unless you decide to run a small local marathon because it is near home (a logical reason), you will probably be best served by entering one of the big-city marathons. With more people in the field, you will feel less lonely running back in the pack, and there usually is more crowd support. If you have never felt loved before, you should try running one of the big-city marathons with spectators lining the course from start to finish, cheering everyone on, slow or fast.

In fact, the back-of-the-packers get most of the cheers. Because they're moving slower, they take a longer time to pass those who are applauding. Often the leaders dart by so quickly, spectators just stare in awe. It is a sad commentary on the popularity of running that most spectators know little about who is leading the race.

Don Kardong, a senior writer for *Runner's World*, once covered the Boston Marathon from his hotel room. The day before the race, he had scouted the course to write down the telephone numbers of pay phones at various intervals along the way. On race day he called each booth at the proper moment and asked whoever answered for a report. "Who's leading?" he asked one person who answered.

"Just a minute," said the respondent, noting that the lead pack had not yet passed the booth. When he returned to the booth, the man announced, "Some cop on a motorcycle."

Thus no one should feel embarrassed at running far in the rear. Another advantage of a big field is that if you stand in the back row, it may take you five or ten minutes to even cross the starting line, relieving you of any latent desire for a fast time. With any luck, the field will be so big that the beginners will also be forced to cover the first several miles at a walk or a very slow jog, thus storing energy for the last few miles.

At the Motor City Marathon in Detroit in 1991, I decided to do just that. With a field of about 2,000 and a wide starting area, it took me about a minute to reach and cross the starting line. I was last among the starting group across the line, although several runners who must have arrived late soon passed me. I walked most of the first mile before eventually breaking into a gentle jog, but I ran the second half of the race faster than the first, and finished comfortably—or at least as comfortable as one can be when finishing a 26-mile race. Starting slow is an intelligent approach to running the marathon—one, I admit, that I don't always take.

The dynamics of race starts began to change toward the end of the 1990s with the arrival of the ChampionChip, a small device that runners attach to one of their shoes. As you cross an electronic carpet at the starting line, your exact start time is automatically recorded. Additional carpets along the course record when you pass set points (and help catch cheaters who don't go the full distance). Finally, as you cross the finish line, your exact time on the course is recorded. This device has been a godsend for runners qualifying for Boston, since all starting delays become irrelevant.

Leading the five-hour pacing team at the 1998 Chicago Marathon, I held my group back until most of the field had gone. We crossed the starting line eight minutes after the official start, and failed to encounter the usual slowdown in the first few miles. In fact, the only delays came between miles 15 and 20 as we caught and passed runners who had gone out too fast and were walking or jogging more slowly than our steady pace.

Another reason to run big marathons, at least your first time, is that these events often are better financed, with better support systems and more volunteers, resulting in more aid stations and everything else you need to make your race more enjoyable. Not to be overlooked are the glitz and glamour that surround many big-city events. Bands playing and balloons in the air may not make you run faster, but these diversions may make you feel better.

Many marathoners probably could learn a lesson from beginners. Having completed one or two marathons comfortably, though relatively untrained, beginners often get caught in the trap of thinking that faster is better, that they have to run each race progressively speedier to justify the time they have spent in training. They forget the first marathoner's joy. But sometimes you have to return to your roots by running *slower* than your potential. Realistically speaking, few of your non-running friends will know or care whether you fail to run a PR. All they want to hear is that you finished.

As with other endeavors, it is a basic tenet of marathon running that rewards come to those who persevere. We all begin with various levels of talent, but we improve in relation to the amount of effort we expend and how we maximize that talent.

Chapter 4

Learning How to

TRAIN RIGHT

Bill Fitzgerald remembers his attitude about people he saw running in the park in the years before he became a runner: "I thought, why would anyone waste their time doing that? It can't be fun. I didn't see any smiles on their faces."

The year was 1986. Fitzgerald was 36. He comments: "That's an age when males frequently encounter their own mortality." Though he had played some sports growing up in suburban Oak Park, Illinois—football, basketball, softball, hockey—Fitzgerald was never quite good enough to make a team. He lived a somewhat sedentary life as a security administrator for Chicago's Water Reclamation District. He had begun to gain weight. "I decided, let's try this thing called jogging," he says.

Fitzgerald went to Portage Park near his apartment and started to jog. A sidewalk wound through the park, covering a distance of about a mile. He planned to go one lap—but failed! "I got mad at myself," he recalls. "I vowed to finish that lap. I returned each day and ran just a little bit farther. Seeing my improvement gave me a sense of accomplishment." When Fitzgerald finally finished a one-mile lap, he felt like he had "won the Boston Marathon."

Fitzgerald continued to run and eventually completed a 5-K race. Friends suggested he run the Shamrock Shuffle, a popular Chicago 8-K held each March. Uncertain how to train for this longer event, Fitzgerald unwisely doubled his training mileage, got shinsplints (a general term for soreness in the front lower leg), and had to miss the race. By the spring of 1989, he had met an experienced runner

33

named C. C. Becker at a local health club. With Becker serving as his mentor, Fitzgerald finished the Shuffle as well as a half marathon in April. At that point he figured he was ready to attempt a full marathon. Becker suggested that Fitzgerald join the Lincoln Park

SECRETS OF SUCCESS

In the fall of 1979, Bill Wenmark, a former ice hockey player from Deephaven, Minnesota, decided to run his first marathon despite having trained only a few dozen miles in preparation. He finished, but it took him nearly six hours, and the experience was less than pleasant. "The three days after the race were the most miserable days of my life," Wenmark recalls. "Every bone ached. Every muscle ached. Even my fingernails ached!"

Nevertheless, Wenmark continued in the sport and currently heads the American Lung Association Running Club (ALARC). He now trains new runners to finish the Twin Cities and Grandma's Marathons. "One of the reasons I'm successful with first timers is that I made every mistake preparing for my first 26-miler," he says.

Wenmark uses a simple schedule involving a long run each weekend with rest days twice a week: Mondays and Fridays. Tuesday and Thursday runs are 6 to 8 miles; Wednesday runs reach 13 miles by the end of the buildup. He also recommends additional cross-training workouts, usually on an exercise bike, but also some strength training.

The training program works. Through the 1998 Twin Cities Marathon, Wenmark had coached 1832 runners to finish their first marathon. Of that number, only 8 failed to finish, and 5 of those succeeded in later tries. Wenmark points to 15 secrets of success for first-time marathoners.

1. Commit yourself. Run your first marathon for the right reasons. *You* must want to run the marathon—not because your boss did it or your spouse did it.
2. Loosen up. Recipe training schedules are fine, but everyone is different. Be willing to adapt your training to your ability and time availability.
3. Seek support. Look for others to run with. Join a class or a running club. Long runs go more smoothly if you don't have to tackle them alone.
4. Get smart. Marathoning is a mental discipline, not just a physical one. Read books. Attend clinics. Ask questions of experienced runners and coaches. Get the best advice.

Pacers. The club met Saturday mornings at the Chicago Area Runners Association (CARA) message board beside the jogging path in Lincoln Park. The Pacers would run 5 to 10 miles then adjourn to a nearby café for breakfast.

5. Think positive. You *are* a special person. Reward yourself with self-praise as you achieve each interim goal en route to the marathon.

6. Don't overtrain. Twenty miles is plenty for your longest training distance. Save the sacred territory between 20 and 26 miles for the race itself. This will make finishing the full marathon distance an extra-special experience.

7. Practice hard. The marathon offers a classic example of success rewarded. If you want to be successful in anything, you must practice.

8. Train thoroughly. Shortcuts don't work. You can't cram for a marathon.

9. Pretrain. Everything will go more easily if you develop a proper level of base training before starting the marathon buildup. Proper preparation will help prevent injury.

10. Try it out. Test anything you might encounter during a marathon in practice. This includes everything from race equipment (shoes, socks, racing gear, sunglasses), endurance drinks or gels, to prerace meals.

11. Drink up. Learn how to drink on the run, specifically how to *stop* running to drink more. If it's going to take you five or more hours to finish, you may also want to practice eating (and more importantly, *what* to eat) on the run.

12. Watch your weight. Seek an ideal weight for your height and build. You don't want to carry extra pounds, but you also don't want to diet—or risk dehydration—to lose too much weight.

13. Cross-train. Doing other aerobic activities occasionally, such as cycling, swimming, or even walking can help you recover on non-running days. Weight training provides the upper body strength needed for the final miles. (Yes, your arms also get tired during a 26.2-mile run!)

14. Slow down. Beginners should avoid speedwork. Concentrate on finishing your first marathon, not finishing it fast.

15. Get an attitude. Learn to love your new lifestyle. Discover the meaning of good health. Focus on the final goal: the marathon finish line.

After one workout, a woman runner told Fitzgerald, "Some guy's starting a class next week to prepare people for the Chicago Marathon." Fitzgerald and the woman attended the first meeting of the class in July. About 35 runners appeared. The meeting was at O'Sullivan's Public House, "a real Irish shot-and-a-beer joint," recalls Fitzgerald. The "some guy" turned out to be Brian Piper, a computer systems analyst and member of the CARA board. Piper outlined a 15-week training program that included a gradual mileage buildup approaching the marathon. The class also featured a series of clinics with speakers offering nutritional and medical advice. Chicago Marathon race director Carey Pinkowski (a top-notch runner in his competitive days, including a college career at Villanova) also appeared to encourage class members.

Piper, like Fitzgerald, was typical of the new breed of runner attracted to running for its fitness benefits. Piper had competed as a swimmer in high school and as a freshman at the University of Iowa. But he quit college swimming because it was too time-consuming, and instead he began to do some running with members of the track team who lived in his dormitory. "I had to struggle to keep up," he says, "but it established running as an alternative activity for staying in shape."

Nevertheless, a year out of college and working for the Regional Transportation Authority in Chicago, Piper found himself 25 pounds overweight. His motivation was the same as Fitzgerald's: to lose weight and get fit. Piper selected the 1981 Chicago Marathon as his goal, then made all the common beginners' mistakes while training and in the race: "I didn't do enough long runs. I ran everything at the same pace. I failed to take enough water. I wore cotton shorts, which resulted in bad chafing. Everything was strictly trial and error. Other than what you read in *Runner's World*, it was hard to get good training advice." He finished his first marathon in 3:54, but he was forced to walk a lot. "There were a lot of 7:00 miles in the beginning, and a lot of 10:00 miles near the end," Piper admits.

Undeterred, Piper set as his next goal qualifying for the Boston Marathon. It took five years, but in 1986 he finally ran a 2:58:25 at the Twin Cities Marathon and was Boston bound. He was then 32 years old. "I began to think that there ought to be some way to help first-time marathoners avoid all the mistakes I had made."

At a CARA meeting in the spring of 1989, Piper suggested to executive director Matt Mimlitz that the organization sponsor a marathon training class. That brought Piper and Fitzgerald together at O'Sullivan's Pub: one the teacher, one the pupil. It would be an encounter from which many runners—both in Chicago and elsewhere—would benefit greatly.

THE ST. LOUIS APPROACH

Piper brought with him to Chicago a 15-week training program borrowed from the St. Louis Track Club, which sponsored its own marathon class. There were training schedules for runners whose base mileage was 30 (novice), 40 (intermediate), or 50 (advanced) miles. The program followed a hard/easy approach, featuring two or three hard days a week and two or three hard weeks a month. Runners did long runs on Tuesdays, Thursdays, and Sundays (the Sunday runs were the longest). Wednesdays and Saturdays they ran easy. Mondays and Fridays were rest days. The pattern went like this:

Monday: No running most weeks for novice runners. Intermediate and advanced runners ran 4 to 5 miles.

Tuesday: Long runs between 6 to 10 miles with the peak coming in the 10th and 12th weeks. Intermediate and advanced runners ran somewhat more mileage.

Wednesday: An easy run of 4 to 5 miles for novices, with intermediate and advanced runners doing a mile or two more.

Thursday: The second longest run of the week. The novice buildup went from 7 to 12 miles. Intermediate and advanced runners did more runs at peak distances of 12 and 13 miles.

Friday: No running for novice and intermediate runners. Advanced runners ran 6 miles this day.

Saturday: An easy run of 4 to 5 miles for each category of runners.

Sunday: The weekend long run. Novices began at 9 miles and reached 21 in the 12th week. Intermediates went from 11 to 22 miles with three runs over 20. Advanced runners went from 13 to 23 miles with five runs over 20.

The unique feature of the St. Louis program was its step up, step back approach in the mileage buildup. Miles did not increase in a continuous ascending line (9, 10, 11, 12, and so forth) but rather in a series of waves: step up to one level, then step back for recovery, then up to a higher level.

This was the schedule that Fitzgerald and the other 34 members of CARA's Chicago Marathon training class followed in the first year. In many respects, the approach was similar to what Fitzgerald had done instinctively when he first started to jog in Portage Park. He had gone a little bit farther each day, and grew stronger day by day until finally he could finish a mile. In the CARA class, he went farther every week until finally he could finish a marathon. All marathon training programs are built on similar progressions. Fitzgerald finished his first marathon in 3:54, coincidentally the same time that his mentor, Piper, had achieved in his first marathon eight years before. "I finished feeling a lot better than Brian," boasts Fitzgerald. "I had better coaching."

Fitzgerald would eventually qualify for Boston by running 3:20:54 in the 1992 Chicago Marathon. By that time the marathon prep class

ST. LOUIS TRACK CLUB MILEAGE PROGRESSION

Week	LONGEST RUNS			WEEKLY MILEAGE		
	Novice	Intermediate	Advanced	Novice	Intermediate	Advanced
1	9	11	13	30	40	50
2	11	13	16	34	44	55
3	10	12	14	36	45	55
4	13	15	18	40	50	61
5	15	16	20	44	53	64
6	10	13	15	36	47	57
7	16	18	21	46	55	65
8	18	20	22	52	59	66
9	13	15	17	41	51	60
10	20	21	22	56	61	67
11	14	16	18	42	52	62
12	21	22	23	57	62	69
13	16	17	17	49	53	61
14	14	14	15	42	47	58
15	26.2	26.2	26.2	44	50	52

had expanded to several hundred runners annually. CARA's new executive director David Patt continued his support of the class, as did marathon race director Pinkowski. Fitzgerald began to share leadership duties with Piper, becoming codirector. In the Chicago Marathon training class's 10th anniversary year of 1998, nearly 1,000 runners participated. To meet demand, the class expanded its midweek clinics to serve four areas of the city: central, north, west, and south. The class featured weekend long runs for each area class on Saturdays. The central and west classes also offered Sunday runs. Drive through Chicago's Lincoln Park on a weekend morning during the summer months and you'll see runners swarming like bees on the jogging paths. Many, if not most, of them are training for the marathon.

A key feature of the Chicago Marathon training class is its volunteer group leaders, approximately a hundred of them, who pace runners during their long training runs. Regardless of whether you want to run a 7:00 pace or a 12:00 pace, someone is there to guide you—and offer midworkout training suggestions. "Our volunteers are the strength of our program," says Piper. "If you have a question, you can get it answered midstride."

Another reason for the popularity of the class is its social aspect: runners meeting runners. "It's easier to run in a group, and it's a lot more fun," says Piper. While running in the 1970s and 1980s may have been the province of baby boomers seeking to delay aging, running in the 1990s has become the province of Generation X, whose plan is *never* to grow old. Increasing numbers of the new crop of marathoners are female. (For example, in the inaugural Rock 'n' Roll Marathon in San Diego in 1998, female marathoners slightly outnumbered the male marathoners.) "We've got the best dating service in town," hints Fitzgerald. "Where would you rather meet your future spouse: Friday night in some smoky bar, or Saturday morning on the jogging path?"

And although enrollees may begin the class and still stay out late on Friday nights, after several weeks they realize that if they expect to run well early the next morning, they need to head home long before their carriage turns into a pumpkin. Usually this message sinks in by the fourth and fifth weeks, at which point the weekend long runs reach 9 and 10 miles.

Although the step up, step back pattern remains the same, the

Chicago mileage buildup now differs from that of the original St. Louis program. It has been a gradual evolution, not a sudden change. After the Chicago class's first marathon in 1989, Piper invited me to speak at its awards banquet. Several years later, with the number of participants increasing, I became a training consultant for the class. Over a period of time, we modified the training approach, expanding the time period from 15 to 18 weeks and also cutting back on the mileage in recognition that not everybody joins the class with a 30-to 50-mile base. Blessed with youthful enthusiasm, many of today's runners choose the marathon as their first race, never having seen the starting line of a 5-K. They also have busy lives, so they don't always have time for midweek runs that last more than an hour. By stretching less mileage over a longer period, we've found that we can reduce runners' risk of injury and increase their chance of success. At the same time, we also provide a separate training program (that includes speedwork) for runners seeking to improve their previous marathon times.

The Chicago Marathon training class follows this approach with its novice runners:

Monday: No running. It's important to rest after the weekend long runs.

Tuesday: Easy runs building from 3 to a maximum of 5 miles by the 14th week of the 18-week program. (This is in contrast to the St. Louis approach with its peak of 10 miles on Tuesdays.)

Wednesday: The second longest run of the week: 3 miles building to 10 by the 15th week.

Thursday: The same as Tuesday: an easy run from 3 to 5 miles.

Friday: No running. It's also important to rest *before* the weekend long runs

Saturday: The key to the marathon program: a long run that builds from 6 miles to 20 in the 15th week, but with step backs every third week to permit runners to gather energy for the next push upward.

Sunday: Cross-training of about an hour for recovery. This could be cycling, swimming, walking, or even some light jogging. Those who do their long runs on Sundays cross-train on Saturdays.

The maximum weekly mileage for the Chicago program is 40 miles in the 15th week when we do our 20-miler. In general, runners cover about as many miles during the rest of the week as they run

THE CHICAGO PROGRAM

Week	Mon.	Tue.	Wed.	Thur.	Fri.	Sat.	Sun.
18	rest	3 m run	3 m run	3 m run	rest	**6**	cross
17	rest	3 m run	3 m run	3 m run	rest	**7**	cross
16	rest	3 m run	4 m run	3 m run	rest	**5**	cross
15	rest	3 m run	4 m run	3 m run	rest	**9**	cross
14	rest	3 m run	5 m run	3 m run	rest	**10**	cross
13	rest	3 m run	5 m run	3 m run	rest	**7**	cross
12	rest	3 m run	6 m run	3 m run	rest	**12**	cross
11	rest	3 m run	6 m run	3 m run	rest	**13**	cross
10	rest	3 m run	7 m run	4 m run	rest	**10**	cross
9	rest	3 m run	7 m run	4 m run	rest	**15**	cross
8	rest	4 m run	8 m run	4 m run	rest	**16**	cross
7	rest	4 m run	8 m run	5 m run	rest	**12**	cross
6	rest	4 m run	9 m run	5 m run	rest	**18**	cross
5	rest	5 m run	9 m run	5 m run	rest	**14**	cross
4	rest	5 m run	10 m run	5 m run	rest	**20**	cross
3	rest	5 m run	8 m run	4 m run	rest	**12**	cross
2	rest	4 m run	6 m run	3 m run	rest	**8**	cross
1	rest	3 m run	4 m run	2 m run	rest	rest	**race**

in their long weekend run. (For instance, in Week 8 the long run is 16 miles; the total mileage that week is 32.) Of course, novice and intermediate runners do somewhat more mileage as they strive for improved times. The training schedule for novice runners is shown above, with weeks numbered from Week 18, the first week of training, to Week 1, the week before the marathon.

The Chicago program follows a very simple schedule, but it works, as thousands of runners have now proved. In fact, tens of thousands of runners follow this same schedule, which is posted on my Web site. There I provide even more detailed information: day-by-day instructions on how to train right to finish your first marathon.

"Running a marathon never will be easy," says Piper. "If it were easy, the challenge would be gone. But learning to train right can increase your enjoyment in both training for and running the race."

Chapter 5

The Truths of
MARATHON ACHIEVEMENT

D espite their lack of coaching credentials, Brian Piper and Bill Fitzgerald succeeded in Chicago by borrowing the best ideas from other marathon coaches from New York to Honolulu. Coaches generally have few secrets. They openly share information. Here are seven truths that can help you achieve success in your next marathon.

Truth Number One: Progressively longer runs will get you to the finish line.

Runners in Chicago begin 18 weeks before the race, with 6 miles for novices, 8 miles for intermediates, and 10 miles for advanced runners. Their maximum long run is 20 miles three weeks before the race, with novices running this far once, intermediates twice, and advanced runners three times.

Although the end point may be slightly different, most training programs center on some progressive buildup. Bill Wenmark, who trains runners for the Twin Cities and Grandma's Marathons, lets his experienced runners go as far as 30 miles for their long run, and Jeff Galloway takes his groups to 26 to 28 miles. Jack Scaff Jr., M.D., in Honolulu considers 15 miles sufficiently far in terms of the long run for first timers, provided their goal is only to finish the marathon. Portland's Bob Williams has runners go 20 to 23 miles on their last long run, but suggests that experienced runners get in six runs of 18 miles or more in the last two months. Robert Vaughan in Dallas favors running for a certain number of minutes as opposed to counting miles; his goal for a long run is 3 hours 30 minutes. Benji Durden (a former world-class marathoner turned coach) of Boulder, Colorado, feels the same.

Numbers aside, what all programs have in common—other than a loving, hands-on approach—is the progression. "It's the same in any sport," explains Piper. "If you were weight training, you'd begin with low weights and few reps. Progressively longer training runs are specific to the sport of marathon running."

Piper considers the psychological reasons for the buildup in weekly long runs to be equal to the physiological reasons. "You need to prepare yourself mentally," he says. "Riding four hours in a car can be very boring. You need to develop psychological strategies for combating that same boredom while running 26 miles."

During the months-long buildup for a marathon, weekly mileage increases along with the length of the long run. Beginners will often *double* their weekly mileage. For more advanced runners, a weekly mileage increase of 50 percent is common, depending on where they begin.

Truth Number Two: Scheduling rest days is the key to staying healthy.

Mileage buildups of the magnitude required to finish a marathon create stress. And one reason for the buildup is that stress creates strength. But too much stress is bad. Many runners have conditioned themselves mentally and physically to run every day with few days off to rest. This may be all right if you run easy, training for health and enjoyment with an occasional 5-K thrown in for spice. If you are peaking for a marathon, however, failure to take rest days is a ticket to injury, suggests Dr. Scaff. This is particularly true for first timers. Says Scaff: "Any person who runs more than five days a week in the first year will have a 100 percent chance of injury!"

Vaughan agrees: "We tell our class it's better to show up at the starting line undertrained, rather than to be injured and not get there."

Dr. Scaff notes that the musculoskeletal system generally requires 48 hours to recover after hard work. "The whole purpose of training is to break the body down so it will rebuild itself stronger than before. It's when you fail to allow time for the rebuilding phase that problems occur." Overtraining can result in muscle injuries and stress fractures (usually tiny breaks in the legs or bones in the foot) that halt training, or in upper respiratory illnesses and frequent bouts of fatigue that limit performance.

To avoid the stress that comes with overtraining, bracket the hardest workouts of the week (specifically the long runs) with easy days, and/or days of total rest. Dr. Scaff also promotes cross-training (walking, swimming, cycling) as one way to reduce the stress of the marathon buildup.

Truth Number Three: Taking one step back allows you to take two steps forward.

Taking rest days is not enough to guard against the dangers of overtraining; most successful marathon programs also include rest weeks in which runners both cut mileage and eliminate the weekend long run. Chuck Cornett of Orange Park, Florida promotes a marathon training program in which every fourth or fifth week features a 50 percent drop in mileage. Our class in Chicago eliminates the long run every third week. Portland's Bob Williams suggests a 25 percent mileage drop every other week, particularly as mileage mounts toward the end of the program.

Williams explains the rationale behind this step-back approach: "When you get up beyond 15 miles for your long run, or 40 miles for your weekly mileage, some people can handle that level of stress, but many cannot. It becomes a grind. The intensity of effort required to cover that many miles can be daunting to some people."

Williams believes psychological recovery is as important as physiological recovery. "Running 20 miles in a workout the first time may be euphoric, but it's also emotionally draining," he says. "You can slow down to go the distance, but you're still spending a lot of time on your feet. Just focusing your mind for several hours of time can be exhausting."

Having regularly scheduled step-back weeks makes it possible to survive the stress load that is part and parcel of the high mileage necessary for successful marathon training. You relax, knowing that you can store strength to push ahead to the next level of achievement.

Truth Number Four: Speed training can be a double-edged sword.
San Diego's Thom Hunt knew the value of speed training when

he prepared for the 2:12:14 PR he achieved in the 1986 New Jersey Waterfront Marathon, but as a coach of other runners, he knows that methods and goals are different for first timers. "They don't need sophisticated training methods," says Hunt. "Their main goal is to finish. Speed training gets in the way. It can unnecessarily raise the risk of injury."

One reason that it is not a good idea to add the stress of trying to run fast to the stress of trying to run progressively farther is that it is one stress too many—even for experienced runners. Danny Perez, a coach from Norwalk, California, offers another reason: "Elite runners often spend 20 minutes a day working on the flexibility it requires to run fast. Beginners don't have time for that. You put them on a track, and they'll explode."

Nevertheless, once you have finished that first marathon, and finished several more in faster times, you may reach a plateau in performance that can be frustrating if you are one of those people who are motivated by improvement. When this happens, speed training can be that "something extra" that offers you the hope of a breakthrough.

"That's when improving the *quality* of training can help," admits Hunt. "Then you might consider fartlek, intervals, hills, and the other tricks of the speed trade." Even then, runners should consider reserving speed training for other times of the year, and not try to do it as part of their high-mileage marathon buildup.

"You want to run fast," warns Hunt, "but you don't want to run hurt."

Truth Number Five: Learning pace and learning to race are the two most critical skills.

"Anybody can run 26 miles if they run the right pace," advises Vaughan. "If they try to run too fast, they'll crash. If they run slowly enough at the start, they'll make it." That strategy works well for beginners, but more experienced runners must fine-tune their pace if they hope to achieve peak performance. Improving pace entails some risk, since even a slight miscalculation can result in failure.

The pacing teams that have become popular in many marathons, including Chicago, take a lot of the guesswork out of staying on pace during a race. One way to fine-tune your pace is to include some training at race pace during your buildup. Whether your pace is 6:00 miles (2:37 at the finish) or 10:00 miles (4:22 finish), you need to know how it feels to achieve that pace. Running occasional races will help you test your limits and determine your approximate marathon pace.

Picking that pace, however, takes skill. (For more information on pace, see chapter 14.) "You need to do some racing," Vaughan says. "Some newcomers are afraid of racing. Running occasional races during the marathon buildup will help you get used to the race experience: how to warm up, where to pin your number, what it feels like running in a crowd, how to take liquids, when and what to eat before and after, whether or not your shoes will cause blisters. It's always best to make your mistakes in unimportant races, so that you can make corrections for marathon day."

Like most coaches, Vaughan warns against racing too often during the marathon buildup period. "Once every third or fourth week seems to be the limit," he suggests. "Otherwise you risk tearing yourself down." Prudence also suggests cutting back overall mileage and skipping the long run during weeks that include a test race.

Truth Number Six: Tapering—reducing your training in order to be better rested for an upcoming big race—is both an art and a science.

Few coaches agree on what day runners should cut back training and begin resting for a race. Depending on the individual, the prerace taper can vary from three days to three weeks. Al Dimicco, who since 1984 has directed a training clinic for the Vulcan Marathon in Birmingham, Alabama, finally settled on a two-week taper for his charges.

"Too many runners want to train right up to the marathon, but you need to let your body recover after all the hard training." Dimicco recommends a 50 percent cutback in mileage during the last two weeks, with very little running the final two or three days prior to the race. "Just enough to keep from going crazy," he says.

Tapering not only permits any damaged muscles to heal; it also promotes maximum glycogen (the fuel used by working muscles) storage within your leg muscles on race day. "You don't want to go into the race depleted of glycogen," warns Dimicco. He believes that it matters little whether you're an elite runner or a beginner; you still need a two- or three-week taper.

Although your mileage drops during the taper, the speed at which you run that mileage should not. The taper period is a good time to practice race pace, but at much shortened distances. One way to cut mileage is to convert "easy" run days into days of complete rest. You may want to jog easily the day before the marathon just to reduce nervousness, but don't go too far. Arrive at the starting line rested and ready to go.

Truth Number Seven: You'll go only as far as your motivation will carry you.

Bill Wenmark is among the most successful coaches when it comes to motivating runners. Bruce Brothers of the St. Paul, Minnesota *Pioneer Press* once wrote of him, "Wenmark could motivate a penguin to fly."

But Wenmark claims he does not supply motivation. "The motivation has to come from within," he says. He feels that people sometimes underestimate the effort it requires to run 26 miles. He says that finishing a marathon requires courage, perseverance, and commitment: "If running marathons were easy, everybody would be doing it—but they're not. You've got to be committed to your training. If you're not focused on being a success, you won't be successful. You'll never succeed if you're not willing to prepare."

While Wenmark believes you can't teach commitment, he knows how to *facilitate* it by providing runners—beginners and experts—with a supportive environment. "People can enroll in a class," says Wenmark, "but unless they have that desire, there's nothing I can do for them. I can't run the marathon for them. I can't train for them. I can't stay out of the refrigerator for them. If you want to succeed in the marathon—or in any other activity in life—you need to be ready to pay the price."

Running 26 miles is one activity for which you get what you paid for. Runners willing to train properly, taking careful note of the seven truths listed in this chapter, will find that the marathon can be an experience that provides much more joy than pain.

Chapter 6

Striving to
IMPROVE

In lectures to beginning marathoners, I always suggest that they pick a finishing time goal a half-hour slower than they expect to achieve. That strategy ensures two achievements: (1) They'll finish that first marathon and probably finish it comfortably, with a smile on their face, and (2) If they ever run a second marathon, they're almost guaranteed to set a PR by finishing faster. That always gets a laugh. But it's very true. Enjoy your first marathon as much as you can. Have fun, because if you continue as a marathoner and attempt to run progressively faster and faster, you may experience some uncomfortable moments, particularly as you push against the edge of your ability. Pushing yourself can be fun—testing yourself at that edge, striving to improve.

How do you improve as a marathoner? How do you run faster? These are key questions for many runners. Getting to the finish line of your first marathon is just a matter of preparation—as we prove every year with the Chicago Marathon training class. Either through talent or with the help of a well-structured and progressive training program (or both), most people who set their minds on becoming marathoners succeed.

If they're hooked on the sport, their next goal is to get better. With every attempt, they seek to run their fastest marathon, whether it's their 3rd or their 33rd race. It's not that simple, but it's also not that difficult.

Here are some tips for those hoping to improve.

TIPS FROM A TOP RUNNER

For the October 1991 issue of *Runner's World*, I coauthored an article with Doug Kurtis, a 2:13 marathoner from Northville, Michigan. The article was touted on the magazine's cover as "26.2 Proven Ways to Run a Better Marathon." Four points in particular apply to the task faced by all of us as we seek to improve our performance. Here, in Kurtis's words, are these major points.

Consistency. The biggest key for me is that I'm built to run marathons: 5'7" and 130 pounds. But another factor is my consistency. My mileage remains the same week after week. There's no downtime, no uptime, no breaks. I could probably run 150 to 160 miles a week, but I would have a much harder time avoiding injuries. I recover well, and rarely get injured. *Message: When you're consistent with your training week after week, there's much less chance of entering a race undertrained or overtrained—both reasons why runners get hurt or perform poorly. This is true for athletes in other sports as well.*

Mileage. I have a strong incentive to do my twice-daily workouts and put in my 105 miles a week. High mileage permits me to run sub-2:20 marathons rather than run somewhat slower. Because of this, I win races and receive invitations to travel all over the world with expenses paid. For someone trying to run 3:20 or 4:20, the incentive might not be quite as high. Each person has to determine what's important to him and use that as a guide to dictate training level. *Message: Everybody has a mileage level that's best for him.*

Intensity. A lot of people believe they have to train hard all the time. They feel they're not getting anything out of a workout unless they're running race pace. That's not true. For me, a 7:00 pace is fast enough, and I often run slower. I'll sometimes start a workout running an 8:00 or 9:00 pace. When I'm training 105 miles a week, there's no way I can run hard every workout. Two things can happen: You can burn out if you run hard every day, or you can be injured. *Message: You can achieve a lot with slow workouts.*

Rest. Usually, I average 15 to 20 rest days a year. I don't plan them in advance, but it's usually when something comes up: travel, or illness, or a family outing. It's good for me, and I probably should rest more often. One of the advantages of keeping your training consistent year-round is that when you do take a short rest, you lose very little of your training edge. *Message: Don't be afraid to take days off.*

THE SECRETS OF IMPROVEMENT

If you're a beginning runner who has just finished your first marathon, you'll continue to improve if you do nothing else but train consistently.

"When you're consistent with your training week after week," as Kurtis says, "there's much less chance of entering a race undertrained or overtrained, both reasons why people get hurt or run poorly." Most established training programs for first-time marathoners last three months or more. Class leaders guide their students through a graduated schedule, the main feature being a long run that gets progressively longer (usually from 6 to 20 miles) as marathon day approaches. Students are usually sent to the starting line undertrained and well rested, because experience has shown that to be the best way to ensure that they finish.

Better to be safe than sorry. And who can argue with success? Thus, most well-coached, first-time marathoners run their races without the training necessary to achieve peak performance, and run comfortably slower than their talents might allow. They finish thinking they probably could have run somewhat faster if they had trained harder. They're right. They can. And so can you.

STEADY DOES IT

Even without adopting a refined training schedule, most marathoners can improve merely by continuing to train at or near the same level. After three months, you will have only begun to reap the benefits of that level of dedication. Your undertrained body will continue to improve, as long as you don't overtrain it. So keep running those long runs on the weekends, whether 20 miles or somewhat less. Keep doing a medium run in the middle of the week. Take those one or two rest days weekly as suggested in the novice training schedule in chapter 4. Fill in the rest of the week with runs at various short distances, and mix in some running at near your marathon pace. The accumulation of miles over a period of time will help you to improve. You will get better.

The important thing is to maintain your fitness at a steady level. Research by Edward F. Coyle, Ph.D., at the University of Texas at Austin, suggests that runners begin to "detrain" (lose their fitness) after 48 to 76 hours, and that it takes two days of retraining to regain the fitness lost for every single day of training that is skipped. That doesn't mean you should never rest, but if you take long periods off, it will take you longer to come back.

That is why Kurtis preaches consistency. You don't need to maintain continuous peak condition, but settle on a consistent level of training that you know you can maintain for 12 months of the year. When it comes time to aim for a specific marathon, you can increase your level of training—slightly. The important goal is to maintain an effective endurance base.

The American College of Sports Medicine (ACSM) guidelines for fitness suggest three to four days of exercise a week, 20 to 60 minutes a day. That's the minimum fitness formula for maintaining good health, beyond which Kenneth H. Cooper, M.D., president and founder of the Cooper Aerobics Center in Dallas, suggests you're exercising for other reasons. For the marathoner, that will be true: Your reason is to stay in shape to run marathons. You'll need to—and want to—run more than the time allotted in Dr. Cooper's formula. But the basic pattern offered in the ACSM guidelines still applies to marathoners.

For four years, I coached the boys' and girls' cross-country teams at Elston High School in Michigan City, and I also worked with the distance runners during the track season. Between seasons I encouraged my runners to keep diaries, and I tried to examine those diaries periodically to monitor the students' conditioning programs. I discovered that the less dedicated ones would train hard for three or four days, but then they would miss three or four days of running. They thought they were staying in shape, but they were actually sliding backward—as they proved when they appeared for practice the first day of the season. The ones who trained consistently improved; the others did not.

As a result, I told them: Never go two days without running. One day of missed training was no problem. That qualifies as rest. But two or three lost days in a row (taking into account Dr. Coyle's research) equaled lost conditioning—and inevitably meant poorer performances once the season began.

FINDING YOUR MILEAGE LEVEL

At his peak, Kurtis was a high-mileage trainer, and that was one of the secrets of his success. You can't compete successfully at the elite level in the marathon unless you average more than 100 miles a week. Most runners would crash if they attempted to reach this mileage level, and Kurtis does not necessarily recommend that everybody do so. He says, "Everybody has a mileage level that's best for them." Determining that level is tricky and may take several years of experimentation, but once you have reached a comfortable level, you can reap the benefits of success.

Norm Green, a Baptist minister from Wayne, Pennsylvania, who ran his first marathon at age 49 (achieving an eventual PR of 2:25:51 at age 52) succeeded on 55 miles a week. During my years of peak performance, I found that I competed well in marathons on a weekly training level around 75 miles. On those one or two occasions when I could edge my training mileage above 100 and hold it there for several months, I achieved peak performances. But I risked injury by doing so. And also boredom, because I found the twice-daily workouts necessary to achieve that mileage robbed running of much of its joy.

Today, I find 20 to 30 miles weekly a more acceptable training level when I'm running 5-K races. When I'm aiming for a marathon, I try to push that level to 40 miles, with most of the extra mileage gained by adding one progressively longer run once a week. Think about it: All you need do to increase your weekly mileage from 20 to 40 is add a single workout of 20 miles.

The best way to determine your optimum mileage level is to keep a training diary. You can find various diaries at bookstores for recording your training, and there are even software programs that let you keep daily workout records in your computer. Or you can simply mark mileage on a wall calendar.

I record my workouts on special diary pages I keep in small, three-ring notebooks. There's a row of such notebooks on a shelf in my office, one for each year. I started the practice while Fred Wilt was coaching me in the 1960s. (Fred was a 1948 and 1952 Olympian from Lafayette, Indiana; he later coached the women's teams at Purdue University.) Each day, I recorded my workouts and related information. At the end of the week, I mailed Fred my diary pages for critiquing. Later, I designed a special diary format similar to his, and had pages printed at a local printer for me and a few others to use.

My diary has spaces for the time of my run, the location, temperature, surface, distance, and what I did to warm up or cool down. There's also room for comments, as well as boxes to record pace per mile in races or interval quarters run in workouts. This system sounds complicated, but it actually takes less than a minute each day to record this information. Then when things go wrong—or right—I can examine my training and determine the reasons. These diaries prove very valuable when I am writing articles for *Runner's World* and books such as this.

During special periods of time—such as when I'm preparing for a marathon or peaking for maximum performance at the World Veterans Championships—I take poster board and a black marker and make my own diary calendars showing three, six, or nine months, whatever the training for that particular race requires. I tack the poster-sized calendar to a cork wall in my basement that I pass each day before and after running. It serves as both a visual record of what I have done, and a reminder of what I have to do. In addition to what I write in my diary, I mark weekly mileage totals and sometimes specific key workouts, such as the distance of my long run.

I use my record-keeping system as motivation, but also as a safety net. If I notice that I have run four consecutive weeks at the 40-mile-plus level (which is high for me now), I may think, "Hmmmm. Maybe I should back off my training for a week to avoid getting injured."

Finding the appropriate training level is not easy—particularly because that level may change as you get stronger or get older—but it is essential if you want to improve as a marathoner.

SLOWING IT DOWN

If there's one difference between fast runners and those who finish back in the pack, it's that the fast runners seem to have no qualms about running slowly. They're not embarrassed about it. Kurtis says, "You can achieve a lot with slow workouts." He was quite happy to train at a 7:00 pace, nearly two minutes a mile slower than his race pace in marathons, and he sometimes started workouts running at 8:00 or 9:00 pace.

I feel the same way as Kurtis, although at this point in my career, I run much slower than that. In fact, I'll do many workouts at a 10:00 pace, or slower. If you station yourself near my house with a spyglass, you may even catch me cruising in at the end of a long run at 12:00 a mile. That pace is quite different from the paces I might run in a 5-K or 10-K, or even a marathon, but my goal is to perform well in important races, not in every daily workout.

The important message in Kurtis's comment is not that he trains slowly, but that he trains differently each day. If I had to cite one mistake made by inexperienced marathoners when they seek to improve their performance, it is that they run too many of their miles at the same pace, and over the same distance. There's little variety, and that limits their improvement.

If I'm running slowly on one day, it's probably because I ran hard the day before—or want to run hard the next day. To improve, you need to add intensity to your program. You may not necessarily need to run sprints on the track, but you need to at least run as fast as race pace. Very few runners can run race pace day after day. Green was one of those rare runners: At his peak, he averaged faster than 6:00 miles in training. I did too, in my peak years. Most runners, however, would break if they attempted to duplicate that feat—which Norm is first to admit. (The last time I saw Norm at a masters track meet in Barbados, he conceded that he had abandoned his practice of running every workout hard.) In order to train at a high level of intensity on certain days, most of us need to train at a low level of intensity on other days. That's where slow running comes in.

SCIENTIFICALLY SPEAKING

From a scientific standpoint, slow running is important for several reasons.

Caloric burn. It varies from runner to runner, depending on size and metabolism, but most of us burn 100 calories for every mile we run. Burn 3,600 calories by running 36 miles and you lose one pound. But it doesn't matter how fast you run those miles. You can even walk and burn the same number of calories per mile. Calorie loss is related to foot-pounds: the amount of effort (that is, energy) it takes to push a body of a specific weight forward. You can run a 5:00 mile or a 10:00 mile, and you'll still burn 100 calories for covering the identical distance.

One means of attaining maximum performance is to achieve optimum body weight and an optimum percentage of body fat. You can do that just as easily with long, steady distance: It will take you somewhat longer than if you ran those miles fast, but you're less likely to become injured.

Sparing glycogen. Exercise physiologists also say that when you run slowly, your body has time to metabolize fat as a source of energy. When you run fast your body burns glycogen, a derivative of carbohydrate, as its preferred energy source. Glycogen is stored in the muscles and is a more efficient fuel in the sense that the body can metabolize it more rapidly than fat. But by training slowly, you apparently teach your muscles to become more efficient at also metabolizing fat, thus sparing glycogen stores for those last few miles in the marathon.

NO RUNNING

With that idea in mind, realize that no running is as important a part of the marathoner's training guide as resting. That may sound somewhat confusing at first, but I can't emphasize enough the importance of rest. Kurtis, who averaged 15 to 20 rest days a year, says he wasn't afraid to take days off. That amounts to one or two days off a month—which isn't much—but some runners don't even rest that much. In *Lore of Running*, Timothy Noakes, M.D., analyzed the training patterns of several dozen expert runners. He looked at reasons they failed and reasons they succeeded. For those who failed, often the reason was that they trained too hard and were too unwilling to take days off.

A prime example is Ron Hill, a British marathoner with a 2:09:28 best, whom Dr. Noakes suspected was as much interested in keeping his streak of double workouts unbroken as he was in winning the 1972 Olympic marathon. An earlier British runner, Jim Peters, trained relentlessly, day after day, almost without pause, once running half a dozen miles at a 5:00 pace the day before setting one of his world records. Yet in two of his most important races (the 1952 Olympics and the 1954 Commonwealth Games), Peters failed to finish. In the 1954 race, on a hot day in British Columbia, he collapsed while leading by several miles, even though he was in sight of the finish line. He retired after that race out of fear that his intense will might cause him to seriously hurt himself. Dr. Noakes suggests that had Peters alternated hard and easy training days, and tapered for his races—common practices among marathoners today—he might have achieved even greater success.

Knowing when to back off and take a complete day off—or even more—is one of the secrets of marathon success. It is not easy, since the traditional work ethic that has proved successful for many people suggests that more is better. That training calendar on my basement wall would be more of a hindrance than a help if it pushed me to run extra miles just to achieve mileage levels I may have planned months ago—without considering whether I have a cold, or failed to get enough sleep the night before, or am overly fatigued because of having spent most of the previous day on an airplane.

Rest is essential to success. In our Chicago class, we program two days of rest into each week for first-time marathoners. Most people reading this book understand that tapering before a marathon—cutting training mileage the last week or two before the race—is important to ensuring success. Less recognized is the necessity for rest and mini-tapers all through the marathon training program. Take a day off; it won't hurt.

Does this message contradict the earlier one related to consistency, the importance of maintaining a steady schedule? Not at all, because who can better afford to take days off than someone who trains consistently?

If you hope to get better as a marathon runner, you need to pay attention to the basic elements championed by Kurtis—consistency, mileage, intensity, and rest—but those are only four of the routes available to you. Let's consider next the benefits and challenges of building up mileage.

Chapter 7

Building Up
MILEAGE

Most marathon coaches agree that building up your weekly mileage is essential for achieving success in any long-distance event. "You need time on your legs," says Susan Kinsey, a coach from La Mesa, California.

But how much time? Atlanta's Jeff Galloway, a former high-mileage Olympian, has made a very successful career of teaching runners to finish their first marathons on the least amount of mileage possible. Three or four days a week of training coupled with some long runs are all you need, according to Galloway. And it works: More than 98 percent of those in Galloway's marathon program finish their first marathon, some on as little as 20 to 30 miles a week. (In recent years, many first-time marathoners in the Galloway program have used a run/walk method to complete the marathon. They use once-per-mile walk breaks, each lasting several minutes, to refresh their legs before they resume running again.)

Coaches surveyed for this book agreed that about 35 miles a week was adequate to finish a marathon, 55 miles to finish well. Most elite runners believe 100-plus-mile weeks are necessary to excel, but some research suggests anything more than 75 miles a week may be a waste.

How many miles do you need to run each week? It depends on your goals, your abilities, and your schedule—and in some cases, who you listen to.

WHAT THE 100-MILERS HAVE TO SAY

Before the 1980 U.S. Olympic marathon trials, a survey of the American contenders showed that nearly all of them trained more than 100 miles a week—somewhat disheartening for the aspiring marathoner now doing 30 miles a week and hoping to work up to 50 or 60.

Bill Rodgers and Frank Shorter, 1976 Olympians and two of the most successful and consistent American road racers at that time, trained 140 miles a week. "I always felt best when doing high mileage," says Rodgers. Alberto Salazar ran 130 miles a week before the 1984 marathon trials. Portugal's Carlos Lopes, the 1984 Olympic champion, ran 140 on average. Joan Benoit Samuelson, the women's gold medalist in the 1984 Games, also ran over 100. Norway's Ingrid Kristiansen ran as much as 125 miles weekly prior to breaking Samuelson's world record in the 1985 London Marathon. Uta Pippig, winner of the 100th Boston Marathon and a German Olympian, was a high-mileage trainer. A survey of the current crop of elite marathoners probably would reveal similar mileage totals.

Tom Fleming, a 2:12:05 marathoner with several second-place finishes at Boston, claims such high mileage is necessary for achieving excellence. "You have to do 140 miles a week to get into the 2:12 bracket," he says. "And you have to maintain that mileage. Most people can't do it. Anyone can run 140 for three or four weeks, but that's not enough. I'd love to be able to have 10 months of 140-mile weeks." Fleming points out that Bill Rodgers ran at that level during his best three years: "His body held up under the stress of the hard training, and the result was that he was the best marathoner in the world."

YOU CAN EXCEL ON LESS

But not every elite distance runner thinks you need to run so many miles. Don Kardong of Spokane, Washington, finished fourth in the 1976 Olympic marathon (2:11:16) with less mileage than most top marathoners, averaging 80 to 90 miles most weeks. "My feeling is that people pick 100 because it's a nice, round number," he says. "But 88 is an even rounder number."

Consider Benji Durden, a top runner from Boulder, Colorado, and a coach of elite and midpack runners. When he ran 110 miles a week at an average pace of 6:30 per mile, Durden had PRs of 29:21 for the 10-K and 2:10:41 for the marathon, and he made the 1980 U.S. Olympic marathon team.

But Durden found the stress of that much training too intense. In 1983 he cut his mileage to a still-demanding 85 to 95 miles a week—and set new PRs. He improved to 28:37 for the 10-K and 2:09:58 for the marathon, finishing third at Boston. "I believe you can be a successful performer on low mileage, as little as 70 to 80 miles a week," Durden now claims. Granted, most of us wouldn't consider 70 to 80 miles a week *low* mileage, but it is for an elite runner.

Craig Virgin, a three-time Olympian and two-time world cross-country champion, was another relatively low mileage runner. While setting PRs of 27:29.2 for 10,000 meters and 2:10:26 for the marathon (in a second-place finish at Boston in 1981), Virgin averaged 90 to 95 miles a week. He didn't run his first 100-mile week until his junior year in college and, except when training for his infrequent marathons, rarely strung 100-mile weeks together.

"I don't think they give any awards for workouts," says Virgin. "To the best of my knowledge, there are no gold medals for 'Most Mileage.' If it was the end of the week, and I had 98 miles in, I didn't go for a third workout that day to get 100. That won't make the difference between winning and losing. It's what you do with that 100 miles a week, and I think people forget about that."

Yet by the end of the millennium, American distance runners—once dominant on the world scene in the era of Shorter, Rodgers, Salazar, and Samuelson—have become second-rate performers. Kenyans, who sometimes run three workouts a day, fill the front ranks of most major marathons. In 1997 and again in 1998, the New Balance shoe company put $1 million on the line for any American man or woman who could break the national record. While the U.S. women's record of 2:21:21 set by Samuelson was very close to the world record, the men's mark of 2:08:47, set by Bob Kempainen, was "soft," nearly two minutes off the world record. Nobody collected the prize. The closest anybody came was Jerry Lawson, a high-mileage runner, who ran 2:09:17 at Chicago in 1997. Then Lawson failed to complete three out of his next four marathons.

WHAT THOSE MILES ACCOMPLISH

The late physiologist Al Claremont claimed that high mileage helps you better utilize glycogen, the starchlike substance stored in the liver and muscles that changes into a simple sugar as the body needs it. Carbohydrates in our diet are our main source of glycogen, one reason spaghetti is such a popular prerace meal for marathoners. Glycogen is the preferred fuel for running, but your levels can become depleted within 60 to 90 minutes. Thereafter, your source of fuel is fat, which is metabolized less efficiently.

Claremont believed high-mileage running in essence teaches your body to burn more fat along with the glycogen, stretching your reserves from 60 to 90 minutes to 2 hours or more. He explained: "Top marathoners are probably so efficient in metabolizing both fats and glycogen throughout the length of their races (because of the vast volume of their training) that they probably rarely deplete their stores. As a result, they don't hit the wall."

William J. Fink, of Ball State University in Muncie, Indiana, suggests that volume training may result in a more efficient use of your muscle fibers. "When a runner doubles his training mileage, we often see no change in his maximum oxygen uptake, the ability to deliver oxygen to the muscles," explains Fink. This, he says, indicates that something else—perhaps improved muscle fibers—causes the better performances.

Jack H. Wilmore, Ph.D., at the University of Texas at El Paso, suggests there is a psychological effect to high mileage as well. "When you do 100 miles a week, your legs are chronically fatigued," he comments. "Then when you finally do taper before an important race, it makes you feel all the stronger. The same would hold true for a 30-mile-a-week runner who, through a gradual buildup, achieved an ability to train comfortably at 60."

Finally, Dr. Wilmore says mileage helps your body adapt to the punishment that occurs during marathons—in ways that scientists can't yet explain. "When I'm out of shape and I race at long distances, everything hurts," he says. "It feels like my connective tissues are coming apart. But when I'm ready for a marathon and have put in the miles, everything moves smoothly."

THE POINT OF DIMINISHING RETURNS

Research from exercise laboratories suggests that many of the long miles done by runners in the past may have been wasted—and, in fact, too many miles may have contributed to chronic overtraining, which then resulted in poorer, rather than better, performances. "You may run far," says David Martin, Ph.D., a U.S. Olympic team consultant, "but you don't run far long."

David L. Costill, Ph.D., founder of the Human Performance Laboratory at Ball State, has measured beginning, average, and elite runners, as well as athletes in other sports. He believes that there exists a finite limit beyond which athletes cease to improve. For runners, he suspects the limit is 50 to 75 miles per week. "The amount of physiological improvement beyond that is almost insignificant," says Dr. Costill.

In one case documented in Dr. Costill's book, *Inside Running*, his lab studied two marathoners who resumed training after six-month layoffs due to injuries. Dr. Costill supervised muscle biopsies and treadmill tests for max VO_2 (the ability of the body to utilize oxygen during exercise) as the pair gradually increased their weekly mileages.

Dr. Costill wrote: "As one might have predicted, the muscles showed dramatic improvements in aerobic capacity with as little as 25 miles of running per week. [Their] max values increased when they increased their weekly mileages to 50 and then 75 miles per week. Beyond that level of training, however, our laboratory tests found no additional gains in endurance. During a one-month period they even trained at 225 miles per week, with no improvement in endurance."

In tests of other athletes, Dr. Costill was unable to detect any differences in oxygen uptake scores between runners who ran 60 miles weekly and those doing twice that mileage. "There may be some psychological reasons for running high mileage," he concedes, "but we haven't been able to measure it."

When working with swimmers, Dr. Costill found that they improved when their mileage was cut. When Ball State swimmers cut their daily mileage from 10,000 yards to 5,000 yards, everyone on the squad set new PRs—some by significant margins.

FITTING THE MILES IN

So what does all this mean to those of us who dream only of qualifying for Boston or setting a new PR? "There's no mystery about how you improve your endurance," says Lee Fidler, a running coach from Stone Mountain, Georgia, with a marathon PR of 2:15:03. "You just increase volume. I ran 110 miles a week ten years in a row, but not everybody can do that. For most people, 60 is plenty."

Although you can finish a marathon on only 30 miles a week, to finish well you need to push your mileage up to the level of 50 or 60 miles per week. Brian Piper, codirector of the Chicago Marathon training class, was running 70 miles a week when he broke three hours and qualified for Boston. To get anywhere near that level of mileage, you should make a gradual progression in increments of 10 percent a week, according to Fidler. Every third or fourth week, drop back close to the starting point to recover. Fidler says: "If you build constantly week after week, you get stronger, but you also find your break point. It's best to approach your break point without reaching it. You advance in steps. Go up two or three steps, drop back one or two steps, then hop back to where you were and start stepping again."

Joe Catalano of East Walpole, Massachusetts, has coached everyone from beginning joggers to his former wife, Patti Lyons Catalano, who had a marathon best of 2:27:51. He believes people vary in their ability to increase mileage: He recommends a gradual climb, adding five extra miles a week for a top runner but fewer for others. "The endurance base is the single most important factor in getting fit," he advises. "People worry about speed, but if you concentrate first on mileage and improving your strength, you can move to the speed phase later."

Thom Hunt, a coach from San Diego whose best marathon time was 2:12:14, often varied his mileage from week to week and from season to season. He usually ran between 85 and 105 miles a week, slightly more when training for marathons. His secret was variation. "I might run 105 one week, 115 the week after that, then go down and run a 90," says Hunt. "Rest is an important part of a training program. There are times of the year when you just go to the beach."

THE PERILS OF THE NUMBERS GAME

What you need to beware of is concentrating on how many miles you're running to the exclusion of everything else. Some runners become fixated on high mileage, feeling that if they fail to reach their weekly mileage goal they remain unfulfilled. They begin worrying by Wednesday or Thursday: "Am I going to make it this week?" At this point, they're running more for their training diaries than for themselves. They're also spending a lot of time running "junk miles"—miles that have no effect on fitness or performance.

Although high mileage may help produce better times, simply adding mileage may not guarantee success either for the world-class athlete or for the dedicated fitness runner who dreams of one day running the Boston Marathon. Quality must be mixed with quantity to produce maximum results. Don Kardong says: "People are too conscious of high mileage and not conscious enough about quality. It's a natural outcome of keeping a running diary. You become very concerned with how many miles you ran this week, but not with how fast you ran them. Quality may be more important than quantity."

Dr. Martin believes that much of the so-called rehabilitative running that elite runners do between hard runs may simply deaden their legs. "One of the secrets to remaining fresh," he says, "is to limit impact time, the number of times your feet strike the pavement."

Some runners jump from 50 to 75 miles to the "magic" 100 by simply adding a second workout to their day. Dr. Martin has his doubts about the gains from multiple workouts. "Run 5 miles each morning, and multiply that by 7, and you get 35 miles," he says. "If you add that to 65 miles of hard training in the afternoon, you can write 100 in your training diary. But does that make you a better runner?"

Invariably, those who achieve the highest level of success for their ability—regardless of whether they are winning marathons or merely running in the middle of the pack—are those who minimize the destructive effects of high mileage and maximize the efficiency of the miles they run.

FINDING THE MILEAGE THAT'S RIGHT FOR YOU

Top marathoners talk about *redlining*, a term borrowed from auto racers. The red line is the mark on the tachometer that delineates the safety zone from the danger zone: If you consistently rev your engine higher, it disintegrates.

In running, redlining means pushing your training to achieve maximum efficiency and your best performances. But if you push past your red line regularly, you risk injury or breakdown.

A beginning runner might redline after a gradual buildup at 30 miles. Or 45. Or 60. There are physiological limits: Too many miles too soon result in injuries such as strained tendons and ligaments, stress fractures, chronically dead legs, and a persistent feeling of fatigue.

There are also psychological limits. Some runners can't cope with dressing, running, and showering all the time—as well as the need for extra rest. Not only does 100 miles weekly require ten or more hours of actual running time; it also requires a lot of recuperative time. One of the coaches in our survey suggested that elite runners need three to four hours of rest daily on top of seven to eight hours of sleep each night.

Scientists can't define the precise point between undertraining and overtraining where optimum benefits occur. And this point certainly differs for different athletes. While one runner might thrive on 30 miles a week, another might need 60, and a third might need 120 to excel. It's also possible that the optimum mileage level may change at different points in a runner's career.

In general, runners who can increase training mileage should expect to improve as long as they don't sacrifice quality for quantity. The key is to increase mileage gradually and to pay careful attention to how your body reacts.

Chapter 8

RUNNING LONG

It is the staple of every distance runner's diet: the long run. If you're a seasoned marathoner, workouts up to 20 miles are de rigueur. If you call the homes of most distance runners on a Sunday at 7:00 A.M., you'll find they're either already out running or just about to head out the door. Running long will get you ready to perform. First-time marathoners use a 20-miler as a springboard to the finish line 6 miles farther down the road. Advanced runners do multiple long runs as one means of improving their PRs. Even 5-K runners find that running long regularly helps them run faster. And even if you're only interested in fitness, a longer-than-usual training run with friends on the weekend can be fun.

But what is the purpose, in both physical and psychological terms, of the long run? What function does it serve in getting you ready for a marathon? What is the perfect distance for running long, how often should you do it, and at what pace?

Most coaches agree that running long is not only enjoyable, but also essential to achieving success in distances from 5-K to the marathon. "The single long run is as important as high mileage in a marathoner's training program," claims Alfred F. Morris, Ph.D., a health and fitness manager for the Department of Justice in Washington, D.C. Tom Grogon, a coach from Cincinnati, ranks it second only to "raw talent."

Robert Wallace, a 2:13 marathoner who placed ninth at Boston in 1982 and is a part-time coach in Dallas, says, "I still love those long, easy runs on Sunday. They're the mainstay of any training program.

65

You don't get results immediately. It's like saving pennies: Put them in a jar, and over a year you accumulate $50 to $60."

Wallace favors slow workouts rather than fast ones for the long runs. "High-quality (fast) runs are too hard on a weekly basis," he says. "Run low-quality and you can get out every weekend. I like to see 10-K runners go 14 to 16 miles; marathoners go 20 to 22 miles, several minutes slower than race pace."

Joe Friel, coach and founder of a running store called Foot of the Rockies in Fort Collins, Colorado, considers the long run essential for building an endurance base. He has his runners do at least one long run every week, or every other week. "Every 10 days would be perfect," says Friel, "but that's tough to fit into a work schedule."

David Cowein, an ultramarathoner from Morrilton, Arkansas, runs long once a month for two to six hours. "I'll usually run trails," he says. "If I did a run that long on roads, I'd be sore the next day, but trails are easier on my body. I'll run far, but I'll also run slowly, walking up hills if necessary."

Runners often do their long runs in groups. "It's great to run with a group, because it can be lonely out there," says Wallace. "Even when I ran fast times, I always trained with the 3:00 and 3:30 runners," he says. "I just wanted to run long and didn't care at what pace."

While working on an article that appeared in the August 1998 issue of *Runner's World*, I posed a number of questions on long runs to a number of top coaches. Each coach agreed that the long run was the key to marathon success. "Shun long runs in training and you'll pay the price for your neglect," warned Al Lawrence of Houston, a former world-class runner from Australia. But not all coaches surveyed agreed on every detail of marathon preparation. Here is what the top coaches had to say about running long.

1. What is the main purpose for the long run?

Running long offers a dress rehearsal for the race. "It's a test," says John Graham, who coaches runners on the Internet.

Atlanta-based coach Roy Benson agrees: "Running long gets you used to the stress of lifting your feet up and down nearly 5,000 times per hour." It allows you to practice skills you will need in the race, such as taking fluids. Long runs build confidence in your ability to succeed, and maybe equally important, you learn *patience*.

"Many runners push too hard on daily runs," says Bob Glover, coach for the New York Road Runners Club. "The long run forces them to slow down and pace themselves wisely—just as they must do in the marathon."

But apart from practical and psychological considerations, there are strong *physiological* reasons to run long. Robert H. Vaughan is an exercise physiologist who trains both elite athletes and first-timers for the Dallas White Rock Marathon. Vaughan offers the scientific reason:

"The long run serves to increase the number of mitochondria, as well as capillaries in the active muscles, thereby improving those muscles' ability to remove and utilize available oxygen. In addition, the long run recruits muscle fibers that would otherwise go unused. This recruitment insures a greater pool of conditioned fibers that may be called upon during the later stages of the race. There are certain psychological barriers and adjustments to central nervous system fatigue that also are affected by the long run."

That's deep, and difficult for a layman to understand—but it's also the single most important reason why you should run long.

2. What is the best long run training distance for marathoners?

There is no "perfect" distance. Twenty miles is the peak distance used in most training programs, if only because 20 is a round number. That's the peak distance we use with our training class in Chicago—even for advanced runners. But in countries outside the United States, 30 kilometers (18.6 miles) is equally round and as frequently used. Most coaches feel that once you reach 16 miles, you're in long-run territory. That's the point where the psychological and physiological changes Vaughan mentioned kick in. But a few coaches prefer talking "time" rather than distance, hours rather than miles. Benji Durden of Boulder, Colorado, points to three hours as the equivalent to running 20 miles.

Running much farther than that increases the risk of injury, particularly for first timers. For experienced runners, the suggested top number is about 23 miles, say the coaches. Jeff Galloway peaks participants in his nationwide programs at 26 miles—but they do a lot of walking to get that far. At the far end of the spectrum, elite Japanese runners do five-hour runs. Former world record holder Rob DeCastello and Steve Monighetti from Australia would peak with a 30-miler five weeks before the marathon, but that's after a

COACHES' CONSENSUS

Runners differ in their backgrounds and their abilities. There is no single workout, or training program, that works best for everyone—and this certainly remains true when it comes to doing long runs. Yet in surveying coaches, I did find a consensus about how far and how often you should run long, specifically during the marathon buildup. The answers and numbers differ depending on whether you are a first-time marathoner or an experienced runner hoping to better your time at that distance. Here is what the coaches advise.

Category	First Timers	Experienced
Longest run	20 miles	23 miles
Frequency	1 time	3–6 times
Pace (per mile)	Race pace	30–90 seconds slower than race pace
Weekly mileage	40 miles	55–60 miles
Walking breaks	Yes	No
Speedwork	No	Yes

Summarizing the feeling of the coaches on two important issues, walking breaks are okay in a marathon if your main interest is in finishing and you don't care about time. Experienced runners seeking to run fast, however, may want to skip the walk breaks (except through aid stations to assure proper fluid intake). Speedwork (training faster than race pace) is considered too risky for first timers. Experienced runners, who do their long runs slower than race pace, are likely to benefit from midweek speed sessions, including long repeats at race pace.

steady diet of 23-milers nearly every weekend. Most runners would self-destruct on that much mileage.

3. *How many long runs at, or near, peak distance should distance runners do?*

If you're a novice, you run only one long run at peak distance: the traditional 20-miler mentioned above. Nearly every training program gradually builds runners up to that distance, rests them two to four weeks, then sends them off to the starting line with a pat on the fanny. And it works! Most runners who follow the marathon training schedules on my Web site jump from 20 miles in practice to 26 in the race fairly easily. The excitement of the event coupled with several weeks' rest during the taper period helps them bridge the gap. First timers often surprise themselves when they discover that running the marathon can be easier than training for it. (That's assuming you train for it correctly.)

But finishing that first marathon and racing subsequent marathons are two different beasts. To improve, you need more long runs, not merely longer runs. Experienced runners don't need to emulate the Aussies and run 23-milers every weekend, but they probably need to run between three and six workouts that are between 18 and 22 miles in the closing stages of their preparation, according to the marathon coaches I consulted.

As with novice marathoners, the reason is psychological as much as physical. "The more peak distance runs runners achieve in their marathon preparation, the more confidence they radiate," states Bob Williams, who prepares runners for the Portland Marathon.

Run long too often, however, and you raise your risk of not only injury, but also staleness. Only experienced runners should venture often beyond 20 miles, and even they will make mistakes.

4. Should you incorporate walking into your long runs, whether you plan to walk in the race or not?

Here's where I encountered some disagreement. Not all the responding coaches bought the idea expressed in the April 1998 *Runner's World* article on "The Run/Walk Plan" by Executive Editor Amby Burfoot. Burfoot recommended that regular walking breaks are helpful both in workouts and in races. "NO!" thundered one coach. "I thought the name of your magazine was *Runner's World*," grumbled another. Al Lawrence was the most diplomatic dissident, when he said, "Runners seem to feel better about themselves when they say I've *run* a marathon, rather than I've *done* a marathon."

Amby can take the heat, but here's the consensus about when to walk.

• Always walk through aid stations. You can grab more fluids and drink more easily while walking.

• Walk if you can't run any further, although it's best to walk *before* you're forced to.

• Do some walking in training, if only to learn how to start running again after being brought to a halt.

• Take walking breaks in training and races if the coach of your program tells you to do so.

5. How much recovery do you need after long runs?

Vaughan summarizes the group consensus when he says, "An experienced marathoner with years of training may recover in 48 to 72 hours, while a novice may require two weeks." Most runners in training will benefit from a day's rest after doing their weekend long run, and probably an easy day after that before taking another hard workout at a shorter distance. Thus, we arrive at the following pattern:

Sunday: Run long
Monday: Rest or easy run
Tuesday: Easy run
Wednesday: Run hard

That doesn't mean that the "hard" run on Wednesday should be another 20-miler. Most first timers should probably choose a medium-length run of between 5 and 10 miles for their midweek (hard) workout. Experienced runners might be more likely to do long repeats, similar to those described on pages 80–81.

Most marathon training programs, including ours in Chicago, allow two weeks between long runs near peak distance. The programs schedule medium-long runs (10 to 14 miles) on the weekends between.

Rest *before* the long run is as important as rest after. If you program a day or two of easy running and/or rest before your long runs so that you are not overly fatigued prior to the long runs, recovery afterward will be easier.

6. Are there any tricks to recovery?

No tricks, just sound training and nutritional practices. The three best strategies cited by our coaches were gels, energy bars and massage. Use the first two during the long runs, the last after. "Taking gels and bars during the long runs speeds recovery," says *Runner's World* columnist Joe Henderson. "You need to keep your glycogen stores continuously high if you want to maintain training effectiveness."

Bob Williams considers dehydration to be one of the major sources of muscle soreness. "Drinking during workouts is as important as drinking during races," he says.

Massages can be expensive, but you make a major time commitment when you decide to run a marathon, so you might as well do it right. Schedule a massage for 48 hours after your long run, since that's often the peak point of muscle soreness. The massage will help you ease your way back into your regular routine. More frequent massages during the final six weeks leading up to your peak long run may help reduce the risk of injury.

7. How fast should you run during long runs?

Speed is of limited importance during long runs, according to the coaches I contacted. More important is time spent on your feet. Set as your goal approximately the length of time you will run in the marathon itself, and don't worry about the distance or the speed at which you cover the distance. "Sub 2:10 marathoners have been known to run their long runs at over 7:00 per mile," says Vaughan.

Rookies in most training programs connected with major marathons run the same pace in their long runs as they will run in the race. "That's because we encourage first timers to select a conservative time goal to guarantee their finish," says Bill Fitzgerald, codirector of the Chicago Marathon training class. "If you can't hold a conversation during the closing miles of your long run, the pace probably was too fast." Glover adds: "If you can chatter, the pace doesn't matter."

Experienced marathoners who continually run long at race pace can get into trouble unless they slow down. They risk both injuries and overtraining. While the law of specificity suggests that you need to do some running at race pace to condition your muscles to the specific pace you will attempt to hold in the marathon, this is best accomplished during midweek workouts at shorter distances. "It's better to err on the slow side," says Lawrence.

Not every long run needs to be done at the same pace, nor does the pace within each run need to be the same. Denis Calabrese, director of USA FIT, who trains marathoners in many cities, believes runners should do the second half of their runs faster than the first half both in practice and in the actual marathon. "The discipline of going out slow rather than allowing the excitement of the marathon to burn you up is very valuable," says Calabrese.

If you're looking for numbers, do your long runs between 30 to 90 seconds per mile slower than the pace-per-mile you expect to run in the marathon, but even slower is acceptable.

8. Is there any advantage in long runs for non-marathoners?

All the coaches we surveyed believe there is. "Endurance is a factor at all racing distances," says Henderson. "Even 5-K and 10-K runners can benefit from one- to two-hour runs, but anything much longer might drain energy away from their more specific work."

Running long regularly also is an effective way to both lose a few pounds and maintain weight. Don't overlook the psychological value of a regular, weekly long run, particularly if it gives you an opportunity to run in the company of friends whom you might not get a chance to see during the week. One reason that many runners continue to run marathons is that training for that long distance provides both focus and structure to their training. It gives them an excuse to do long runs, which is something that they want to do anyway.

Whatever the reason, the long run is here to stay as a regular part of our training diets.

Chapter 9

SPEEDWORK
for Distance Runners

Dark clouds hovered on the horizon as I drove eastward late on a spring afternoon toward Eagle Lake in Michigan. The temperature was in the 60s, but dropping. Thunderstorms had rattled through the area sporadically during the past few hours. Only a few drops of rain had hit my windshield, but I found out later that others in the class had driven through downpours.

It was a Thursday in mid-April, and I was running with Ron Gunn's Marathon 101 class. Gunn is the athletic director at Southwestern Michigan College, and he regularly conducts training classes for beginning and experienced runners. That spring's version of Marathon 101 was designed to prepare people for June's Sunburst Marathon in South Bend, Indiana. Class members were scheduled to run 16 miles that day in their progression to a maximum long run of 20 miles before tapering to marathon day. But I didn't want to run that far, or that hard. I had already done my long run earlier in the week, so I decided to cut that night's distance to 11 and do some speedwork.

We were to run a preprepared course circling Eagle Lake, along which Gunn had chalked mile marks so we would know how far we had to go. While driving toward the lake, I decided to slice 5 miles from the planned workout and start at the 11-to-go mark. (Gunn drives class members to different starting points, depending on how far they want to run.)

I started slowly, as part of a planned warmup. I ran the first two miles at an 8:30 pace, allowing several class members to move out ahead of me. I weighed how I felt: decent, but fatigued and a bit stiff from my long run earlier in the week. I also planned to run a 15-K race in Kalamazoo, Michigan, on Saturday. It made sense to cruise comfortably and save energy for that race, the last formal test of my conditioning before the marathon. But at the 9-to-go mark, I started to push hard. I shifted gear into what Jack Daniels, Ph.D., once called "cruise control." This is fast (but controlled) running, a phrase familiar to most serious runners.

I swept past several class members and continued at that pace until I crossed the 8-mile mark on the road. I punched my watch: 6:09 for the mile. I floated through the next mile, taking nearly ten minutes, then spurted again. Twice more I did the same at a nearly equal pace. Finally, I finished with two slow miles, coming in with a pair of runners I had caught who had started at a different point along the course.

Later, I recorded that workout in my diary as: 4 × 1 mile (one-mile jog between each fast mile) with a two-mile warmup and a two-mile cooldown, a classic speed workout featuring repeats.

WHO NEEDS SPEEDWORK?

Speedwork! That's a scary word, a frightening concept to a lot of marathoners, who reason that there's nothing speedy about the pace at which they run 26-mile races. If that is so, why do speedwork, with its ultimate threat of injury? Most marathoners want to run far, not run fast. One runner who picked up a copy of my book with that title (*Run Fast*) at a race expo where I was selling copies grunted, "I don't want to run fast."

Fair enough. If you're a marathoner, you probably need to do speedwork only if you want to improve your performances.

Speedwork is an effective way to train, even though by running fast at Eagle Lake I ruined my race in Kalamazoo that weekend. With sore muscles, I failed to run any one mile as fast as I had that Thursday in practice. Bad judgment on my part? Perhaps, but I rationalized that my goals were long range: the marathon later that spring, and still other races beyond. But in all honesty, I had operated on instinct when I chose to run fast, because it was a good night for running.

That's not a bad reason, but the more pressing reason to include speedwork in your training program—even for marathons—is to improve performance. "Speedwork coupled with overdistance can bring a runner to any goal," states Paul Goss, a coach and duathlete (duathletes typically compete in races that include both running and cycling; triathletes add a swimming leg) from Foster City, California.

According to Alfred F. Morris, Ph.D., a health and fitness manager with the Department of Justice, "It is important for runners to learn to run fast, so that the marathon pace feels comfortable." Adds Frank X. Mari, a coach from Toms River, New Jersey: "You will never see full potential as a marathon runner until you develop your full potential as a sprinter." Coach Keith Woodard of Portland, Oregon, adds: "You have to be able to run fast at short distances before you can run fast at long distances."

As mentioned in earlier chapters, first-time marathoners need give little attention to speedwork: Their main goal is to gradually (but gently) increase their mileage so that they can finish a 26-mile race. Improving marathoners probably should also focus their attention on determining what level of high-mileage training works best for them. But after you've been running for several years and you begin to shave seconds instead of minutes off your PRs, or if you start to slip backward, it's time to turn to speedwork.

Most experienced marathoners know the value of speedwork, whether or not they practice it regularly. "Speed was my weakness, and I always felt I needed to concentrate on it even more than distance," says Julie Isphording, a 1984 Olympic marathoner. One time when I was visiting Cincinnati on business, I met her and a friend at 5:30 A.M. downtown near my hotel, and we ran across the Ohio River into Covington, Kentucky, to a high school track. The three of us had to climb a fence to get in, and it was still dark, but Isphording ran 8 × 800 meters, jogging 400 between. Soon after, she won the Los Angeles Marathon. (Another favorite workout of hers is 5 × 1600 meters, also jogging 400 between.)

HOW YOU BENEFIT FROM SPEEDWORK

Although long-distance runners concede that speedwork forms an integral part of any well-designed training regimen, not all marathoners use it as part of their training. One reason is unfamiliarity. Many of today's adult runners didn't compete in track or on cross-country teams in high school or college, so speedwork and running tracks feel foreign to them.

There is also an element of fear, both of the unknown and of injury—with some reason, since by training at a high intensity you can hurt yourself. It also can *hurt*, and the burning sensation you get in your lungs, and the ache in your legs may seem more threatening than the less piercing fatigue you encounter on the roads. Usually after a hard workout on the track, particularly early in the season, my legs are sore for several days.

Also, you can't carry on a decent conversation while zipping through a speed session. When I did those early morning interval halves at the Covington track with Isphording and her friend, I was hanging on for dear life. Only later, jogging back across the river into downtown Cincinnati, could we resume our conversation.

Nevertheless, there are 10 good reasons why every long-distance runner should do speedwork on a track.

1. Performance. This is the most valid reason. With speedwork, you will run faster. That's guaranteed. Numerous laboratory studies prove that adding speed training to an endurance base can take seconds off your 5-K times and minutes off your marathon bests. And runner after runner will testify to the value of including regular speed sessions in your long-distance program. Melvin H. Williams, Ph.D., a professor of exercise science at the Human Performance Laboratory at Old Dominion University in Norfolk, Virginia, only began training seriously in his mid-thirties. After half a dozen years of mainly long-distance training, his performance times stalled in the 2:50s for the marathon. After he cut mileage and added speedwork, he dropped his PR to 2:33:30 at age 44. "By training faster," says Dr. Williams, "you improve specific muscles used at higher speeds. You also improve your anaerobic threshold, which allows you to run a faster pace and remain aerobic. If you can run faster at short distances, you can increase your absolute ability at longer distances, too."

2. Form. One of the best ways I know—in fact, the *only* good way—to improve form is by running fast in practice. If you can learn to run more efficiently (exercise physiologists prefer the term *economically*), you will perform better at all distances and levels. I'm not sure why speed training improves your running form. Maybe you recruit different muscles. Maybe you force yourself to move more smoothly. Maybe by learning how to run at speeds faster than race pace, you're more relaxed when you do run that pace in a marathon. Maybe it's all of these reasons. Whatever the reason, running fast works.

3. Variety. Running the same course and the same distance at the same pace day after day can become tedious. To keep running exciting, you need variety. "Keeping workouts varied is one way to ensure success," says coach Joe Catalano, from East Walpole, Massachusetts. Catalano has his runners do speedwork on the roads, on trails, and on the track. Many road-running clubs organize weekly speed sessions as a benefit to their members.

4. Excitement. Running alone through scenic trails provides its own pleasure, but tracks can have a level of activity that can stimulate you during your workouts. "Usually I preferred to do my fast running at a track where something is going on, even if it's only soccer practice and nobody's watching me," says Doug Kurtis of Northville, Michigan. "It's often hard to run when nobody's around."

I used to train frequently at Stagg Field on the campus of the University of Chicago. There always seemed to be half a dozen activities going on simultaneously: rugby in the infield, tennis behind the stands, several softball games on an adjoining field, kids playing in the sand of the long jump pit, people doing yoga, and track athletes practicing multiple events. There was an electricity about being in the middle of this whirlwind of athletic activity that I found enormously appealing.

5. Convenience. "There are tracks in every city and town," says Catalano, "so it's very convenient to find one to do your workouts." Another important point: You can obtain maximum benefit in minimum time by doing speedwork.

"My clients don't have much time," notes Robert Eslick, a coach of adult runners from Nashville, "so short workouts appeal to them."

Here's a workout Fred Wilt, one of my former coaches, taught

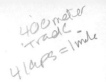

me. Head to the track and run eight laps, which is two miles (3200 meters). Run the first four laps (1600 meters) at a comfortable warmup pace. Then, without stopping, run the next 200 meters hard, the following 200 easy, and repeat this pattern for a total of three more laps (eight laps total for the workout). You're done, and your workout will have taken less than 20 minutes. That interval workout would be expressed as 4 × 200 (200 jog). The final 200 jog serves as your cooldown, and then you're in the car heading home for dinner. (The same workout—once you learn the pattern—can be done on the road or on trails as well as on a track.)

6. Concentration. One of the skills that separates the good runners from the almost-good runners is an ability to focus their attention for the entire period of the race, whether it's a mile or a marathon. Dissociating is a good strategy for beginning marathoners, but not for people who want to run fast. When your mind wanders during a marathon, inevitably you slow down. If you stay focused, you learn how to concentrate all body systems to sustain a steady pace, conserve your energy and maintain your running form. Eslick suggests that repeats between ¾ mile and 1½ miles simulate the concentration and pacing feel needed in a marathon. It takes total concentration to run fast on a track; once you master this skill, you can transfer it to your road runs.

7. Safety. You can't get hit by a car while running on a track, and you probably won't be chased by a dog either. If you're in the company of others, the danger of being mugged is reduced. On a hot or cold day, if you become overheated or overchilled or overfatigued, you can just walk off the track and head for your car or the locker room: You don't have to worry about being caught three miles from home and trudging those final miles at a diminishing pace. Also, there are usually drinking fountains at running tracks, and toilets nearby.

8. Companionship. Willie Sutton was once asked why he robbed banks, and his response was, "Because that's where the money is." Well, tracks are where the runners are. On a track you can seek company and training partners, and partners are important if you want to push yourself. It sometimes becomes difficult to motivate yourself to train hard when you're by yourself. With someone running those interval quarters with you, you may get a better workout and improve. But beware: A companion danger is that you may train *too* hard, resulting in staleness (a.k.a. "burnout") or injury. On balance, however, your running will improve if you find running partners with whom you enjoy training.

9. Motivation. Your running also will improve if you can find a coach to guide you in your training. A second variation of the Willie Sutton rule is that you find coaches at tracks. Because it's difficult to watch runners and monitor their strengths and weaknesses when they are scattered all over a road, most coaches prefer to gather people in groups for speedwork sessions. Probably the single most important asset a coach can offer any runner is motivation. Any runner can select one of the many training programs offered in this book or on the Internet, but only a skilled coach can motivate you and guide you to follow that program properly.

10. Pleasure. Just as it feels good for a tennis player to hit the ball perfectly over the net or for a golfer to loft a well-aimed chip shot to the green, it also feels good to run fast. There's a certain tactile pleasure in doing any activity well, an experience that in running I call "feeling the wind in your hair." One way to achieve the pleasure of fast running is to run short distances interspersed with adequate periods of rest. In other words, speedwork. And because speedwork inevitably will help you to improve your performance on race day, that boost will add to your pleasure, too.

VARIETIES OF SPEED

I defined speedwork in *Run Fast* as "any training done at race pace or faster." In that book I was offering advice for runners seeking to improve their 5-K and 10-K times, so I related race pace to how fast they ran those distances. If you run the marathon in 3:30, you run at an approximate pace of 8:00 per mile, but to go out and run half a dozen miles at your marathon pace—which most experienced runners could achieve easily—would not necessarily constitute speedwork. Speedwork for marathoners is training done at a pace significantly faster than you would run in a marathon. Your 10-K pace still remains an excellent benchmark.

To further define speedwork, I probably should add that it usually involves *bursts* of fast running (at race pace) followed by periods of slower running, or rest. That's essential, because most runners probably can achieve race pace for long distances only when well motivated and rested—in other words, during the race itself. To achieve race pace in practice, they need to cut their race distance into segments, and rest between those segments. If you were a competitor at 5000 meters, you could run 12 × 400 meters in a workout, resting short periods after each 400, and simulate some of the stress of your race as well as practicing race pace. A marathon runner probably wouldn't do 26 × mile in a single workout, but the principle is the same.

There are different ways to do speedwork. Some ways work better for marathoners than for runners competing at shorter distances. You can run repeats, intervals, sprints, strides, fartlek, or do tempo runs. You can run these workouts on the track, down the road, or on a path in the woods. You don't even need a measured distance and a stopwatch; you can measure intensity using a pulse

LONG REPEATS

Most marathon coaches believe runners should do their long runs slower than race pace. To do otherwise is to risk injury. Yet they agree on the need to do *some* running at the pace you plan to run your marathon so you can familiarize both your mind and your muscles with that pace. So when and how do you run race pace?

The answer is long repeats.

Just as milers go to the track and do interval workouts of 10 × 400 or 15 × 200 at fast pace, jogging or walking in between each rep for recovery, experienced marathoners can do long repeats as a form of speed training. Runners training for 5-K and 10-K races can also benefit from long repeats, although this workout is not advised for first-time marathoners.

Long repeats are best done on the roads on a course featuring mile markers. If there is no such course nearby, you can always use your car to make measurements, even though they won't be precise. Good distances for long repeat workouts are the half-mile, mile, 1.5-mile and 2-mile. Run one of those distances at race pace once, rest for two to three minutes by walking and/or jogging slowly, then repeat. Over a period of weeks and months, you can gradually increase the number of repeats, but you should always run monitor or even by perceived exertion. In *Run Fast*, I devoted a chapter to each of the speedwork variations, describing each in detail. In summary, here are the various types of speedwork and their applicability to marathon training.

Repeats. In a repeat workout, you run very fast, usually over a very short distance, and take a relatively long period of time to recover before repeating that distance. The fast (or hard) run in repeats is referred to as a repetition, or a *rep*. The runner recovers almost fully between repetitions, either jogging or completely resting. When I coached high school distance runners, I often had them walk a timed five minutes between reps. That allowed them to recover sufficiently so they could run each repetition at near maximum speed. There's nothing magic about five minutes, but resting for that precise amount of time at each workout offered them a familiar benchmark.

Interval training. In interval training, you carefully control the race pace, because familiarization is one of the most important reasons for this workout.

Here are several patterns for runners training for different race distances. Over a period of weeks and months, begin at the lower numbers and increase to the higher numbers.

Goal Race	Starting Workout	Goal Workout
5-K	3 × half-mile	6 × half-mile
10-K	3 × mile	6 × mile
Half-marathon	2 × 1.5-mile	5 × 1.5-mile
Marathon	2 × 2-mile	5 × 2-mile

Taper the workout two to three weeks before your important race. If your goal is not a specific race, you can vary your training by alternating between different repeat distances week to week. Or if your goal is a fast marathon, begin with the 5-K repeat distances and gradually progress to those for the marathon.

period of rest time, or interval, between the fast repetitions. Usually there are more reps than in repeat workouts, and the distance (or time) of the interval is shorter. Key to this kind of workout is that your heart rate is not allowed to drop too low before you surge into action again. Please note that the "interval" is the period *between* reps, not the repetition itself. Interval training is a more stressful form of training than most other forms of speedwork because you are never quite allowed to relax, so the result is a steady buildup of fatigue. For this reason, many veteran long-distance runners shy away from this type of speedwork.

Sprints. A sprint is just that: an all-out run for a short distance. The maximum distance a runner can run at full speed is probably around 300 meters, and that only if the runner is extremely well trained. Most sprints run by distance runners in practice are probably shorter than that: 50 to 100 meters, a straightaway on a running track or a fairway on a golf course. The object of running sprints in training is to develop style as well as speed, economy more than endurance. It's also a good way to stretch muscles and learn to lengthen your stride.

Why should marathon runners run sprints, when at no time during the race will they run anywhere near that speed? The reason is that sprints develop speed. And speed is basic to success in running, regardless of the distance. If you can develop your base speed at distances of 100 meters to a mile, inevitably you will become a faster marathon runner.

Strides. Strides are simply slow sprints. I frequently use strides as part of my warmup to get ready for a faster workout, or before a race. Typically, I might jog a mile or two, stretch, then do 4 × 100 meters near race pace. Or I'll sometimes do strides at the end of a workout. Or on a "rest" day I'll do an easy workout that consists mainly of stretching and a few strides. Particularly during summer months, I like to do these stride workouts barefoot on the fairway of a golf course in the early morning before the golfers appear.

Surges. Surges are fast sprints thrown into the middle of a long run or a long race. Well, not too long a race. You probably don't surge too frequently in a marathon, or you'll surge yourself into the pickup bus for runners who can't finish. Although surging at the right time might win you an Olympic gold medal (as Joan Benoit proved in 1984), it's probably not a good race strategy for midpack runners whose goal is to spread their energy evenly throughout the race to maximize their performance. Nevertheless, surging is an effective and enjoyable training strategy.

Surging is also one way to get yourself out of those "bad patches" that develop in the middle of even the best-trained runner's marathon. Sometimes a surge to a slightly faster pace allows you to recover as much as if you jogged along slowly. You may surge for any distance. Tim Nicholls, a coach from Pembroke Pines, Florida, recommends one-mile surges, as well as two-mile repeats, but a surge can be as short as 100 meters.

Fartlek. Fartlek is all of the above thrown into a single workout, usually done away from the track, preferably in the woods. It's a Swedish word that roughly translates to "speed play." Fartlek includes fast and slow running—maybe even walking. Basically, you jog or sprint or stride as the mood strikes you, generally alternating fast and slow running. One of my favorite T-shirts was one I saw worn by a woman in a race. On the front of the shirt it said "fartlek." On the back of the shirt it said, "It's a runner's thing."

Although fartlek is best practiced on wooded trails, marathoners can adapt this type of workout to their own needs on the roads. This is an unstructured form of speed training that appeals particularly to experienced runners who have become very adept at reading their bodies' signals and thus don't need the discipline of a stopwatch and a measured distance.

Tempo runs. Exercise scientists now tell us that doing tempo runs is the most efficient way to raise your lactate threshold, that is, your ability to run at a fast pace without accumulating lactic acid in the bloodstream, which eventually will bring you to a halt. You train at the theoretical point between aerobic and anaerobic running.

A tempo run is one in which you begin at an easy jogging pace, gradually accelerate to near your 10-K race pace, hold that pace for a period of time, then gradually decelerate to your earlier jogging pace. A 40-minute tempo run might follow a pattern like this: jog for 10 minutes, accelerate for 10 minutes, hold near 10-K pace for 10 minutes, decelerate for 10 minutes. There's nothing magic in the pattern of $10 + 10 + 10 + 10 = 40$. A tempo run can follow any pattern as long as you take yourself up to near the edge of your lactate threshold.

I find tempo runs to be not only the most effective form of speed-work, but also the most enjoyable. I love to do tempo runs on the trails of Indiana Dunes State Park near Chesterton, Indiana, about a 20-minute drive from my home. The surface of Trail Two circling the marsh near Wilson Shelter is smooth, flat, and conducive to very fast running. Maybe it's partly the scenery (often I spot deer in the woods), but I usually finish my tempo runs invigorated and ready to beat the world.

All forms of speedwork can make you a better runner, and a better marathoner. If you want to improve at any level of running, you have to learn to run fast.

Chapter 10

Defensive Running
STRATEGIES

When it comes to automobile accidents, one of the most dangerous strips of ground is Chicago's Dan Ryan Expressway. Whoever designed this expressway with its intersecting lanes failed to consider the mindset of Chicago area drivers. They speed, they weave, they cut each other off in their desperate attempts to get where they're going 30 seconds faster than the other guy. Maybe if these motor maniacs ran a couple of miles before jumping into their cars, they'd be less likely to inflict damage on each other.

One evening while heading home after a marathon training class, I was driving in a middle lane on a four-lane stretch of the Dan Ryan when I noticed in my rearview mirror that two cars were approaching rapidly. Either the drivers were racing each other or they were simply clueless. One passed on my left; the other passed on my right. Then each decided he wanted to occupy the same lane. I can still see the moment in instant replay. Their sides touched. Locked together, the cars began spinning in front of me.

I reached deep into my bag of defensive driving techniques. I stayed in my lane. I hit the brakes, but gently. I was as worried that I would be hit from the rear as that I would hit the two cars spinning in front of me. I watched as they skidded off to my left, crashing into the guardrail.

I believe in defensive driving, which is why I stay especially alert when driving the Dan Ryan Expressway, which I can't avoid when heading home to Indiana.

As a runner, I also know what I need to do to avoid injury—not necessarily encounters with automobiles, but injuries that may be caused by overuse, training errors, and so forth. You can call these defensive running techniques. If you want to have a long running career, determine what activities most often cause you to become injured, then avoid them—just as I try to avoid high-risk highways.

ARE INJURIES INEVITABLE?

Some physicians order injured runners to give up running. Several doctors offered me that advice, until I stopped going to doctors who weren't themselves runners. For most of us, stopping running permanently is not an option. We want to learn to run injury free.

We also want to run long distances. And to run marathons is to court injury—if not from the race itself, then from the high mileage that's necessary for training. Jack H. Scaff Jr., M.D., founder of the Honolulu Marathon and director of the highly successful Honolulu Marathon Clinic, says marathon running, by definition, is an injury. Dr. Scaff isn't advising people not to run marathons; he's just stating what he considers to be a fact.

The late Michael L. Pollock, Ph.D., who directed the University of Florida Center for Exercise Science in Gainesville, identified intensity as the most common cause of running injuries. "People who only walk or jog short distances at slow paces don't become injured," said Dr. Pollock.

Stan James, M.D., the orthopedist from Eugene, Oregon, who performed arthroscopic surgery on Joan Benoit months before her Olympic Marathon victory, claims that most running injuries are the result of training errors. Avoid those errors, suggests Dr. James, and you can run injury free. Lyle J. Micheli, M.D., of Boston's Children's Hospital agrees: "Many of the injuries we see could have been prevented. There is usually some type of training error."

Nevertheless, most successful training programs—including the ones presented in this book—are based on variations of the progressive overload theory. You gradually overload the system with progressively more mileage or the same mileage at faster paces. To achieve peak performance, you train to just under the point that your body would break down if you went further.

FINDING YOUR BREAKING POINT

For most elite runners, their breaking point is somewhere beyond 100 miles per week, but not everyone is blessed with superior athletic ability. Podiatrists tell us their waiting rooms are filled with average runners who run 30 miles or more a week. Above that magic 30 miles seems to be where chondromalacia, plantar fasciitis, Achilles tendinitis, and other major injuries occur.

Logically, you just wouldn't run beyond that 30 miles a week, but that won't suffice for marathoners. The ideal, then, is to determine within a tenth of a mile, if possible—the weekly mileage at which your body self-destructs. Then you can train to the edge of disaster, occasionally pushing slightly (and I emphasize the word *slightly*) over that edge to determine whether months and years of steady training (or a new pair of shoes) have allowed you to nudge your breaking point to a new level.

Pushing to that edge has to be done gradually. Elite runners spend many years gradually adapting their bodies to accept the stress of 100-mile weeks. They don't increase from 70 miles a week one month to 140 the next. First-time marathoners who try to double their weekly mileage from 35 to 70 too rapidly are likely to get into trouble.

When I began coaching track at the local high school in Michigan City, Indiana, a student named Tony Morales rejoined the team midway through his junior year. He had run well as a freshman under a previous coach, but had suffered a series of discouraging injuries and had missed most of his sophomore year.

The previous coach told me, "Tony has a lot of talent, but whenever I got his weekly mileage up over 35, he'd get injured."

"Then I'll train him at 34 miles a week," I said.

That statement didn't endear me to the previous coach, but that's what I did, and Tony was able to run pain free. By gently pushing his limit over a period of nearly a year, Tony eventually nudged his training mileage to nearly 55 a week. As a senior, he made the All-Conference team in cross-country.

But midway through the season, Tony developed mild tendinitis in his upper thigh that limited his performance over a period of several weeks. Maybe if we had stopped at 54 miles a week this injury would not have occurred. Or maybe not. That's the secret to injury prevention: to straddle the line between undertraining and over-training.

ARE YOU OVERTRAINED?

Overtraining isn't an injury, per se. You're not hurt. Nothing is swollen; nothing is broken. You don't limp. It's just that when you run, your legs feel dead most of the time, your workout and race times have both started to deteriorate, and you enjoy running less and less. By overdoing it, you may be predisposing yourself to injury. If you overtrain, something bad will happen—not *can* happen, *will* happen.

Marathon runners probably are more prone to overtraining than other runners, simply because of the volume of training required. It stands to reason that if you train more, you increase your chances of becoming overtrained.

Probably the key cause of the symptoms of overtraining is the loss of glycogen, the sugarlike substance that fuels your muscles and provides the readily available energy that permits them to contract efficiently. Glycogen debt can occur if you're not eating enough carbohydrates to match the amount of calories burned—or if you're not *synthesizing* enough glycogen. Excessive training appears to inhibit the body's conversion of fuel into energy, although why this occurs is not fully understood. This condition might be compared to having fouled spark plugs in your automobile. The engine still runs, but not as well as it would if you bought new plugs.

Some runners increase their training levels to reduce weight. They sometimes train for marathons to provide the incentive to slim down. But one common mistake is to combine an increase in mileage with a decrease in calorie consumption. Frequently, I get questions to my "Ask the Expert" column for *Runner's World* on the Internet from runners training for marathons who complain of energy loss. Inevitably, when I inquire, I discover that they were either dieting or following a regimen such as the Zone (40-30-30) Diet, which provides insufficient carbohydrates for high-mileage training. (For more information, see chapter 13.) They became overtrained as much from their eating habits as from their training habits.

The overtrained runner may maintain speed but with poorer form and with greater expenditure of energy. David Costill, Ph.D., of the Human Performance Laboratory at Ball State University in Muncie, Indiana, cited one runner who, early in his training, could run a 6:00 mile pace at only 60 percent of his aerobic capacity. Later, when he became overtrained, the same runner had to use 80 percent of his capacity to maintain that pace.

As athletes enlist all available muscle fibers in an attempt to maintain their training pace, they invariably exhaust their fast-twitch muscles faster than their slow-twitch muscles. This is one reason runners lose speed: Their fast-twitch muscles have become exhausted through intensive training.

But glycogen depletion is not the only problem. Another is microscopic damage to the muscle fibers, which tear, fray, and lose their resilience, like a rubber band that has been snapped too often. Despite analysis of blood and urine samples, researchers find it difficult to identify how, or why, chronically overtrained muscles lose their ability to contract. Harm Kuipers, M.D., Ph.D., of the University of Limburg in the Netherlands researched the effect of overtraining for nearly a year by training racehorses on a treadmill, alternating hard days of interval sprints with easy days. Horse trainers warned that the animals would become overtrained, but this failed to happen. Finally, with time running out, Dr. Kuipers began training the horses hard on their easy days. "Almost immediately," he said, "the horses began to exhibit symptoms of being overtrained." The message to runners is, If you want to avoid overtraining, don't eliminate easy days.

RECOGNIZING THE SIGNS

The simplest defensive running strategy you can use is your training diary. Determining where you made a mistake—that "training error" described by Dr. James—is the main reason for keeping a training diary. Learn the cause of that mistake and you are less likely to repeat it.

Your training diary can also provide clues that you're over-training. For example, if you've noted that you feel tired all the time, you may be training too hard. "Perceived exertion may give us our most important clues," suggests William P. Morgan, Ed.D., of the University of Wisconsin at Madison. Here are some other symptoms to watch for:

Heavy legs. Your legs lose their snap—and speed. A run at an 8:00 pace feels like a 7:00 pace. Depleted muscle glycogen may be the cause. "You feel like you're running with glue on your shoes," says Dr. Costill.

Increased pulse rate. This is easily measured: Record your pulse each morning before you get out of bed, and cut back your training on days when it's higher than usual. After doing a research project for Athletics West, Jack Daniels, Ph.D., and psychologist Scott Pengelli advised that club's athletes to cut training on days when their pulse rates were high.

Sleep problems. You have trouble getting to sleep and may wake several times during the night. Then you have to drag yourself out of bed in the morning. On rising, your pulse is also elevated, as above. "Sleep dysfunctions often are a sign of overstress," says Dr. Costill.

Diminished sex drive. The romance has gone out of your life. Somehow you seem to have lost interest in sex. You're too tired to tango. Whether this is related to lowered testosterone levels caused by training, or just plain exhaustion, no one knows for sure. But overtrained runners of both sexes look and feel like zombies, according to Costill.

Fear of training. You have trouble pushing yourself out the door to run each morning. So you sit and stretch longer. Your body is telling you to back off. "This is part of the psychological effect of overtraining," says Dr. Costill.

Sore muscles. Your muscles, particularly your legs, seem sore and stiff. "They may even be sore to the touch," says Costill. The reason is muscle damage, caused by too much pounding on the roads. Some muscle soreness is natural after hard training sessions, but if it persists, you're working too hard.

I like to believe that individuals who sign up for my marathon training class in Chicago have a relatively low rate of injury. My coleaders, Brian Piper and Bill Fitzgerald, agonize over every single individual lost to injury, but I'm certain that local marathoners who don't join the class get hurt more frequently than those who do. When a class member does get hurt, it's often for one of three reasons: (1) They started the program with insufficient base mileage. (2) If first-time marathoners, they followed the intermediate program rather than the novice program, because they had been running for several years and didn't want to consider themselves "novices," or "joggers." (3) They ran their long runs at race pace or faster, believing it would get them in better shape to set a PR.

BEWARE THE COMMON COLD

Another early warning sign of overtraining is the common cold, particularly right before an important race.

Precompetition colds are common, claims Gregory W. Heath, D.H.S., an exercise physiologist and epidemiologist at the Centers for Disease Control in Atlanta. He notes that runners normally experience only half as many upper respiratory infections as the general population. Up to a certain point, exercise boosts your immunity. But you lose this protection, claims Dr. Heath, if you race, and particularly if you race in marathons.

David C. Nieman, Dr.P.H., a health professor at Appalachian State University in Boone, North Carolina, surveyed participants in the Los Angeles Marathon and found that 40 percent caught a cold during the two months before the race. By doing high-mileage training, runners lowered their resistance and became more susceptible to whatever cold bugs were floating around, even in the warm climate of Los Angeles.

Dr. Nieman discovered that if runners train more than 60 miles a week, they double their risk of infection. He also found that in the week following the race, 13 percent of marathon finishers caught colds, compared with 2 percent of runners who didn't race. Although Nieman's research failed to indicate this, I suspect that most of those 60-mile runners who became victims of cold bugs were individuals who normally trained much less, but had cranked their mileage way up for the marathon. Those who regularly run 60 miles a week and whose systems have adapted to that high load may not be at increased risk, because they're not necessarily over-trained.

It makes sense, nevertheless, to save your high-mileage training for months when the risk of infection is less (spring through fall). Obtaining a flu shot at least once a year, usually in the fall, is important. You may not be able to avoid the flu entirely, but the shot may help ward off its worst symptoms.

Also, build a strong training base so that a week lost to a cold or flu won't be a serious setback. You should start your taper early enough to prevent last-week problems. Finally, you need to be particularly wary following the race. "Spread of many viruses is hand-to-hand rather than airborne," says Heath, who recommends avoiding people with colds, washing your hands after contact, and particularly, isolating yourself as much as possible before and after competition (avoiding crowded movie theaters, for example).

I caught a bad cold the week before the 1998 Chicago Marathon. It was less a result of the stress of training and more from the stress of a busy life. My wife and I had spent the weekend before visiting our daughter Laura. She and her husband Pete have two children. Kids are notorious for bringing germs home from school.

After I got back to Chicago, I had the mother of all colds, and I had to give final lectures to my marathon training class in four locations on the next four nights. I arrived at our biggest clinic at the Scholl Center on the near North Side with my nose running so much I could barely carry enough tissues in my pocket to contain the flow. Several hundred runners attended this last lecture, and I worried that each one of them would catch my cold and compromise their marathon. Afterward, class members approached me to thank me for helping them with their training. I tried to avoid shaking any hands, but didn't entirely succeed. My cold was gone by race day, but I hope I didn't infect too many others. Perhaps by confessing this indiscretion, I can be absolved of my sin. Since we carefully taper class members the last three weeks before the marathon, it's likely that the runners' immune systems had rebounded from the hard training enough to avoid my germs.

It's important to cut your training during a cold and cease it entirely if you have the flu (with elevated temperature), because you may increase your chance of an injury while in a weakened condition. You can run a marathon with a cold without it greatly affecting performance (dehydration may be your worst problem), but running a marathon with the flu is definitely unwise. You may finish, but you can significantly compromise your immune system, and incur health problems that can extend not merely weeks, but months and even years, according to Dr. Nieman.

EASE INTO THE SEASON

One of the first lines of defense against injury is to quash your instinct to start training at full steam. Coaches have noted that many athletic injuries occur in the spring. "Usually I find that after a very sedentary winter, runners want to get out and start training at the same mileage level as in the fall," says one coach of adult runners. "As a result, they get hurt."

In my work on the "Ask the Expert" column for *Runner's World*, I discovered that high school runners, particularly, were susceptible to injuries in both the spring and fall a few weeks after track or cross-country season had begun. This was because they failed to train properly between seasons, and then they were forced to do too much too soon. The most common injury: shinsplints. "It's like an epidemic at the start of each season," claims Debbie Fray, an assistant coach at Valparaiso High School, who frequently runs with our club at Indiana Dunes State Park. Running through the park one Sunday, she told me, "Kids go from zero miles to high miles, and they get injured."

Cross-training can lull you into a false sense of security. Don't overvalue off-season training that doesn't involve running. During the winter, I cross-country ski—and it gets me into fabulous cardiovascular shape. But when the snow melts, I have to be cautious about bringing the same intensity to the running trails as I did to the ski trails. The one or two times I pushed right into running, I suffered injuries. In 1984, I entered several cross-country ski races in Norway, then headed south to Italy, where I ran surprisingly well in the famed Cinque Mulini race north of Milan. "Wow," I thought, "I'm in great shape." But two weeks later, I was limping.

My cardiovascular system had been in better shape than my running muscles. It was like putting a Porsche engine into a Volkswagen chassis: The chassis couldn't handle the power.

Since then I've used two strategies to help prevent this problem. First, instead of shifting completely from running to skiing as soon as snow covers the ground, I maintain a maintenance level of running, at least every other day. And once the snow melts, I cut the intensity of my training during that transition period between winter and spring.

ADD SOME VARIETY

Cross-training can be an important means of preventing injury—if used wisely. Hector Leyba of Raton, New Mexico, a track coach and a sub-3:00 marathoner, skis winters and bicycles summers. "Cross-training helps my endurance," he says. "After many years pounding the streets, I feel I need variety."

One of the main causes of running injuries is the stress caused by the literally thousands of times your feet hit the ground when you run. If you've ever seen any slow-motion photography of what happens to the leg muscles during a single running stride, you'd wonder how we survive even a single lap on a track, much less a marathon. Swimming, skiing, cycling, and walking don't generate this ground impact.

It follows that if you want to maintain a high level of intensity in your training, you can shift to swimming, skiing, cycling, walking, or other activities on your off days. Or select nonimpact exercises that mimic running movements. Melvin H. Williams, Ph.D., of Old Dominion University, and a top ranked 50-plus runner, spends one day a week cross-training, and does supplemental training on his off days. His one-hour off-day routine includes running in deep water wearing a flotation belt and riding standard and recumbent exercise bicycles. On the standard bike, he likes to stand up on the pedals frequently, figuring that this more closely exercises the muscles used in running, but without the impact. His recumbent workout exercises the quadriceps, which are sometimes overlooked in running. Again, he uses an interval approach: hard and easy. When Williams runs less than his usual one hour, he uses cross-training to fill out the exercise period to a full 60 to 70 minutes.

Dr. Williams has selected exercises that simulate running as much as possible, but most cross-training fails to exercise the muscles specific to running. In order to succeed as a runner, you need to train as a runner.

There is also the danger that you can cross-train yourself into an injury if you over-cross-train. Coach Roy Benson of Atlanta warns that runners who cross-train on days between hard running bouts may do too much because they're using different (read "unfatigued") muscle groups. "If you're not careful," says Benson, "you can convert an 'easy' day into a 'hard' day, and it will eventually catch up with you. It's a myth to believe that you can't get hurt cross-training."

One woman training for the marathon wrote my "Ask the Expert" column worried that she would lose fitness during the three-week taper. She wondered if she could cross-train to compensate for the lost miles while tapering.

My response was that if she was used to cross-training, she could continue with her alternate activities, but it was unwise to suddenly add new cross-training activities during the premarathon taper. The whole purpose of the taper is to rest your muscles—all your muscles—by exercising significantly less. Cross-training the week after the marathon because you're too sore to run is also a very bad idea.

Nevertheless, if you're prone to overuse injuries, substituting less stressful cross-training for some of your running may decrease your injuries and therefore your down time. And if you can avoid gaps in your training caused by injuries, inevitably you'll perform better as a runner.

USE SPEEDWORK CAUTIOUSLY

Every running expert I know recommends speed training as the most effective means of improving as a runner. But this can be dangerous advice if applied too zealously, particularly in training for a marathon. "Don't read what an elite athlete does in terms of mileage and attempt to do the same," advises John E. Tolbert, a coach from New Haven, Connecticut. "Get advice and train at your own level."

It isn't the speedwork itself that causes marathon runners to injure themselves in training, but speedwork coupled with the progressively longer distances run during the marathon buildup. Early in my career, I learned that I could improve either by increasing the intensity of my workouts or the distance, but I couldn't do both at the same time without risking injury. Marathoners should include speedwork in their training program only after an initial buildup to high mileage and a subsequent cutback.

In his book *Your First Marathon*, Jack H. Scaff Jr., M.D., who directs the Honolulu Marathon Clinic, advised that racing or speedwork should make up no more than 10 percent of your mileage. "After you've run a marathon," he warned, "you need 260 miles of training before you enter your next event, or start doing speedwork."

Although I dislike formulas and don't want to suggest 10 percent as the absolute limit to speedwork—particularly because when your mileage is cut at peak training, speedwork could become a predominant part of your training—Dr. Scaff's basic advice is sound.

CHOOSE RUNNING SURFACES CAREFULLY

I'm a believer in trail running, partly because I love to run in the woods, but also because there's less chance of getting injured on a soft trail surface. Yet I've noticed that runners who are not used to varying trail surfaces are prone to injury when they take to the woods. This was borne out by my cross-country team at the beginning of the fall season, and the track team when it trained on trails after the long winter hiatus. The less dedicated runners, who had failed to work out during the off-season, tripped over roots or twisted ankles stepping in holes, but this never seems to happen to those runners who train on trails year-round.

In addition to running trails, I like to train on the smooth fairways of golf courses. To avoid interfering with golfers, I rise very early in the morning during the summer—a marvelous time to train if you can motivate yourself to get out of bed. Living as I do near Lake Michigan, I also find that the beach (particularly the day after high waves have flattened it) provides an ideal training surface.

In training top Dallas runners, including five-time Olympian Francie Larrieu Smith, coach Robert Vaughan avoids interval running on a track. "We do all our interval work on grass," he says. "We do repeats on the track, anything less than six reps. Anything more, we run on grass." Since switching to grass, Vaughan has virtually eliminated the problem of stress fractures, even though his runners do two speed workouts a week.

Asphalt may be slightly less unyielding than concrete, but let's face it, neither surface is soft. Nevertheless, if you're going to race on roads, you need to train on the roads to accustom your muscles to the impact. When preparing for a marathon, I usually do a much higher percentage of my running on the roads than if I were training for shorter events, such as track and cross-country races.

FOOTWEAR: NOT TOO SOFT, NOT TOO FIRM

One way to diminish road shock is to wear properly cushioned shoes. Running shoe companies spend millions of dollars on research and technology to design shoes that help prevent injuries. Various energy-absorbing materials, and air built into or pumped into your shoes, can decrease the impact of running on either asphalt or concrete.

One possible reason that men's marathon times have improved by nearly 20 minutes in the last half century may be better footwear, and, as a result, fewer training injuries. A word of caution, however: Shoes that are too spongy (so soft that they offer little support) may destabilize the foot and contribute to injury. One shoe company in recent years came out with a marvelously comfortable shoe that was half the weight of other shoes. But the shoe was so spongy, I suspected it could contribute to injuries.

Spending more money does not guarantee you will obtain the shoe most likely to help you prevent injury. When I visit the office of Franklin Wefald, M.D., a cardiologist in Elkhart, Indiana, I find that he spends as much time pumping me for running advice as I do pumping him for medical advice. During one visit, he asked me what shoes I would recommend. I learned that he owned a very expensive model. Physicians earn good money, and Dr. Wefald had not skimped when selecting a running shoe. But the expensive shoes he purchased were designed with extra features to protect much heavier runners. That's why they cost more. By paying too much for a pair of shoes that were stiffer than he needed, he had actually increased his risk of injury.

MAKING THE MOST OF YOUR MILES

Sometimes even a conservative runner who tries to ease gradually into a routine of high mileage just can't do so without injury. This is where the unfairness doctrine enters in.

The unfairness doctrine says that just when you increase quantity to the point where you feel you really are getting in shape, something happens. You catch a cold. You twist an ankle. Your knee starts aching. You suffer a stress fracture.

You may be one of those runners who just can't handle high mileage. If so, there are still ways to improve.

Mixing miles. In the marathoning world, this means running different distances on different days. A runner who can't safely do more than 35 weekly miles need not run 5 miles every day, seven days a week. That runner may be able to train more efficiently by running more than 5 miles on some days and less than 5 miles on others, or even taking days off.

By altering your daily running schedule, you can increase the intensity and duration of certain workouts without necessarily increasing your weekly time commitment. (In fact, you might save time.)

Here is a week's training schedule that involves mixing miles.

It is of paramount importance to choose your footwear very carefully. Among other considerations, heavier runners certainly do need shoes that offer more support than those designed for lighter runners. You may also need more than one type of shoe. I have a built-in rack on one basement wall where I stack my various athletic shoes, each pair for a specific purpose.

I wear heavy, protective shoes on those easy days when I run slow. When I run fast, I prefer a light shoe, and I often wear racing flats for my speed workouts, and a semilight pair for long runs. When I run smooth trails, I wear a flexible, light shoe; uneven trails may require shoes with studs on the bottom. At the track, I may don spikes for repeats. I also have cycling shoes and ski boots and Aquasocks for the beach.

Every shoe has its own place in a runner's shoe inventory, and

Sunday—15 miles
Monday—1 mile
Tuesday—10 miles
Wednesday—3 miles
Thursday—read a spy novel
Friday—6 miles
Saturday—rent a video

Mixing miles is simple. But there are other ways to prevent injury and still excel in your marathon goals.

Speeding is another variation that can help runners improve. When you're unable to push past a certain mileage because of lack of talent, time, or determination, simply run those miles faster. A runner limited to 35 weekly miles might have a training program like this.

Sunday—15 miles steady pace
Monday—2 miles recuperative jogging
Tuesday—fartlek in woods: 6 miles total
Wednesday—2 miles easy jogging
Thursday—100-yard sprints on golf course
Friday—rent a video: *Chariots of Fire*
Saturday—6 miles hard, or race

For real improvement, combine the principles of mixing and speeding while also running farther.

certain shoes that work well in one setting may not perform well in another. Runners who wear inflexible road shoes in the woods may increase their chance of injury on the uneven ground. Cross-training shoes may be suitable for weekend warriors who exercise infrequently, but I'm not convinced they belong in the inventory of any serious endurance athlete.

When I run on grass or sand, or sometimes in deep water, I'll go barefoot, because I believe that it stretches and strengthens the muscles in my feet. I've even raced without shoes, running 5000 meters barefoot on London's Crystal Palace track in 1972 in 14:59.6, a masters record that lasted a quarter century until it was broken recently. Telling you that I run barefoot won't endear me to the shoe companies, but it's all part of my defensive running approach.

KEEP MUSCLES LOOSE AND STRONG

Stretching and strengthening is another way to minimize injury. The best time to stretch a muscle is after it's warmed up. Track runners typically jog a mile or two, then stretch or do calisthenic exercises before beginning the intense part of their workout.

Long-distance runners are less likely to pause in the middle of a long run to stretch, although this practice is becoming more common. I'll stretch before long runs and in the middle of intense workouts, but my preferred time to stretch is after the workout, usually while relaxing in a whirlpool, even though some experts advise against this approach. Every runner should adopt a stretching regimen that is convenient and comfortable.

Strength training is important for both conditioning and injury prevention. I lift weights and/or use exercise machines regularly in the off-season when I'm not racing regularly, but I limit strength training during the competitive season. It is wise to cut back on your strength training during the marathon mileage buildup. I recommend no lifting the last six weeks before the race at the time when you are peaking near 20 miles. You may be able to continue lifting safely, but why take a chance? If a specific injury threatens, I'm quick to seek advice from a trainer or physical therapist about what strength training will help.

Part of my long-term success as a runner has come from avoiding those injuries that require extensive rehabilitation. During a half century of running, I've had very little downtime. A sore Achilles tendon now and then, a strained knee once, plantar fasciitis on another occasion. Nothing much. No surgery. Either I'm smart, or lucky, or I have what Dr. Costill describes as a "bulletproof body," one that is biomechanically sound. (Or maybe it's a combination of all three.) Although two of these factors are out of your control, you can be smart about your training by including stretching and strengthening as part of your routine.

PREVENT REINJURY

After suffering an injury serious enough that standard remedies such as ice, aspirin, and rest fail to provide relief, a runner needs not only to seek medical advice, but also to consult his training diary to identify the training patterns that contributed to the injury. Coming off an injury or a period of reduced training mileage, runners often reinjure themselves, claims Russell H. Pate, Ph.D., chairman of the Department of Exercise Science at the University of South Carolina in Columbia. "Runners think, 'I can do 80 miles a week again,' but their bodies aren't ready," he says.

After following the daily training of 600 runners for a year, Dr. Pate identified two major predictors for injuries: a previous injury and heavy training. "If you got injured once and don't modify your training, you probably will get injured again.

For those doing heavy training, three factors determined whether runners would be reinjured: frequency, mileage, and whether or not they ran marathons. A critical problem was the runners' approach to training. "Too rapid a buildup is a critical factor in injuries," says Dr. Pate. "You need to know your limitations." Once you determine that, you can modify your training to prevent future injuries.

One additional strategy I use in preventing injury is to obtain therapeutic massages. I am a frequent client of Patty Longnecker, a certified massage therapist, who owns Harbor Country Day Spa in New Buffalo, Michigan. Typically, I schedule a massage once every two weeks, more frequently if I am training hard for a specific race. And I'll often schedule a massage for after the race, particularly if it's a marathon. Although the free (or low-cost) post-race massages available at marathons feel good, it's better to obtain a massage 24 to 48 hours after the race while your muscles are recovering.

Professional athletes often get more frequent massages. Tennis player Pete Sampras has daily massages from a personal trainer. In the 1980s, Nike sponsored a club called Athletics West for several dozen athletes who trained in Eugene, Oregon. Team members, including Alberto Salazar and Mary Slaney, were able to benefit from massages three times a week. If I were a professional athlete whose income depended on my performance, I would get massages more frequently than I do now. Therapists sometimes suggest that massage can soothe and heal fatigued muscles, but research on the subject is scanty. I'm convinced that the most important benefit from massage is the relaxation effect. A relaxed muscle is less likely to get injured.

ADJUST YOUR PROGRAM TO YOUR AGE

Basic training principles apply to all runners, but the specifics may vary greatly. Although running offers a marvelous means of diminishing the effects of aging, the body eventually begins to slow, and as you get older, certain cautions are in order.

Instead of one day's rest following a hard speed session or long run, you may need two days, or more. And standard training programs may not work for you if they predispose you to injury. Tom Cross, a coach from Tulsa, Oklahoma, describes a discussion he had about training with three other runners, all over 60, who had just finished an 8-K race with times faster than 35:00.

"We decided that we should just keep a steady pace and forget about the frills," says Cross. "At our age, the consensus was: Don't run intervals, don't try hills, just be consistent. Run the same every day, although the pace might vary depending on the distance. This is what older runners learn, because the secret of endurance is to stay uninjured. All you need to do is run steadily every day, and whether or not you improve, you'll at least maintain your ability as well as you can."

REST—IT'S GOOD FOR YOU

"Dynamic repair" is a fancy title for rest coined by Bob Glover, a supervisor of coaches for the New York Road Runners Club. Glover considers rest to be a commonly overlooked component of any successful training program, and he believes that less training is sometimes best. "When in doubt, the coach should suggest less, and I've gotten softer and softer every year," he says. "By minimizing injury and getting a person to improve gradually, instead of rapidly, you'll have the most success. The old coach's mentality was to get out there and crack the whip: survival of the fittest. But how many people ended up on the junk heap along the way?"

Inevitably, if you can avoid injury, you can run long distances for the longest time. Defensive running may be the best training strategy.

Chapter 11

Planning for

PEAK PERFORMANCE

A iming at key races is the best way to achieve peak performance in long-distance events, says Russell H. Pate, Ph.D., chairman of the Department of Exercise Science at the University of South Carolina in Columbia.

Yet Dr. Pate (a man with several top 20 Boston Marathon finishes to his credit when he raced in the mid-1970s) concedes that the buildup to a goal carries with it a degree of risk, which escalates as the race gets closer and the workouts more intense. "Experience indicates that high-intensity workouts are more demanding and stressful," he says. "Training hard for prolonged periods is risky in terms of overtraining and even riskier in terms of injury."

This is where progressive training aimed at a certain event—sometimes called *periodization*—comes in: You start from a low point of conditioning and build to a high point. You compete in a race or a series of races. You then relax your training and begin to contemplate your next goal.

More than any other event, the marathon lends itself to this approach. Although some runners run a dozen or more marathons a year, most distance runners are content to run one or two during any given 12-month period. Many runners will run a single marathon in a lifetime. Usually, these races are selected well in advance, allowing ample time for a buildup to peak performance.

How do you plan for peak performance? How do you adjust your training schedule in anticipation of a specific race? How do you guarantee that you can follow that planned schedule and maximize your chances for success—and enjoyment?

"There is no magic formula," warns Keith Woodard, a coach from Portland, Oregon. "There is no magic mileage, no magic mold to put runners into. Runners are too individual for that." Nevertheless, there are certain guidelines all runners can follow to help achieve peak performance.

TIMING IS EVERYTHING

If you're planning to run a marathon in the next month or so, skip ahead to the chapters on nutrition and tapering that will do you more immediate good. You don't have *time* to execute the advice that follows here. Stick a bookmark here, so you'll remember to return. After you've finished that race and have begun to plan your next major running campaign, then come back and read this chapter.

If you expect to peak for a specific race—whether a mile or a marathon—you need time. You need time to plan, time to establish a base, time to progress and time to taper properly.

How much time? For a short-distance event on the track or an important 5-K or 10-K on the roads, you probably need at least 3 months of preparation (although 6 months or more would be better). If you're talking marathon, 3 months is probably enough time for most first timers; our program in Chicago lasts 18 weeks. But for experienced runners seeking improvement, 6 months is probably minimum, and 12 would be better. Former world-class marathoner Benji Durden of Boulder, Colorado, designed an 84-week schedule for me to use in my book *How to Train*. It involved a preliminary buildup to one test marathon, then a peak buildup to a second PR effort. Those with Olympic aspirations must think four years ahead. I planned 18 months ahead for one of my best races, a sub-2:30 marathon I ran to win a gold medal at the 1981 World Veterans Championships in New Zealand.

Doug Renner, a coach from Westminster, Maryland, suggests you develop a two- to four-year game plan. "Goals must continually be refined," Renner says. "Runners need to know the big picture, rather than just haphazardly go from race to race."

You want enough time to execute a well-organized plan that will bring you to the starting line in the best shape of your life. If you don't do that, you're not peaking.

WHY YOU NEED A GOAL

Before you make a plan, you need a goal. "The ability to adhere to a specific well-thought-out and long-term training program is the most necessary factor leading to success in the marathon," advises Clark Campbell, a coach and professional triathlete from Lawrence, Kansas.

In other words, when you have no destination, you can take any road. If you want to float along from week to week, training the way you feel, racing whenever you want to, that's fine. Running need not always be the relentless pursuit of one Big Event after another. We all need downtime to renew ourselves psychologically, to gather ourselves for the next push. Sometimes I'll take a year or more off from serious training and racing. I've spoken often about the Bowerman approach, which features hard days and easy days; I'll often plan hard years and easy years. Sometimes *not* having a goal might even be considered having a goal.

Usually I set goals at the beginning of each year, when I'm starting a new training diary. Sometimes my goals will be a set of times I want to better at various distances—or maybe there are a number of races I want to do well in. Most frequently, I attempt to peak for the World Veterans Championships, which comes at two-year intervals. Other times, I'll peak for a marathon.

Marathons lend themselves to goal setting, because of the extra effort required both to train for them and to compete well in them—and simply because of the magic of the marathon itself. But setting a goal involves not merely selecting an event or events but also deciding what you expect from your participation in that event. Is your goal just to finish? Is your goal a PR? Is your goal victory—or at least placing high in your age group? Or maybe you're just out to have a good time? You need to determine your principal goal first, and only after that can you begin to make plans.

It is also possible to have subgoals, or a series of goals. You may want to run some preliminary races—and run them well—as interim contests before the main race that interests you most. Sometimes I select a primary goal (such as running a fast marathon), expecting to use it as a stepping stone to a greater goal (running a faster marathon). Michigan marathoner Doug Kurtis says, "Marathoners need short-term goals, other races leading up to the marathon. I'm amazed when I meet people and their first race is a marathon. It's hard to focus on a marathon two or three months away, so focusing two or three weeks ahead on a 5-K can help keep you motivated."

On the other hand, if your goals are too many or too diverse, you may have difficulty achieving your main goal.

DEVELOPING YOUR GAME PLAN

Once you set your goal, you can make a *plan* to achieve that goal. Here's where training diaries come in handy, particularly for those of us who have been running for more than a few years. Whether or not I actually pull individual diaries down from the shelf, I'll at least mentally review what has worked for me in the past and what hasn't. Even if I decide to take a totally different approach—say, low-mileage training instead of high-mileage—it will be pursued after considerable reflection.

I do a lot of my preliminary planning on airplanes returning from major events. If, as so often happens, it's an overseas flight, I have plenty of time trapped in a tight seat with nothing better to do than think. Invariably the food is terrible, and I've already seen what is probably a bad movie, so what better time for considering future goals? Sometimes I'll pull out a notebook and jot down dates and times. Or I'll tap away at my laptop computer, which I frequently take with me on trips.

Inevitably, however, I fine-tune my plan after returning home. On a large sheet of poster board, I draw a homemade calendar with large blocks for each date. I'll list major events in appropriate boxes, usually drawing a red border around the important box, the day on which I want to hit my peak. I may list certain workouts I want to run, or distances (daily or weekly) I want to achieve. Or I may use the calendar to record how my training is going. I'll record the distance of my long runs and my weekly miles, and I may plot key speed workouts in advance, or record them after they occur. I'll do the same with races and my times at those races. (This is in addition to my regular diary, where I record more specific details about individual workouts every day.)

The Internet has provided runners with many planning tools. For several years I would ask runners in my marathon training classes how many had Internet access. The first year I asked it seemed half the people raised their hands; the following year it was more like 75 percent. Now I no longer ask, because it seems like practically every runner has Internet access, or knows a friend who can obtain training information for them off the World Wide Web. Many runners go to my Web site and print or download one of the training programs for novice, intermediate, or advanced runners. It's quite easy to modify the dates and numbers to fit your specific marathon training needs. In fact, I do this myself. To get ready for the 1999 Walt Disney World Marathon, where I was leading a pacing team for *Runner's World*, I used one of the *Marathon Training Guides* from my class in Chicago and simply scribbled in changes. In planning for a marathon PR, you're limited only by your imagination—although it helps to have the support of a good coach.

Planning is where time and goal come together. If you have a specific period of time in which to achieve a specific goal, you can plan accordingly—to a point, of course. You can't predict whether the wind will be in your face or the weather will be too warm. But you can plan almost every other aspect of your marathon training so you'll reach the starting line ready to perform to the best of your ability. If you can plan to achieve that goal, it won't matter how fast you run or whom you beat.

Dr. Pate advises, "Figure out the key sessions you need for your program. Get them in there, then surround them with those kinds of recovery activities that allow you to continue over a period of time. Build your program on priorities. The highest priority is attached to the key, hard sessions.

"The secret to success in long-distance running is not what type of workouts you do, whether high or low intensity, but how those workouts are structured into a specific program and incorporated throughout a training year—and for the length of a career as well."

You might want to reread that paragraph. It may be the most important message you encounter in this book.

TAKING TIME OFF

How important is rest? It's more important than most of us realize, says Paul Goss, a top-ranked duathlete and coach from Foster City, California. Boulder's marathoner Durden makes rest an integral part of his training programs.

While you're choosing your goal and planning your attack, you may want to take time to relax: a planned vacation, not necessarily away from running, but away from training at maximum effort. *Rest* is a word you have encountered before in this book, and it is a word you will encounter again.

Rest isn't always entirely optional, of course. If you've completed a marathon, you may be forced into a period of recuperation that could last a week, a month, or more. This time is necessary not only to allow sore muscles to recover, but also to permit rejuvenation of the spirit.

It may take more time for the spirit to recover than the muscles. Psychiatrists write about postmarathon depression. At a premarathon lecture in Chicago, Joan Benoit Samuelson referred to it as PMS. At first many of the women in the audience thought she was talking about premenstrual syndrome. When Joanie explained she meant postmarathon syndrome, women as well as men gave a nervous laugh.

At least in the aftermath of a marathon, there usually is a period of well-deserved euphoria following a peak performance, particularly one that involved much preparation. First-time marathoners are more susceptible than others because they have passed—for better or worse—through a unique experience. They wonder: "What do I do next?" and often there is no immediate answer.

One year, Ron Gunn of Southwestern Michigan College and I took a large number of runners from his beginning running class to the Honolulu Marathon. The morning after the race, we planned a short walk along the beach from our hotel to the Royal Hawaiian Hotel for brunch. Nearly everybody appeared wearing the "finisher" shirt they had won the previous day. Inevitably, of course, that revered shirt gets thrown into the dirty laundry.

Regardless of whether or not you immediately select your next goal, take ample time to rest before setting out to achieve it.

STABILIZING YOUR TRAINING

In many respects, the base period (when you run easy without worrying about pace or distance) is an extension of the rest period. Usually within a week after finishing a marathon, muscle soreness will almost completely disappear and you can begin to run comfortably again. But you need time to stabilize your training. Don't rush immediately into all-out training for your next goal. If you do, you're liable to crash some weeks or months later.

Runners tend to have a comfortable base level of training, a weekly maintenance mileage that they can accomplish almost effortlessly. For me, this base level is about 25 or 30 miles. I don't have to aim at running that far; it just happens. If I'm just going out the door five or six days a week without thinking about where I'm going or how far or how fast, I'll end the week with this level. That's my base maintenance level to which I return periodically: It's enough to maintain a reasonable percentage of my peak fitness level.

While training at this level, I often cross-train. If I've just finished a fall marathon, I'll swing eagerly into the cross-country ski season. I'll also spend more time lifting weights, since inevitably I eliminate strength training during my final race countdown.

I rarely peak for winter events, but after a spring marathon I might do some cycling or swimming, compete in some triathlons, or run some summer 5-K races—which I like because hot weather offers you a built-in excuse for slow times. I'll sometimes run these races on impulse, only deciding to enter on race morning.

Quite often, my peak performances coincide with late-summer track meets. Once past the track season, I divert time and energy in the fall to road races such as the Scenic Ten (10 miles) in Park Forest, Illinois, or the Blueberry Stomp (15-K) in Plymouth, Indiana, or the

National Heritage Corridor 25-K along a towpath beside the I & M Canal near Channahon, Illinois. Sometimes I run a fall marathon with minimal preparation, with no goal other than having a good time, or leading a pacing team.

Running many different races can take the edge off the period of base training, but it's important to slack off and give yourself some time when you're not too serious about anything connected with running—either racing or training. When it comes time to concentrate your training toward a peak goal, you then move into a new phase.

RACKING UP THE MILES

Practically every beginner's program depends on gradually increasing distance, usually weekly up to the day you do your longest run. Nobody has been able to come up with a better program, and I doubt anybody ever will. It's the old story of Milo (the ancient Greek wrestler) and the bull. You start lifting a calf when it is young, and by the time the calf grows into a heavy bull, you have the strength to throw people out of the ring in the Olympics.

The same is true with running: You take people running 15 to 25 miles a week, and by adding a few miles a week over a period of 18 weeks, you get them up near 40 to 50 miles weekly. You take people capable of running an hour (or half a dozen miles) continuously and help them to progress to where they can run for three to four hours (or about 20 miles).

If you're talking *peak* performance, however, you need to do more than spend three months adding a mile a week and increasing your final long workout to 20 miles. You need to take sufficient time (or have a sufficient base) to arrive at that level probably at least two months before the marathon—and hold at that level.

A single 20-miler isn't enough. For peak performance, you need to develop the ability to run 20-milers repeatedly (two or three times) without undue fatigue and without overtraining.

Some runners go beyond marathon distance in their training. At one point I progressed to 31-mile workouts, but I eventually decided that it was counterproductive, at least for me. It took too much time, and I had to slow down too much to achieve that distance.

During peak marathon training, however, I added a second semi-long run to my training week, usually about two-thirds of the distance of the longest run: 10 miles if my long run was 15; 13 to 15 miles if my long run was 20. Olympian Julie Isphording refers to these workouts as "sorta long" runs. It's possible to increase your long and semilong runs simultaneously, but a more sensible approach is to stabilize your long run near 20 miles, then begin a progression featuring a second workout.

Don't forget that word I promised to use again in this chapter: *rest*. Every third or fourth week, depending on how I felt, I would take an extra day or two of rest. I would back down from my weekly mileage and maybe skip my long run that week. That allowed me to gather strength so that I could progress to a still higher level.

Pumping Up the Intensity

Another standard approach for elite runners is to increase the intensity of their training sessions. One way to increase overall intensity is to do your long runs faster. When I peak for spring marathons, this happens naturally. As the weather warms, I can run more fluidly in shorts and a T-shirt than I can in the multilayered outfit I wear in colder weather. Similarly, before fall marathons, I find I can run more comfortably (and faster) as the weather cools, at least to a point. Some natural speeding is acceptable as you increase distance and improve fitness, but to push too fast, too far, too soon raises the specter of overtraining and injury.

One training option for long runs that I have begun to appreciate recently is a 3/1 pattern favored by John Davies, bronze medalist for 1500 meters in the 1964 Olympic Games, and currently a coach in Auckland, New Zealand. Davies suggests that runners do their long runs at a gentle pace for the first three-quarters of the distance (12 miles in a 16-mile run), then push the pace over the last quarter (the final 4 miles). This strategy pushes you to finish faster than you started, which is good both psychologically and physically. Davies doesn't advise 3/1 long runs every weekend, only every other weekend: again, the hard/easy approach.

Another sensible approach is to run all your distance workouts at a steady pace and to increase intensity in separate speed sessions. In fact, most experienced runners decrease their mileage at least slightly when moving from the distance phases to the speed phases of their peak training plans. Various forms of speedwork, particularly interval training, lend themselves to progressive training of this sort.

A typical speed progression would be to start with running 10 × 400 in 90 seconds with a 400 jog between, then over 10 successive weeks lower the time one second a week until you are capable of running 10 × 400 in 80 seconds. Another approach would be to begin at 5 × 400 and add an extra repetition at the same pace each week until you achieve 10 × 400, or more.

But don't make the mistake I once made when I increased the speed and the number of reps simultaneously. While training in Germany in 1956, I began at 10 × 400 in 70 seconds, and tried to add a 400 a week and drop a second a week. A few weeks before reaching my goal of 20 × 400 in 60 seconds, I suffered a sudden drop in performance.

Don't let the numbers frighten you. Progressions such as those I've described work only if you begin conservatively, and don't pick an end goal beyond your capabilities. Many runners would find it difficult to run a single 400 in 90 seconds much less use that as their starting point. No matter. We all play with the hands we are dealt and succeed or fail at various levels depending on our abilities.

HILLS FULFILL A PURPOSE

Hill training is another means of increasing workout intensity. You can run sprints up hills as a form of speed training or shift to hilly courses for your long runs. Preparing for the Chicago Marathon, which has a relatively flat course, I select flat courses for my long runs. When I'm preparing for a hillier marathon, such as Boston, I train over hillier courses, at least during the closing stages of my training. I also include some downhill repeats, since Boston is a point-to-point course that drops in elevation. This can make for very fast times, but you need to be prepared for the pounding your legs (especially your quadriceps) get on the downhill portion of the race.

Because Joe Catalano coaches in New England, where the Boston Marathon is the annual focus of many runners, he has his runners do their long workouts on hilly courses, because he feels that the combination of hills and distance increases endurance. "Many people shy away from hills," says Catalano, "especially when they go long. They make it easy on themselves—but that limits their improvement. It's a matter of strength: The more you repeat something, the stronger you get. We run long every week for best results. Wait more and you fail to improve. We start novice runners on courses as short as 3 to 6 miles. Very gradually we build: 8, 10, 12, 14, 16, then level off. We'll start on a series of small hills spaced apart. Then as the runners get stronger, we seek steeper hills closer together." One advantage of the Boston area, he says, is that it's fairly hilly.

The advantage of training using an overload, or progressive, stage similar to that proposed by Catalano is that as you get tougher, you toughen the workout. This approach provides a strong psychological "carrot" for the runner trying to peak for a specific race. After the long runs to develop endurance, after the fast runs to develop strength, you use a shot of speed training to fine-tune your speed.

CONSIDER OTHER FACTORS

Blind application of any number-based training system can cause problems. One variable not mentioned in many coaching articles is weather. Whether it's cold or hot, windy or rainy can affect how fast or how far you run during any given workout. The number of miles you have run doesn't necessarily reflect the quality of your training.

The late Barry Brown, a top masters runner, was an investment consultant who commuted by air between offices in Bolton Landing, New York, and Gainesville, Florida. Brown trained with a pulse monitor so he could measure the relative intensity of his workouts, regardless of other variables.

He once described to me an interval workout featuring mile repetitions, which he ran averaging 5:20 per mile in cool weather in New York, then averaged 5:40 in hot weather in Florida the following week. "The intensity measured by my pulse rate was exactly the same," he told me. "But if you just looked at the numbers in my diary, you would have thought I was taking it easy in the second workout."

A flight attendant with Delta Airlines lived in Boulder, Colorado, was based in Atlanta, and often flew to San Juan, Puerto Rico. Managing and measuring the intensity of her training schedule required the full-time attention of a coach.

Fatigue, diet, and sleep can affect the intensity of your training. Monitoring intensity is probably the trickiest aspect of any training program, even for an experienced runner, and that is one reason a knowledgeable coach can help you shave minutes off your marathon time. Self-trained runners who are well motivated can get themselves in trouble too easily. If they train in a group, where group dynamics sometimes take precedence over good sense, they can encounter similar problems.

For these reasons, I do not recommend doing interval training—or any form of speedwork—year-round. Nevertheless, it's a type of training that lends itself well to progressing toward a specific goal.

REVIEWING THE PLAN

At various points during the premarathon buildup, I like to review what I am doing. Am I on schedule? Am I training too hard and need to back off? What level of fitness have I achieved, and how will that affect my pace in the marathon?

In some respects, this review is ongoing, because every day on my way out to train I pass my training calendar on the wall, where I can see at a glance the number of weekly miles I've run and the distance of my long runs, and whether I'm on schedule or not. My smaller diary provides me with the details of my training, and I sometimes thumb backward through it if I'm planning to progress in certain workouts (in either distance or intensity). I also look for key words and phrases, such as "tired," or "dragging," or "legs dead," which, if they occur too often, are a clear signal to me that I need several easy days or a week of low mileage to avoid injury or overtraining.

One year at the Chicago Marathon, a runner approached the booth where I was selling books and said that he would log onto the marathon training program on my Web site to see what he was supposed to run that day. After the workout, he would log back on to make sure he had done the workout correctly. You're tempted to laugh, but what he achieved was positive reinforcement for his training. A lot of runners today who don't have easy access to good coaching in their area use the Internet as their coach.

During any review, I'll decide only to decrease the level of my training; I never decide to *increase* the level. If you think you're behind your premarathon schedule, you either need to lower your performance expectations or choose another race later in the year.

One way to determine your fitness level is to enter a race over a well-established distance. It's easy enough to find a 5-K or 10-K race to jump into, although I would prefer to test myself at either a 10-miler or a half-marathon. A 25-K would be ideal, but there are only a few of those around. (One of the best in my area is the Old Kent River Bank Run in Grand Rapids, Michigan, although its May date eliminates it as preparation for most spring marathons.)

I don't like to race too often during my peak buildup for any major event, but particularly not before a marathon. To race properly, I find I need to rest several days before the race, and it takes me several days after the race to recover. Before you know it, you've lost the equivalent of a week of productive training. For that reason, I try to limit any test races in the premarathon buildup to one a month. We used to list three to four test races for runners taking our marathon training class, but then we decided against it for fear that runners felt obligated to run all of them.

Invariably someone in each early lecture would ask what my codirectors, Brian Piper and Bill Fitzgerald, and I used to refer to as "the triathlon question." There was a late-summer triathlon in Chicago, and some individuals would want to enter both that and the marathon. "You can do both," we would usually tell them, "but it's difficult to do both well. You need to establish which race is most important to you and concentrate your main energy on that event. This may mean cutting back on the biking and swimming you might normally do before a triathlon, and doing the triathlon as a hard workout rather than a race. Or do the marathon as an afterthought: 26 miles of low-pressure running without worrying about time."

Nevertheless, some racing is helpful. If you're a beginner, you'll learn where to pin your number (front rather than back) and what it feels like to go to a starting line. Your time in test races can help you predict your marathon time and guide you in selecting a pace. But in making comparisons, beware of overconfidence. You may also need to make adjustments depending on conditions, including weather and the difficulty of the course.

THE REWARD: THE PEAK

Eventually, if you have planned well, you will reach a peak in your training. Running becomes easier and less of an effort. You are able to finish your weekly long runs at the same pace you started—and you don't feel as tired or worn out the next day. If you are running speedwork on the track, your times are faster. You feel good. You look lean and mean. One of the best indicators of my fitness level was when my wife's mother would look at me and say, "You're too skinny!" It was then that I knew I was in shape.

All of these signals offer positive feedback and will provide a psychological boost when you run your big race. If you know you're in shape, you're more likely to feel confident that you can achieve a peak performance. To achieve peak performance, mental strength may be as important as physical strength, but you achieve mental confidence by training yourself physically.

Most first-time marathoners train to reach a quick peak—that final 20-miler before the race. But if they're well coached, they won't try to achieve a peak performance in their first marathon; they'll save that goal for future races.

Most experienced marathoners like to reach a peak, then hold that training level for four to six weeks. Once you get to the point at which you have the time and ability to run several 20-milers, you are more likely to achieve the peak performance you want. You will probably also chop minutes off the time you ran in your first marathon.

The final touch for any program designed to achieve peak performance is the taper, the gradual cutback of training immediately before the race. This is such an important subject that I've devoted an entire chapter to it.

The one factor critical to your taper is rest, something many dedicated runners have trouble doing. You need to arrive at the starting line Rested, Refreshed, and Ready to run, the three Rs of peak performance. But more on this in the following chapter.

Chapter 12

The

MAGIC TAPER

After months and months of training, after the steady buildup of weekly miles and a string of long runs on weekends, the big event is near. Many questions may spring to mind: What do you do the last weeks before the marathon? How do you prepare yourself physically and mentally? How much should you rest? How do you cut back on training, or taper? How *long* should you taper?

In the critical weeks just prior to the race, many marathoners make a serious mistake. They fail to utilize one key ingredient in any training system that's mentioned many times in this book: *rest*.

FEAR OF TAPERING

David L. Costill, Ph.D., of Ball State University, believes that runners sometimes train too hard in the weeks immediately preceding a marathon. "They feel they need one last butt-busting workout and end up tearing themselves down," he says.

In decades past, runners rarely tapered, or cut back their training, for more than a week, even for a major marathon. But now that so many marathons have their own training classes, and with the increasing availability of coaches, especially for beginning runners, the word has gotten out. You need to cut back on your training for several weeks to obtain a peak performance. In his research with swimmers, Dr. Costill noticed that they often set PRs by tapering as much as three to six weeks before an event.

He also found that swimmers performed better when undertrained. So when Dr. Costill worked with a group of runners, he started their taper three weeks before a track race. During this period they ran only two easy miles daily.

Two problems developed. Psychological tests showed that the runners, addicted to running and worried about losing conditioning, became anxious. Also, in a preliminary 5000-meter trial, the runners—apparently so well rested that they misjudged their abilities—started off too fast and faded at the end. But in a subsequent trial, the runners paced themselves better and ran their best times.

Dr. Costill eventually concluded that runners can best achieve success in long-distance running by preparing far in advance. "Base is important. Runners need to start their marathon training early enough so that they can afford to taper two or three weeks before the event. You need to realize that it is the training you do *months* before—rather than weeks before—that spells success."

That's a message we all should heed, but the drive that pushes us to success often pushes us to train too hard at the end. This is particularly true of seasoned marathoners. You become comfortable with your regular training routine, whether it's 40, 50, 60, or more weekly miles, and don't want to cut back.

You may not know what to do with the extra time. And you don't want to give up your long Sunday run with friends, even the last weekend before the marathon. Then there's the problem of diet. If you cut down on the number of miles you run, you'll also need to cut the number of calories you eat if you don't want to gain weight. And while many marathoners might believe that rest could benefit their performance in *this* marathon, they're afraid of the effect of two or three weeks' rest on their overall conditioning.

CUT BACK—IT'S GOOD FOR YOU

Nevertheless, if you want to run well in the marathon, in the weeks leading up to the race you will need to change your habits in four areas.

Cut total mileage. Many of us are slaves to our training logs. We find security in the consistency with which we run week after week, month after month, recording a steady succession of miles in our diaries and on our calendars. That's fine, since steady and consistent training brings results, but for the last two to three weeks before the marathon, mileage doesn't count. In fact, high mileage may hinder your performance.

According to Owen Anderson, Ph.D., editor of *Running Research News*, "Scientific evidence suggests that temporary training reductions bolster leg muscle power, reduce lactic acid production, and carve precious minutes off race times. In contrast, hard workouts just before a race can produce nagging injuries and deplete leg muscles of their key fuel for running—glycogen."

How much should you cut mileage? That's a tough question, because all of us are different, and our goals differ. As a general rule, I'd say cut total mileage by at least 50 percent. Later in this chapter I'll present specific programs for how to do this.

Cut frequency. The simplest way to cut total mileage is to reduce the number of times you train. When I was training at the elite level and running twice a day, I cut my mileage by eliminating one of those daily workouts for the last ten days before a race.

You may not train twice daily, but if you follow a hard/easy pattern in your training, you have a similar option. Just eliminate the easy days. Instead of running an easy three-miler on your in-between days, don't run at all. Take a day off. Your body will be able to recover more fully from the hard workouts, and you won't lose any conditioning.

Cut distance, not intensity. Research suggests that you need to continue to train at or near race pace on the hard days. At McMaster University in Hamilton, Ontario, a group led by Duncan Mac-Dougall, Ph.D., compared different ways of tapering for well-trained runners who averaged 45 to 50 miles a week. For the taper week, some athletes didn't run, others ran 18 to 19 miles at an easy pace, and another group cut their mileage but continued running fast. The researchers decided that a taper including small amounts of fast running was superior to slow, easy miles.

Dr. MacDougall also worked with runners training for a 10-K race who started their taper with 5×500 at race pace, then progressively eliminated one 500 for the next five days, ending with a one-day rest. (In other words: 5×500, 4×500, 3×500, 2×500, 1×500, rest.)

Dr. MacDougall commented, "We still don't know what the optimal tapering plan actually is, but we do know that if you're going to be tapering for a week or so, it's important to keep the intensity of your workouts fairly high as you cut back drastically on your mileage."

Translated to the marathon, this would mean maintaining the pace of your runs but cutting their distance. A hard eight-mile run would become a six-mile run at the beginning of the taper, then later get cut to four or two. But you should keep the pace near the comfortable pace you've used for most of your training. In speed workouts, cut the number of repetitions similar to the McMaster's taper.

Cut back on calories. Finally, watch what you eat. If you're running less, you're also burning fewer calories. This could mean you gain a pound or so—no big deal, unless you also fill in your spare time by making extra trips to the fridge.

Robert Eslick, a coach from Nashville, says, "I tell my runners to watch their intake for the first three days of the marathon week to avoid weight gain and then to eat a little more than their normal intake, with the emphasis on carbohydrates, the last three days." Sound advice.

To keep from piling on extra pounds, you could eliminate junk food from your regular diet during your taper week. Get rid of the soft drinks and sugar sweets that you may have used to *boost* your calorie intake during regular training. Rely on complex carbohydrates instead—potatoes, apples, pasta, bread, and so on.

TAPERING FORMULAS THAT WORK

Knowing precisely how to modify your training during the last two to three weeks before a marathon takes experience. Even for seasoned marathoners, it may take a few bad starts before finding a specific routine that works. There are too many variables in the equation: How long you may have prepared for any one specific long race, how effective your training has been, whether you enter the closing stages undertrained or overtrained, and how confident you are.

A good coach who is familiar with your abilities and training patterns can tell you how to taper. A coach who has worked with you on a day-by-day basis could tell you precisely how to modify your training for the final countdown. Although I frequently get involved in writing training schedules for *Runner's World* and for various books, one single program cannot be expected to fit all runners. Nevertheless, here's my spin on the last three weeks before the Big Race.

Week three. Three weeks (21 days) before the race, you need to begin at least thinking about your taper. Ideally, this is a week when you *stabilize* your training. If you planned properly, you should have reached your high point in mileage, intensity, or both in the previous week. Most experienced runners plan to peak with three weeks to go. Avoid the trap of thinking that one additional week of training just might get you in really good shape. It's more likely to injure you or lower your resistance so you're at risk of catching a cold or the flu—a big liability when you have a race to run.

If you're an experienced runner and plan only a two-week taper, you can run as hard this week as you did the week before, but no harder. If it's the week for your final 20-miler, resist the temptation to push to 21 or 22. If your weekly mileage last week was 50, keep it there. Don't try for 55.

In Chicago, we do our final 20-miler on the Saturday or Sunday before the three-week taper begins. On successive Sundays, we go from 20 to 12 to 8 miles with the 26-mile race falling on the fourth Sunday of our program. The more I work with both beginning and experienced runners, the more comfortable I become with this pattern.

Most runners, even experienced ones, will benefit from a slight decrease in their mileage, to about 75 percent of the mileage the week before. The runner who ran 50 miles last week should cut back to somewhere between 35 and 40 miles. An easy way to cut total mileage is to convert one or two of your easy days into rest days. Change one or two others into half workouts, decreasing your distance. But don't cut intensity or pace yet. You can cut the number of repeats during speed workouts, for example, but don't run them slower.

Week two. If you didn't cut mileage last week, cut it now. You need at least 10 days to taper. In my peak years, I tapered 10 days before marathons, or even before important track races. Now that I am older and wiser, I take more time. If you feel you must run a final 20-miler two weeks before the race, it should be your final workout at this distance.

If you did cut your mileage to 75 percent in week three, now you should cut it to nearly 50 percent of your normal mileage. The marathoner who normally runs 50 miles a week should run 25 miles this week.

But don't reduce your pace yet. You don't want to forget too soon what it feels like to train at near-marathon pace.

Remember that along with the decreased mileage, you'll be

burning fewer calories, so if you're worried about gaining a pound or two, cut back on your intake of "empty" calories.

Week one. If you've resisted the idea of cutting your mileage before, at least cut it now. Even macho, supermileage, another-lap-around-the-park, give-me-100 zealots will concede that maybe a little taper is helpful at this point. Okay, if you wouldn't taper for three weeks, how about three days? Did you really believe running 20 miles the final Sunday before your race was going to help you? I once did, but I've long since changed my mind.

Speaking of diet, begin carbo-loading seven days in advance. Forget what you read years ago about depletion and three days of a low-carbohydrate diet before switching to a diet high in carbohydrates. (The theory was that the depleted muscles—"starved" for carbohydrates—would then be able to suck up even more carbos than normal and thus provide the marathoner with even more energy on race day.) Stick with a high-carbohydrate diet throughout the week. You don't need to eat spaghetti all seven days: Focusing on fruits, vegetables, and grains will keep you above 60 percent carbos even if you have lean meat as a main course. If you haven't eliminated between-meal junk snacks, do it now.

This is also the week to *eliminate* hard training. There's no room in your training plan for hard, fast, or long runs. Forget them. If you run anything at or near race pace, don't run far. I enjoy doing "strides," which are controlled sprints at race pace. But by definition, strides are short: 150 meters at the most. Soft surfaces are best. Instead of jogging between strides, I'll walk. Before Boston, I'll head out to the Charles River and do my strides on the grass beside the bike path; in Chicago, there's plenty of grass in Grant Park near the start of the race. Most runners find prerace training areas without much prodding.

Now is not the time to cross-train. According to Tom Grogon, a coach from Cincinnati, "One problem that often develops is that people in training sometimes use these easy/lower mileage weeks to do something else equally stressful." Grogon recalls one tapering runner who rebuilt his barn and another who spent his "rest" time swimming and biking—and none of these activities exactly qualify as resting. Grogon recommends using the extra time to catch up on family and work responsibilities.

Days three to one. For the final three days of the countdown, I shift to almost total rest. Notice I said "almost." During the final three days, I rest two, run one. This is my usual premarathon pattern:

Three days before is a day off.

Two days before is a day off.

One day before, I may do some light jogging and perhaps do a few strides, particularly if I've traveled a long distance to the race.

If possible, I prefer to travel at least two days before the race, not the day before. Travel fatigues me, and I prefer to get to the race city early. For international races requiring an overnight jet flight, I need to arrive *much* earlier. For a short overseas track race, I'll sometimes arrive a couple of days before I compete; for marathons I need nearly a week to adjust. One rule of thumb is to arrive one day early for every time zone crossed—if the cost of hotel rooms isn't prohibitive. Ask yourself: How important is this race? Then plan accordingly.

24 hours. The important point to remember about the last 24 hours is that if you have prepared properly, nothing much you do on this day—except what you eat and drink—will have much effect on your race. As for training, if what you do allows you to relax—including those strides mentioned earlier—do it. Mental preparation is probably more important than physical preparation at this point.

One way to pass time the day before the race is to hang out at the exhibition of running equipment that's as much a part of the marathon mystique as the pasta party. But don't spend all day on your feet, particularly on the hard concrete in most exhibition halls. If you want to chat with your friends, do it in your room, or sitting in soft chairs in the lobby.

Another option is touring the course. Some runners feel it is important to see the course in advance, so they know what to expect. But having been in the running business this long as both a participant and as a reporter, I've either run over most of the courses I race or ridden them on press trucks. I don't need to see them one more time, or even one time, particularly if it means committing myself to sitting for several hours on a bus. With several thousand people around you on race day, you're not going to get lost.

To me the hills always seem steeper and the miles longer when you're riding over them rather than running them. But if there are key points of a course I feel I need to see—such as a series of hills—

I might make an effort to see them, but usually I'm content to wait until race day.

THE FINAL FEAST

My all-time favorite running book title is *Spaghetti Every Friday*, written by Houston runner Bob Fletcher, who ran 50 marathons on 50 successive weekends. This title refers to the ritual spaghetti dinner the night before most major marathons. Often you can eat on the cheap at these affairs, but sometimes they're noisy and impersonal. My nominee for the best prerace pasta party is the Chicago Marathon, but I'm biased because I grew up in Chicago.

To avoid crowds, I'll sometimes sneak off to a local Italian restaurant—if I can find one without a 30-minute wait. Boston has some of the best Italian restaurants in the world in its North End. Or I may pick a Chinese restaurant where I can eat a rice dish. Honolulu, as you might suspect, has excellent Asian restaurants.

Wherever or whatever you eat, your last meal needs to be high in carbohydrates. But don't overeat, thinking more is better. The night before the 1982 Avon Women's International Marathon in San Francisco, I sat next to a top runner who piled a world-record amount of pasta on her plate. Then she went back for seconds! She was only 5 feet 5 inches tall and weighed 109 pounds, so I don't know where she stored all that food. And I don't recall that she ran too well the next day.

Basically, don't eat any more at the prerace pasta party than you're used to. Even though the second and third helpings are free, don't necessarily avail yourself of them. Eat a normal-size meal and drink what you usually drink. I notice a lot of runners walking around expos with water bottles in their hands. If you feel that's what you need to do to ensure that you go to the starting line well hydrated, do it, but you may spend most of the last 24 hours before the race going to the bathroom. Most experts advise against beer, because it's a diuretic, but if you're used to having an occasional beer with your meal and you think it will relax you, it probably will.

Research at Ball State University suggests that eating two small meals four hours apart the night before the race may be better than eating one larger meal. Logistically, that used to be difficult to do, but with so many energy drinks and bars on the market, carbo-loading has become easier. Dr. Costill suggests that a high-carbohydrate snack just before going to bed may help assure a full supply of glycogen in your muscles. Avoid soft drinks with caffeine that may keep you awake. My caffeine limit is normally one cup of coffee or one soft drink, but I won't even have that the night before a marathon.

With or without caffeine in my system, I may sleep fitfully or awaken in the middle of the night. This used to worry me; it no longer does. I thought I was losing energy by lying awake in bed, but as long as you're horizontal you're still getting rest. More important than the night before the race, is the night *before* the night before. For a Sunday race, make certain you sleep well on Friday, and don't worry about Saturday.

Another important and delicate question. Sex the night before: Yes or no? It depends. It's your choice and your mate's choice. My general recommendation is to follow the advice in the previous paragraphs on marathon-related items, but try to keep the rest of your life normal. Casey Stengel, the famous New York Yankee manager, used to claim that it wasn't sex before the game that caused declines in his baseball players' performance the next day, it was chasing all over town to find it.

One final item in my premarathon countdown: I always pin my number on my singlet before I go to bed. In deference to the sponsors, I no longer fold around the numeral to cut wind resistance (as elite runners used to do obsessively several decades ago), but I will fold the bar strip under. I usually bring extra safety pins in case there aren't enough in my race packet, as I don't want the number flapping in the wind.

With my singlet so pinned—and I'll try it on to make certain I haven't pinned the front to the back—I'll position it on a chair in my hotel room along with my shorts, warmup clothes, and any other gear, with my shoes (socks inside) positioned under the chair pointing in the right direction, as though I were seated in the chair. I once felt somewhat foolish doing this, but I've talked to enough runners to realize that I am not alone.

Be sure to check to make sure you have all of the necessary gear before you leave home, and you may want to carry your shoes onto the plane just in case the airline loses your bag.

When it comes to the marathon, you don't want to leave anything to chance.

Chapter 13

The Distance Runner's
DIET

It was tough for those of us who ran long distance in the 1960s. We were poorly served nutritionally because of our own lack of knowledge, and an equal lack among event organizers. We didn't know what to drink—or *whether* to drink. Race officials rarely provided fluids on the course, and frequently scheduled starting times so we ran during the hottest part of the day. Our motto could have been, "Mad dogs and marathoners go out in the midday sun."

Somehow we survived, and the sport began to prosper—but only after major changes were made in the distance runner's diet.

THE DARK AGES OF SPORTS NUTRITION

A page from my 1963 training diary is particularly frightening. While being coached by Fred Wilt, I kept meticulous records of everything from temperature and humidity to what I ate. It was June 30, at the National Amateur Athletic Union (AAU) 25-Kilometer Championships in Detroit. The race started at 1:30 in the afternoon. It was 94 F°; the humidity was high, and there wasn't a cloud in the sky. I recorded the weather as "hot!!" There was no drinking water on the course past 10 miles.

Most astounding was my prerace meal. For breakfast at 7:30 A.M., I had orange juice and cereal, which was a good start, but my choices for lunch several hours later seem strange today. I had more orange juice, bread, milk, and a *six-ounce steak*! Little wonder I suffered problems that day. I kept pace for half the distance with the

126

eventual winner, Peter McArdle, of the New York Athletic Club, then faded badly to barely salvage third.

Coach Wilt and I knew even then that good nutrition was essential for success in endurance events, but we hadn't yet fit together all the puzzle pieces. I usually had problems in the closing stages of marathons because I ran out of energy, so I experimented with several nutritional means of boosting energy stores. At various times, I taped dextrose tablets to the back of my shorts to take during the race, or drank a high-energy drink called Sustagen, a milkshake-like supplement often used for the elderly. It made me belch through the first half of the Boston Marathon one year and didn't help much during the second half.

Actually, where diet was concerned, some of the veteran runners from New England knew better. In the 1950s, New England was a hotbed of road-running activity. In fact, it was the *only* bed. When I first arrived at Boston in 1959, I learned that the traditional breakfast for marathoners was "porridge," what I knew as oatmeal. I made fun of this strange New England meal in an article I wrote for *Sports Illustrated* in 1963 called "On the Run from Dogs and People" (later expanded into a book with the same title).

I should have kept my mouth shut. Or rather opened it and started to eat. Oatmeal is high in carbohydrates and, sweetened with honey and coupled with orange juice, was exactly the kind of premarathon meal I should have been eating.

Getting a Handle on Proper Eating

By the end of the 1960s, we began to get an idea of what diet worked best for distance runners. In 1966, David L. Costill, Ph.D., established the Human Performance Laboratory at Ball State University in Muncie, Indiana, and I became one of his first guinea pigs. One of his early experiments involved fluid replacement. One summer, I ran two hours on a treadmill on three successive days in Dr. Costill's lab—the equivalent of three 20-milers—drinking either nothing, water, or Gatorade.

When allowed to drink at the rate of 50 milliliters every five minutes, my core body temperature remained several degrees lower than when I ran without fluids. The replacement drink provided a glucose boost that theoretically would permit me to run cooler and faster.

Dr. Costill continued his research on race nutrition. Within a few years, in some of the earliest experiments on carbohydrate loading, his assistant Bill Fink was cooking large pots of spaghetti in the Ball State lab to feed to runners. The word soon leaked out to the sports world: Steaks were out, pasta was in. Several years later, I had an assignment to write an article for the *New York Times Magazine* on a quarterback for the Kansas City Chiefs. I noted with interest that Hank Stram, coach of the Chiefs, was already promoting spaghetti as a better pregame meal for his 280-pound linemen than the traditional lean beef. Today, just about any runner knows that spaghetti is a better premarathon meal than, say, scrambled eggs or steak, but that knowledge was a result of the pain suffered by us guinea pigs.

We now realize that the preferred fuel for the endurance athlete is carbohydrates, because they are easy to digest and easy to convert into energy. Carbohydrates convert quickly into glucose (a form of sugar that circulates in the blood) and glycogen (the form of glucose stored in muscle tissue and the liver). Proteins and fats also convert into glucose/glycogen, but at a greater energy cost. The body can normally store about 2,000 calories worth of glycogen in the muscle, enough for maybe 20 miles of running.

Can better nutrition create better athletes? Ann C. Grandjean, Ed.D., director of the International Center for Sports Nutrition, frowns at the question and gives an indirect, one-word answer: "Genetics!" What she means is that great athletes are born with the ability to succeed, a gift of good genes that allows them—when properly trained and fed—to run and jump and throw faster and higher and farther than their less genetically gifted opponents. In suggesting better nutrition for long-distance runners, sports nutritionists can't promise you success—but at least you won't fail because of poor nutrition.

How important is good nutrition? Frederick C. Hagerman, Ph.D., of Ohio University in Athens, served as a nutritional consultant for the Cincinnati Reds baseball team. Dr. Hagerman led off a conference in Columbus, Ohio, on "Nutrition for the Marathon and Other Endurance Sports" before the 1992 men's Olympic marathon trials by saying that the second most important question asked by athletes is, "What should I eat to make me stronger, better, and faster for my sport?" (The most important question, he said, is, "How do I train?") Dr. Hagerman claimed that too many athletes have no idea how to eat properly to maximize their performance.

There are three important areas of the distance runner's diet. One is overall nutrition, the ability to maintain high energy levels during training. The second is prerace nutrition, what you eat in the last few days before running to ensure a good performance. Third is what you consume (mostly liquids) during the race itself to make sure that you maximize performance—and get to the finish line on your own two feet. This chapter covers the first two, training nutrition and prerace nutrition. Your body's needs during the race are covered in chapter 16.

THE SPECIAL NEEDS OF RUNNERS IN TRAINING

When you run long distances, your energy requirements increase. In an article on endurance exercise in *The Physician and Sportsmedicine*, Walter R. Frontera, M.D., and Richard P. Adams, Ph.D., comment, "During sustained exercise such as marathon running, total body energy requirements increase 10 to 20 times above resting values." Runners need to eat more of the proper foods to fuel their muscles. They also need to drink more, particularly in warm weather.

At the sports nutrition seminar in Columbus, Linda Houtkooper, Ph.D., a registered dietitian at the University of Arizona, made clear that endurance athletes in particular should get most of their calories from carbohydrates.

No argument there. The only problem is that with 35,000 items in the supermarket, marathon runners sometimes need help determining which foods are highest in carbohydrates. Unless you plan to eat spaghetti three meals a day (and even pasta contains 13 percent protein and 4 percent fat), you may need to start reading labels.

Dr. Houtkooper explained that the body requires at least 40 nutrients that are classified into six nutritional components: proteins, carbohydrates, fats, vitamins, minerals, and water. "These nutrients cannot be made in the body, and so must be supplied from solid or liquid foods." She listed six categories that form the fundamentals of a nutritionally adequate food selection plan: fruits, vegetables, grains/legumes, lean meats, low-fat milk products, and fats/sweets (in descending order of importance).

The recommendations for a healthy diet suggest 15 to 20 percent protein, 30 percent fat and 50 to 55 percent carbohydrates. But all carbohydrates aren't created alike. There are simple and complex carbohydrates. Simple carbohydrates include sugar, honey, jam, and any food such as sweets and soft drinks that gets most of its calories from sugar. Nutritionists recommend that these simple carbos make up only 10 percent of your diet. It's complex carbohydrates you should concentrate on—the starch in plant foods—which include fruits, vegetables, bread, pasta, and legumes.

Endurance athletes in particular benefit from fuel-efficient complex carbohydrates because of the extra calories burned each day. You need to aim for even more total carbohydrates than the suggested 50 percent. You can eat (in fact, may *need* to eat) more total calories without worrying about weight gain. The average runner training for a marathon and running 25 to 30 miles a week probably needs a daily caloric intake near 3,000 to maintain muscle glycogen stores. As your mileage climbs beyond that, you need to eat more and more food, not less. In all honesty, this is why a lot of runners run, and why they train for marathons. Their common motto is, "I love to eat."

High-mileage athletes may want to supplement their diets with high-carbohydrate drinks to ensure sufficient energy for their daily long runs. But you also need more protein, suggests Liz Applegate, Ph.D., a professor at the University of California at Davis, author of *Power Foods*, as well as a nutrition columnist for *Runner's World*. Dr. Applegate suggests that runners training for a marathon need a minimum of 70 grams of protein a day—more if you're a high-mileage trainer. You need 400 grams of carbohydrates a day if you're on a training program such as mine, 500 if your weekly mileage peaks above 50, 600 if over 70, and so forth. Eating such a high-carbohydrate diet allows you to continuously restock your muscles with glycogen, the fuel that is as important in training as it is in racing. Because of the number of miles you run, you can also afford a somewhat higher ratio of simple versus complex carbohydrates in your diet—although some nutritionists might argue with me on this point.

Here's where I part company with the popular "Zone" (or

40/30/30) Diet, the numbers referring to its mix of 40 percent carbohydrates, 30 percent protein, and 30 percent fat. People have lost weight following the Zone Diet, although researchers suggest it is mainly because in following this regimen, they also cut calorie intake. When it comes to losing weight, all nutritionists agree that the best approach is to combine diet and exercise. And the most effective weight-burning exercise is running. You'll burn approximately 100 calories a mile. Run 36 miles (3,600 calories burned), and you can lose a pound. Follow my marathon training program, and you'll run approximately 500 miles over a period of 18 weeks. Theoretically, at least, you can lose 15 pounds by training for a marathon. This assumes that you don't increase your calorie consumption to meet your body's increased energy needs.

Some people seeking to finish their first marathon, however, are more than 15 pounds overweight—or they think they are. So they also attempt to lose some additional weight by dieting. To a certain extent, this isn't a bad idea, assuming you choose your diet prudently. Those who choose the Zone Diet, or any other fad diet that lowers carbohydrate intake, make a major mistake. That's because most fad diets fail to provide enough energy for endurance activities. Follow the Zone Diet, and if you're eating 3,000 calories a day, according to Dr. Applegate, you'll ingest only about 300 grams of carbohydrates a day, much less than the 400 recommended. "One problem," says Dr. Applegate, "is that individuals following the Zone Diet Monday to Thursday start running out of energy by the weekend when they're about to do their long run. They need to take a day off on Friday, not to rest from their running, but to rest from their diets. These Zone Diet runners either crash during the workout or binge on carbos to survive, which makes them feel guilty."

The only aspect of the Zone Diet that Dr. Applegate likes is its emphasis on protein. She feels that runners who graze on bagels and jelly beans and entirely avoid meats or other protein sources aren't doing themselves any good either.

Frequently, I receive questions for my "Ask the Expert" column in *Runner's World* from runners training for a marathon who claim that they have no energy, that they have to struggle to get through their long runs, particularly as the mileage begins to escalate toward the end of their training plans. They aren't eating enough carbohydrates;

HIGH-CARBOHYDRATE FOODS

The traditional prerace meal for marathoners is spaghetti. With a wife of Italian origin, I also reap the culinary benefits of a tradition that literally demands frequent doses of pasta. But spaghetti (or macaroni, or other forms of pasta) every day can become boring, particularly when you're trying to carbo-load the week before a marathon. Fortunately, there are many foods you can eat that will guarantee that your diet is high in carbohydrates both during training and before races.

In *Nancy Clark's Sports Nutrition Guidebook*, the author, a dietitian, lists the following carbohydrate-rich foods.

Fruits
Apples
Apricots, dried
Bananas
Fruit Roll-Ups
Oranges
Raisins

Vegetables
Broccoli
Carrots
Corn
Green beans
Peas
Tomato sauce
Winter squash
Zucchini

Grains, Legumes, and Potatoes
Baked beans
Lentils
Potato, baked

Rice
Spaghetti
Stuffing

Breads, Rolls, and Crackers
Bagel
Bran muffin
English muffin
Graham crackers
Matzo
Pancakes
Pita bread
Saltines
Submarine roll
Waffles
Whole-grain bread

Breakfast Cereals
Cream of Wheat
Granola (low-fat varieties)
Grape-Nuts

Muesli
Oatmeal
Raisin Bran

Beverages
Apple juice
Apricot nectar
Cola drinks
Cran-Raspberry juice
Orange juice

Sweets, Snacks, and Desserts
Cranberry sauce
Fig bars
Fruit yogurt
Honey
Maple syrup
Pop-Tarts
Strawberry jam

Clark also warns that some foods that runners assume are high in carbohydrates may have a high percentage of their calories hidden in fat. These foods include croissants, Ritz crackers, thin-crust pizza (as opposed to thick-crust), and granola. When in doubt, Clark advises, read the labels.

they're starved for fuel. My advice is to avoid *any* kind of fad diet. Sound nutritional practices will get you to the starting line, and that includes eating plenty of carbohydrates, since they are the most efficient form of fuel.

You don't need to patronize Italian restaurants to ensure an adequate supply of complex carbohydrates. I sometimes choose a Chinese restaurant, because rice is also high in carbohydrates. And Nancy Clark, R.D., director of nutrition services for SportsMedicine Brookline in Boston, and author of *Nancy Clark's Sports Nutrition Guidebook* (among the best books on the subject) points out that you can get plenty of carbos in most American restaurants. If you eat soup (such as minestrone, bean, rice, or noodle), potatoes, breads, and vegetables along with your main dish, and maybe grab a piece of apple cobbler off the dessert tray, you can end up eating more carbohydrates than fats or protein. (For a list of good high-carbohydrate choices, see "High-Carbohydrate Foods" on the opposite page.)

CHECKING OUT YOUR DIET

I don't spend a lot of time agonizing over what I eat, but the last time a dietitian evaluated my diet, I averaged 12 percent protein, 19 percent fat, and 69 percent carbohydrates over a typical three-day period. Fifty-two percent of my total calories came from complex carbohydrates, and 16 percent were from simple carbohydrates.

The nutritional analysis of my diet also showed I was getting more than the recommended daily allowances of vitamins and minerals, so I don't normally take supplements. And my cholesterol count usually hovers within a few points of 185, with a favorable HDL ratio. If I have succeeded with my dietary goals, I believe there are two reasons.

A healthy breakfast. You can think of a good breakfast as a fast start out of the blocks. Each morning I drink two or three eight-ounce glasses of orange juice and usually eat a high-fiber breakfast cereal with skim milk, piled high with raisins, bananas, and whatever other fruits are in season: strawberries, raspberries, blueberries. A couple of times when we were out of milk, I substituted orange juice on my cereal. Yes, it sounds disgusting, but don't knock it until you've tried it.

I used to add two slices of toast spread with margarine or butter, and sometimes a soft-boiled egg, although as my mileage totals declined over the last several years I began to cut back on my calorie consumption to maintain a steady weight, and those items have dropped out of my diet. Sometimes on Sundays, between my long run and church, my wife and I will treat ourselves to a special breakfast with coffee cake (or pancakes, waffles, or French toast), bacon, and scrambled eggs with mozzarella cheese. Research suggests that if you are going to do any "dangerous" eating of high-fat foods, you're best off doing it on days when you burn a lot of calories and can quickly metabolize those foods.

Joanne Milkereit's refrigerator. Okay, this needs some explaining. Joanne Milkereit was the nutritionist at the Hyde Park Co-op, an upscale grocery store near the University of Chicago, when we collaborated to write the *Runner's Cookbook* back in 1979. (She now works as the director of dietetic internship at the Medical University of South Carolina.)

While we were working on the cookbook, Milkereit told me that all runners should tape the following words on their refrigerators: "Eat a wide variety of lightly processed foods." Go back and reread this phrase. Think about it. By wide variety, she means you sample all the food groups. When foods are lightly processed, you don't destroy all the vitamins.

What does she mean by lightly processed? Beware of foods that come wrapped in plastic, or that you can buy at a fast-food restaurant—although several restaurants have started to offer such fare as low-fat burgers, carrot sticks and nutritious salads. Another food rule comes from Pete Pfitzinger, a 1984 and 1988 Olympic marathoner. He once told me, "I don't put anything in my mouth that's been invented in the last 25 years." That may be a bit too extreme, but if you pay attention to these two messages, you probably can't go wrong with your diet.

Judy Tillapaugh, R.D., of Fort Wayne, Indiana, believes that although runners understand the value of carbo-loading before a marathon, they don't give equal attention to day-to-day meal plans. "Endurance athletes need to continually replace energy stores with a diet high in carbohydrates, low in fat, and with enough protein to maintain muscle," says Tillapaugh. "Some weight-conscious runners don't eat enough."

And you need to spread your calories throughout the day by snacking, choosing healthy fare such as fruit, graham crackers, yogurt, or bagels. If you need 3,500 calories daily, you can't pack them into one or two meals. Athletes often neglect breakfast, then wonder why they're tired while running in the evening.

Does a good diet mean no treats? My measured intake of 16 percent of calories from simple carbohydrates might be considered high for "healthy" people, but not necessarily for a competitive runner. "Athletes are told to avoid junk foods," says Dr. Grandjean, "but the reality is that if you are eating 4,000 calories a day, once you have taken in those first 2,000 calories—assuming you've done a reasonably intelligent job of selecting foods—you've probably obtained all the nutrients you need. You don't need to worry about vitamins and minerals, because you've already supplied your needs. You can afford foods high in sugar, so-called 'empty calories,' because you need energy. Your problem sometimes is finding enough time to eat."

Sports nutrition thus comes down to a management problem.

DISTANCE RUNNERS NEED CALORIES

The importance of general nutrition—as opposed to prerace nutrition—is that you need adequate energy for training. And unlike the general population, you may need to eat more to help maintain your weight. If you're a 150-pound person running 30 miles a week to prepare for a marathon, you need approximately 3,000 calories a week more than a sedentary person, and most of those calories should come from carbohydrates. Since carbohydrates are bulkier than fats or protein, the sheer volume of food high-mileage runners must eat can become a problem.

Dr. Grandjean says that among the athletes she advises, distance runners are most knowledgeable about nutrition because their energy needs are so high. And those most talented, the ones already on top, often have the best nutrition. Fred Brouns of the Nutrition Research Center at the University of Limburg in the Netherlands studied cyclists competing in the Tour de France, both in the laboratory and during the race. Brouns discovered that those who finished near the front were those who were most successful at managing their diets. "Endurance athletes must pay close attention to food intake if they expect to keep energy levels high," says Brouns.

In the Tour de France, cyclists frequently burn *5,000 calories a day!* There's no way these competitors can ride five or six hours a day and have time to eat that much, so they take much of their calories in liquid form while riding. Although most runners don't have anywhere near the energy requirements of a Tour cyclist, some high-mileage runners like to use high-carbohydrate drinks as a dietary supplement.

Nancy Ditz, the top U.S. finisher at the 1987 world championship and 1988 Olympic marathons, took an intelligent approach to diet. Between those two marathons, Ditz decided she wanted to leave nothing to chance when it came to race preparation. Following the suggestion of her coach, Rod Dixon (the 1983 New York City marathon champion and Olympic runner from New Zealand), she sought nutritional advice.

Ditz didn't go to a standard dietitian, but spoke with Jerry Attaway, an assistant coach with the San Francisco 49ers. Attaway managed that team's strength training, rehabilitation, and diet programs. He determined that, based on Ditz's energy expenditure while training 100 miles a week, she needed a higher percentage of carbohydrates than she was getting.

"Even though I was eating a pretty good diet, my carbohydrate intake still wasn't enough," Ditz recalls. She started using Exceed, a high-carbohydrate drink. (Such drinks are most effective when consumed immediately after exercise, when they can be most quickly absorbed.) Her calcium intake needed to be higher, so she also started drinking buttermilk with meals.

Ditz feared Attaway might ask her to cut out one of her favorite treats—cinnamon rolls at breakfast—but instead he eliminated mayonnaise on her sandwich at lunch. "That was a minor behavioral change for a major change in my ratio of fat to carbohydrate," she says. (In two tablespoons of mayonnaise, you get 202 calories that are 100 percent fat!)

Attaway identified foods that did the most damage to Ditz's diet, then asked, "Which do you *really* like?" He let her keep those, then eliminated the rest.

Ideally, long-distance runners interested in maximizing their performance in the marathon should find someone as knowledgeable as Jerry Attaway to tell them how to eat. If I had to offer a single piece of dietary advice to every person who reads this book—regardless of whether or not you have Olympic aspirations—it would be to consult a dietitian. (The American Dietetic Association's referral network can help you find a sports nutritionist. Dial 800-877-1600. Or check the ADA Web site: www.eatright.org.) Have that dietitian analyze your diet and recommend what to eat and what not to eat.

EATING BEFORE THE RACE

Pasta has become the ritual prerace feast for marathoners. No major marathon is without its night-before spaghetti dinner, which has assumed almost ceremonial aspects.

The spaghetti dinner, of course, has more than a ceremonial purpose. In eating high-carbohydrate pasta, we want to make sure our bodies have adequate glycogen, the fuel supply stored in the muscles that allows the most efficient form of energy metabolism. The more glycogen you can store, the faster you can run for longer periods of time, because when muscle glycogen is depleted, muscles contract poorly. But a well-fueled athlete also needs a full supply of glycogen for the liver, a "processing station" that sends fuel through the bloodstream to the muscles. So in addition to having your fuel tank full, you also need a full carburetor.

Various diets have been devised in an attempt to ensure maximum glycogen storage. The term *carbohydrate loading*, or *carbo-loading*, was originally coined to describe a dietary regimen that involved depletion and replenishment. This early form of carbo-loading became popular in the mid-1970s following research in Scandinavia. The regimen began with a 20-mile run to exhaustion one week before the marathon to deplete muscles of all available glycogen. For three days following that purge, the athlete followed a high-protein, low-carbohydrate diet designed to keep glycogen stores artificially low. Midweek, the athlete switched to a low-protein, high-carbohydrate diet to overload the muscles with glycogen during the final three days before the race. The theory was that if you depleted your body of glycogen, you would absorb more when you did eat carbohydrates—like a sponge that, squeezed dry, absorbs more water than a damp one.

I never could quite figure out how a sponge 100 percent saturated with water could absorb more than 100 percent after being squeezed dry, but this early form of carbo-loading seemed to work for some marathoners—at least sometimes. I experimented with it and had both good and bad results. (One problem scientists have in measuring anything as complicated as the effect of diet on performance is that so many other variables are present.)

Most experts today believe that runners should avoid the carbo-loading regime featuring depletion and replenishment. The problem is the depletion part of the cycle and the 20-miler one week before the marathon. Enlightened coaches say that 20 miles is too long and hard a run so close to a marathon. They recommend more than a weeklong taper, which wouldn't allow any depletion runs. Also, the high-protein diet three days following the depletion run was so severe that runners often became depressed while following it. I certainly did. Eating became no fun—and as an upbeat psychological mood may be as important to performance as glycogen stores, the depletion phase soon lost favor.

And later research by Dr. Costill suggested that the depletion phase was unnecessary because you could achieve equally high glycogen levels with only the three-day, high-carbohydrate approach. Forget about squeezing the sponge dry. We don't need to do that. Most of us shouted "Hallelujah" and never went back.

So the current advice is to concentrate heavily on eating carbohydrates those final days before the marathon. When someone says "carbo-loading" today, that's usually what they mean, not the seven-day depletion/replenishment cycle. For someone like me, used to following a high-carbohydrate diet, carbo-loading requires only a few changes in the regular daily routine. This is good, because you don't want to subject your system to any radical changes just before you're about to run 26 miles.

If you're racing out of town, you may even want to take along some snacks to eat between the pasta dinner and the race the next morning. Dried fruits can be particularly useful, especially if you're competing in a foreign country where you're not used to the food.

LAST-MINUTE LOADING

Carbo-loading shouldn't stop with the pasta dinner; scientists tell us it should continue on the starting line to ensure maximum pre-race nutrition. W. Michael Sherman, Ph.D., of Ohio State University, tested trained cyclists pedaling indoors, feeding them five grams of carbohydrates per kilogram of body weight three hours before exercising. Both power and endurance increased when athletes ate before exercising. (For a 165-pound cyclist, that would be about the amount of carbohydrates in 12 bagels or 7 baked potatoes.) Dr. Sherman explains: "The cyclists were able to maintain a higher output for a longer period of time before fatiguing."

Other studies have shown improved performance four hours after eating. "We can safely say that if you have a carbohydrate feeding three to four hours before a marathon, you can enhance performance," says Dr. Sherman.

Admittedly, marathoners do not tolerate solids in their stomachs as well as cyclists do. Dr. Sherman suggests runners either delay eating their prerace pasta until late evening, or rise early for a high-carbohydrate breakfast, such as pancakes or toast and orange juice. Liquid meals featuring high-carbohydrate drinks may work best for races near dawn. Dr. Sherman warns, however, that runners should try this first in practice or before minor races.

In fact, practice may let you adjust to a different type of prerace nutrition than you thought possible, including solid food an hour before the race. "You can train your body to do almost anything," says Tillapaugh, who says her favorite snack before races is a bagel or low-fat crackers.

Doug Kurtis, the multimarathon runner from Michigan, however, usually ate his last meal the night before. "Rarely will I eat anything the morning of a race," he says, "unless there's a late start, such as noon at Boston. I'd rather lie in bed an extra hour than get up just to eat. Some runners can eat and be ready to run an hour later, but I find I need three to four hours to digest my food before I feel comfortable running. I've experimented with eating two to three hours before, but it just didn't work."

"The main thing is not to do anything out of the ordinary," says Ed Eyestone, a 1988 and 1992 Olympic marathoner. "Yet you have to be flexible enough to go with the flow and eat what's available. If you're programmed to eat pancakes precisely seven hours before a marathon, you may be disappointed."

Experience has taught me that eating as close to three hours before a race gives my stomach sufficient time to digest the food and allows me to clear my intestines without the fear of having to duck into the bushes at the five-mile mark. Closer to race time than that, however, and I'm asking for trouble. Timing can be a problem if you're running a race like the Honolulu Marathon with its predawn start. But I've gotten up as early as 2:30 A.M. to eat breakfast before that race, and I notice I'm not always alone in the hotel coffee shop.

I'll order orange juice, toast or maybe a Danish roll, and/or some applesauce along with a single cup of coffee. Some experts warn against coffee, because it's a diuretic (and brings about water loss through increased urination), but it helps clear my bowels. If you're running an international race—and I've run marathons in Berlin, Athens, Rome, and other major cities—you may not be able to get a typical American breakfast, but the continental breakfast of coffee and rolls (with or without jelly) works quite well.

If the coffee shop doesn't open early enough, those snacks in the suitcase may come in handy. I'm less fussy. Practically every hotel has a soft drink machine on each floor, and frequently a can of pop is my last meal before a morning marathon.

I'll stop drinking two hours before the race, as it takes approximately that long for liquids to migrate from your mouth to your bladder. Another one to two cups just before the start will help you tank up for the race, and this liquid will most likely be utilized before it reaches your bladder. If you drink too much in that two-hour period, however, you may find yourself worrying about how you will relieve yourself several miles into the race. Following his bronze-medal performance at the 1991 World Championships, Steve Spence told *Runner's World* that he drank so much that he had to urinate three times during the race without breaking stride. Personally, I'd prefer to avoid that. Experience teaches you how.

Chapter 14

Predicting
PACE AND PERFORMANCE

How do you pick the pace that's right for you? How can you anticipate a reasonable finishing time?

Unless you have some idea of what you're capable of, you won't know how fast you should be running each mile. Run too slowly at the start, and you may find yourself too fresh at the end with a slower finishing time than you had anticipated. That's all right if you're a first timer intent only on finishing, but not if you're a seasoned runner hoping to improve. But start too quickly and you risk hitting the wall.

If you chart your times during workouts—speed workouts as well as your long runs—you probably have an approximate idea of how fast you can run. Your times in preliminary races will also give you a clue. But there are more precise ways to predict your performance in a marathon and also more precise ways to determine how fast you should run each mile. Once you get into the race itself, maintaining that perfect pace may be a problem. Fortunately, in recent years (spurred by the success of the *Runner's World* pacing teams), more and more marathons have begun to provide pacing assistance for midpack runners, not only through training programs leading up to those marathons, but also in the race itself.

MEASURING HUMAN PERFORMANCE

With the increased interest in fitness sports during the last quarter century, there has been a simultaneous rise in the number of laboratories that are dedicated to measuring human performance. Scientists have become interested in why some athletes outperform others.

The most common measuring device found in any running-oriented human performance laboratory is the treadmill, a moving belt on which you can run in place while various measurements are made. The most common measurement is maximum VO_2, the volume of oxygen a person can consume during exercise. This relates both to the heart's capacity to pump oxygen-rich blood to the muscles, and to how efficiently the muscles extract and utilize that oxygen.

Maximum VO_2, often referred to simply as max VO_2, is calculated based on the number of milliliters of oxygen that your body can absorb during 60 seconds, per kilogram of body weight (ml/kg/mn). Within certain limits, the higher your max VO_2, the better you will be able to perform. A talented runner with a max VO_2 of 70 could be expected to run a 10-K in around 31 minutes, and a marathon in 2:23. An average runner, say someone with the ability to run a 10-K in about 45 minutes, probably has a max VO_2 of around 45. Untrained or sedentary individuals would have still lower levels.

But other factors can also affect performance. One is running technique, or efficiency, what exercise scientists often refer to as "economy." Runners succeed only partly because of their superior cardiovascular systems. You need only look at the people near the front of the pack to understand that. Most of them are smooth, efficient runners who waste little energy covering ground. An economical runner might run a marathon 10 to 20 minutes faster than someone with an equal max VO_2 who is a less efficient runner.

In general, however, if you know your max VO_2, you can predict your performance. If you can *improve* your max VO_2, you may be able to improve your performance.

OXYGEN POWER

Alas, not everybody has the opportunity to determine their max VO_2. Most human performance laboratories are geared to doing research, not testing joggers for their own information. Most medical centers do what are known as "symptom-limited" exercise stress tests to diagnose heart conditions, but they usually stop short of testing for max VO_2. They don't—and usually *won't*—measure it for you. So how do average runners determine their max VO_2?

Jack Daniels, Ph.D., exercise physiologist at the State University of New York at Cortland, and coach of that school's highly successful cross-country team, has developed oxygen power tables to help predict performance. Dr. Daniels, formerly a top-ranked pentathlete, is among America's most respected sports scientists and coaches. He has also worked as a coach/adviser to world-class runners such as Jim Ryun, Alberto Salazar, and Joan Benoit Samuelson. For several years, Dr. Daniels worked in Eugene, Oregon, for Athletics West, Nike's sponsored team.

Dr. Daniels developed his oxygen power tables in collaboration with Jimmy Gilbert, one of his former runners and a programmer for NASA in Houston. By doing treadmill and track measurements on runners of various abilities (and collecting available data on others), Daniels and Gilbert were able to relate max VO_2 scores to performances. The two researchers developed a set of tables, which they published in a book titled *Oxygen Power*. (Copies of the book can be obtained from Dr. Daniels at Box 948, Walden Pond Lane, Cortland, NY 13045.) Using these tables, a runner can use any recent performance to predict something called VDOT. This value combines max VO_2 with running economy into a single value that *approximates* max VO_2. The VDOT can be used to predict with some accuracy how fast you can run at distances from 800 meters to 50-K. A runner can also equate performance at one distance to a performance at another. For instance, if you have the ability to run a 10-K in 40 minutes, you can probably (assuming proper training) run the marathon near three hours. (Notice I said "probably.")

Charts such as those developed by Dr. Daniels can be useful in predicting performance. If you know how fast you run a 10-K, or any other distance, you can predict your VDOT. If you run a 10-K in 49:00, you probably have a VDOT of 41.0. If you improve your time to 48:30, it's probably because your VDOT also has improved, to 41.5.

The table on pages 146–47 is an adapted and condensed version of the Daniels oxygen power tables for five commonly run distances: the mile, 5-K (3.1 miles), 10-K (6.2 miles), half-marathon (13.1 miles) and marathon (42.2-K or 26.2 miles). This oxygen power table includes 65 rows, showing VDOT values that might be achieved by runners at various levels, from a beginning jogger to a world-class athlete. The first level (VDOT 30) shows someone capable of running 63:46 for a 10-K. The final level describes performances that are better than the current world records.

PREDICTING PERFORMANCE

You should not attempt to measure your ability using the oxygen power table if you are a beginning runner. You need to condition your body before you test your abilities.

If you are reasonably well-conditioned, have been training for several months, and have no serious medical conditions that would prevent you from running as hard and as fast as you can (as determined by an exercise stress test), you are ready to test your oxygen power.

The basic test distance is one mile, although seasoned runners may prefer 5-K, the most common competitive race distance. To test yourself over one mile, you can go to any 400-meter track and time yourself for four laps with a stopwatch. (Since a mile is slightly more than 1600 meters, you may want to make adjustments by either running the additional 10-yard difference between 1600 meters and one mile, or adding several seconds to your time.)

If you are an experienced runner, you may prefer to test your max VO_2 in a race, possibly a 5-K or 10-K. It can be easier to push yourself to maximum performance while running in the company of others. If you go this route, be certain that the race organizers have accurately measured the course. Choose a race where the course is certified by the USATF Road Running Technical Council. Most major races provide well-measured courses, because experienced runners demand them. Races often note their certification number on the entry blank. But smaller races that are more "fun runs" may be measured with less precision. I recently organized a low-key 5-K race in my hometown. The course chosen was one on which I frequently train; I figured it to be *about* 5-K. (If you ever want to achieve a 5-K PR, show up some Fourth of July in Long Beach, Indiana, and you're almost guaranteed success.)

To get a more accurate idea of your max VO_2 level, you may want to test yourself over a series of distances, adding half-marathon or marathon times to those for the mile, 5-K, or 10-K. Don't be surprised, however, if the chart indicates a higher VDOT for your speed at some distances than others. If you have more fast-twitch muscles (for short, explosive effort) than slow-twitch muscles (for sustained effort), you're more likely to run the mile comparatively better than the marathon. If the reverse is true, your marathon time may be better. Your level of conditioning may also affect your ability to perform at the longer distances. Obviously, the best predictor of your marathon performance will be a VDOT level based on longer distances rather than shorter ones.

When you have completed your test run, whether on a track or on the road, look at the table and find the number closest to the time you ran. Locate the corresponding VDOT, which is your approximate max VO_2. The table will also tell you how fast you might run at other race distances—assuming you train properly for those distances.

Having established your oxygen power level, you may now use that level as a guide to predicting your theoretical race pace over other distances.

How accurate are the Daniels and Gilbert numbers? From a theoretical standpoint, they're *very* accurate. From a realistic standpoint, however, they're flawed, because people with lower max VO_2 may have trouble meeting the times predicted for all distances. A person who jogs a mile in 9 or 10 minutes may have trouble finishing a 10-K, much less running it in nearly 60 minutes. And running a marathon in anything under five hours may be out of the question—at least until the runner has trained for that distance.

In general, the better trained you are as a runner, the more accurate you're apt to find the Daniels and Gilbert numbers.

OXYGEN POWER TABLE

VDOT	Mile	5-K	10-K	Half-Marathon	Marathon
30	9:11	30:40	63:46	2:21:04	4:49:17
31	8:55	29:51	62:03	2:17:21	4:41:57
32	8:41	29:05	60:26	2:13:49	4:34:59
33	8:27	28:21	58:54	2:10:27	4:28:22
34	8:14	27:39	57:26	2:07:16	4:22:03
35	8:01	27:00	56:03	2:04:13	4:16:03
36	7:49	26:22	54:44	2:01:19	4:10:19
37	7:38	25:46	53:29	1:58:34	4:04:50
38	7:27	25:12	52:17	1:55:55	3:59:35
39	7:17	24:39	51:09	1:53:24	3:54:34
40	7:07	24:08	50:03	1:50:59	3:49:45
41	6:58	23:38	49:01	1:48:40	3:45:09
42	6:49	23:09	48:01	1:46:27	3:40:43
43	6:41	22:41	47:04	1:44:20	3:36:28
44	6:32	22:15	46:09	1:42:17	3:32:23
45	6:25	21:50	45:16	1:40:20	3:28:26
46	6:17	21:25	44:25	1:38:27	3:24:39
47	6:10	21:02	43:36	1:36:38	3:21:00
48	6:03	20:39	42:50	1:34:53	3:17:29
49	5:56	20:18	42:04	1:33:12	3:14:06
50	5:50	19:57	41:21	1:31:35	3:10:49
51	5:44	19:36	40:39	1:30:02	3:07:39
52	5:38	19:17	39:59	1:28:31	3:04:36
53	5:32	18:58	39:20	1:27:04	3:01:39
54	5:27	18:40	38:42	1:25:40	2:58:47
55	5:21	18:22	38:06	1:24:18	2:56:01
56	5:16	18:05	37:31	1:23:00	2:53:20
57	5:11	17:49	36:57	1:21:43	2:50:45
58	5:06	17:33	36:24	1:20:30	2:48:14
59	5:02	17:17	35:52	1:19:18	2:45:47
60	4:57	17:03	35:22	1:18:09	2:43:25
61	4:53	16:48	34:52	1:17:02	2:41:08
62	4:49	16:34	34:23	1:15:57	2:38:54

VDOT	Mile	5-K	10-K	Half-Marathon	Marathon
63	4:45	16:20	33:55	1:14:54	2:36:44
64	4:41	16:07	33:28	1:13:53	2:34:38
65	4:37	15:54	33:01	1:12:53	2:32:35
66	4:33	15:42	32:35	1:11:56	2:30:36
67	4:30	15:29	32:11	1:11:00	2:28:40
68	4:26	15:18	31:46	1:10:05	2:26:47
69	4:23	15:06	31:23	1:09:12	2:24:57
70	4:19	14:55	31:00	1:08:21	2:23:10
71	4:16	14:44	30:38	1:07:31	2:21:26
72	4:13	14:33	30:16	1:06:42	2:19:44
73	4:10	14:23	29:55	1:05:54	2:18:05
74	4:07	14:13	29:34	1:05:08	2:16:29
75	4:04	14:03	29:14	1:04:23	2:14:55
76	4:02	13:54	28:55	1:03:39	2:13:23
76.5	4:00.2	13:49	28:45	1:03:18	2:12:38
77	3:58.8	13:44	28:36	1:02:56	2:11:54
77.5	3:57.5	13:40	28:26	1:02:35	2:11:10
78	3:56.2	13:35	28:17	1:02:15	2:10:27
78.5	3:54.9	13:31	28:08	1:01:54	2:09:44
79	3:53.7	13:26	27:59	1:01:34	2:09:02
79.5	3:52.4	13:22.1	27:49.9	1:01:14	2:08:20
80	3:51.2	13:17.8	27:41.2	1:00:54	2:07:38
80.5	3:49.9	13:13.5	27:32.5	1:00:34.9	2:26:57.5
81	3:48.7	13:09.3	27:23.9	1:00:15.6	2:06:17.1
81.5	3:47.5	13:05.2	27:15.4	59:56.6	2:05:37.2
82	3:46.4	13:01.1	27:07.1	59:37.9	2:04:57.8
82.5	3:45.2	12:57.0	26:58.8	59:19.3	2:04:18.8
83	3:44.1	12:53.0	26:50.6	59:01.0	2:03:40.3
83.5	3:42.9	12:49.1	26:42.5	58:42.9	2:03:02.2
84	3:41.8	12:45.2	26:34.6	58:25.0	2:02:24.5
84.5	3:40.7	12:41.3	26:26.7	58:07.3	2:01:47.3
85	3:39.6	12:37.5	26:18.9	57:49.9	2:01:10.5

A SECOND OPINION

Here's another method of predicting performance. These figures come from George Myers, a retired engineer who lives in Sarasota, Florida. Myers has an extensive sports background. While attending Iowa State University, he placed second in the 1952 National Collegiate Athletic Association (NCAA) wrestling championships, and later took up bicycle touring, marathons, and triathlons. Myers had too much upper-body mass to have great success as a runner, but he loved to run. He also enjoyed playing with numbers. After participating in about 150 races (including 20 marathons), and talking with coaches and other runners, Myers decided to develop his own race prediction table, based more on experience than on scientific research.

Myers contends that not all runners slow their 10-K pace as much as you'd think when they run a marathon. "Fast runners slow down less than slower runners," he insists. Although the pace of a fast runner who is capable of 30:00 for a 10-K might slow by 10 percent to 2:19:15 for the marathon, Myers projects that a runner capable of 40:00 for a 10-K will run the marathon in 3:09:53, a slowdown of 12.5 percent.

"Runners do slow down on a straight line or linear basis from the 10-K to the marathon," says Myers, "but this is true only if the runner is conditioned to run the given distance. A 40-minute 10-K runner cannot run 3:10 for the marathon unless he trains for that distance."

Even well-trained runners may have trouble maintaining a steady pace during a marathon. Once you get out past 20 miles, all the rules change. Other factors may cause a slowdown irrespective of the miles you've run in training. While leading pacing teams for *Runner's World* in several marathons, I was able to witness firsthand how fatigue overcomes fitness. Everybody is happy the first half dozen miles, and most runners maintain the pace through the half-marathon and to 16 miles. But around mile 16 everyone goes through a reality check. At the 1998 Chicago Marathon, I had recruited a friend, Mary Burke, to assist me with pace-leading chores. Until about 17 miles, Mary had been leading us in chants and entertaining us all. I was content to go along for the ride. Then suddenly I noticed Mary, chin on chest, hanging off my shoulder and chanting more to herself than to others: "Dig in! Dig in!"

				Half- Marathon		
5-K	10-K	15-K	20-K		25-K	Marathon
13:40	28:00	42:37	57:39	1:01:00	1:13:06	2:09:22
14:38	30:00	45:42	1:01:52	1:05:28	1:18:30	2:19:15
15:37	32:00	48:47	1:06:05	1:09:57	1:23:55	2:29:12
16:35	34:00	51:52	1:10:19	1:14:27	1:29:21	2:39:15
17:34	36:00	54:58	1:14:34	1:18:15	1:34:49	2:49:22
18:32	38:00	58:04	1:18:50	1:23:29	1:40:19	2:59:35
19:31	40:00	1:01:10	1:23:06	1:28:02	1:45:49	3:09:53
20:29	42:00	1:04:16	1:27:24	1:32:35	1:51:22	3:20:15
21:28	44:00	1:07:23	1:31:41	1:37:09	1:56:55	3:30:43
22:26	46:00	1:10:30	1:36:00	1:41:44	2:02:30	3:41:16
23:25	48:00	1:13:37	1:40:19	1:46:20	2:08:06	3:51:54
24:23	50:00	1:16:45	1:44:40	1:50:56	2:13:44	4:02:37
25:22	52:00	1:19:53	1:49:00	1:55:34	2:19:23	4:13:25
26:20	54:00	1:23:01	1:53:22	2:00:13	2:25:04	4:24:19

MYERS PERFORMANCE PREDICTION TABLE

Everyone goes through what the British runners call "bad patches" in marathons, where it's hard to maintain concentration and hard to maintain pace. Those of us who have led pacing teams note that usually the team begins to disintegrate around 20 miles, with some runners moving ahead and some dropping behind. By 22 miles in that race, Mary had recovered. She moved smoothly ahead to finish well inside our goal time.

George Myers's prediction times in the table above assume a fast course, good weather, and a well-prepared and well-rested runner.

STILL MORE PREDICTORS

Let me offer you a simpler method of using your 10-K time to predict marathon performance, one suggested by Melvin H. Williams, Ph.D., of Old Dominion University in Norfolk, Virginia. Dr. Williams suggests multiplying your 10-K time by 4.66. According to this theory, a runner capable of 36:00 for a 10-K should be able to run a 2:47:45 marathon. The Daniels and Gilbert table would predict

2:46:15; Myers would suggest 2:49:22. David Cowein, a coach from Morrilton, Arkansas, suggests a simpler strategy: multiplying your 10-K time by 5, which results in an even more conservative prediction of 3:00. In working with beginning marathoners in Chicago, I always recommend the 5 × 10-K time approach to prediction. And I usually tell class members to add a half hour to that predicted time if they want to ensure a comfortable finish in their first marathon.

If space were available, I could offer you half a dozen other tables developed by knowledgeable individuals. One I use most often myself is in the book *Runningtrax: Computerized Running Training Programs*, by J. Gerry Purdy, originally published in 1970 and still available from *Track & Field News*. Purdy's tables suggest a 36:10 10-K is equivalent to a 2:59:00 marathon, although Purdy makes no claims to being in the prediction business.

So what method should you use? There's no concrete answer. If you're a highly talented and well-trained runner who runs fast, you will probably find the Daniels and Gilbert table most accurate; if you are less gifted and have less time to train, you may prefer one of the more conservative charts. Achieving success as a long-distance runner remains as much an art as a science. You need to apply both art and science if you expect to succeed.

Cowein also warns that you should pick a realistic goal: "No matter how well you feel on race day, if you're a 3:00 marathoner, you're not going to run 2:30. Be honest with yourself." Indeed, most of the drop-off by 20 miles we see with the *Runner's World* pacing teams may be the result of runners not accurately estimating their own abilities.

THE RIGHT PACE

Once you have an estimate of your finishing time, you can determine the best pace for achieving that time. Again, experts differ, and there are various ways to predetermine your race pace. The simplest is to run at the same speed mile after mile for the full distance. That's the approach of the pacing teams—and it works!

To run a 4:30 marathon—as I did leading a pacing team at the 1999 Walt Disney World Marathon—you would simply run 26 consecutive 10:18 miles. And I did a pretty good job: five of the 26 miles I ran at Disney were within one second of that precise time.

Robert Eslick, a coach from Nashville claims, "All in all, I think it's no secret that even pacing works best."

Coach Tom Grogon of Cincinnati agrees: "I want my runners to run at a relatively even pace. Given this, they should view those who bolt out early as foolish people whom they will catch at the end." To save yourself the bother of calculating all the splits for your next marathon, check "The Right Pace" on my Web site at www.halhigdon.com.

If you really enjoy catching people, you can try running "reverse splits." This means running the second half of the race faster than the first half. This was the approach taken by Brazilian Ronaldo da Costa when he set the world record of 2:06:05 in the 1998 Berlin Marathon. He strolled through the first half in 1:04:42, then flamed the second half in 1:01:23 to break the old record of 2:06:50 (set by Ethiopian Belayneh Dinsano) by 45 mind-boggling seconds! It almost makes you wonder if the second half of the course was downhill—but I've run Berlin, and it's a loop course.

The advantage of the reverse-split theory is that you'll be speeding up when most runners are slowing down. You'll pass others, rather than have others pass you. This can be stimulating mentally, and you'll also probably suffer less postrace muscle soreness and fatigue, because saving your fast running will let you retain your most efficient running form longer.

This strategy works best on courses with little variation in terrain. Encounter a hill (uphill or down) and you may need to alter your planned pace. For example, because of its hilly nature, the Boston Marathon keeps runners from attempting an even pace. Boston is a point-to-point course from suburban Hopkinton into the city. The course drops sharply in the first mile and continues downhill for most of the first 6 miles before flattening through mile 12. Then there is a series of ups and downs with the low spot on the course near 17 miles. Four hills over the next 4 miles—culminating with the notorious Heartbreak Hill—slow even the best-conditioned runner. Then there's a final steady drop between miles 21 and 26. The course will defy most pace charts.

But George Myers, my engineer/analyst friend from Sarasota, Florida, has also studied marathon pace from the point of view of the slower runner. He determined that most runners should allow a slowdown toward the end of the race.

Myers got the idea for creating a pacing table from one designed by Joe Henderson, a senior writer for *Runner's World*. Henderson contended that most published marathon pacing guides incorrectly assumed people could run all 26 miles (not to mention the final 385 yards) at an even pace. Few runners can do that, Henderson claimed, so he developed a table based on the more common pattern of a slow beginning, a fast middle, and a sag at the end.

With the exception of a few individuals such as da Costa, even world-class runners slow down in the last six miles, as their core body temperatures rise (even in relatively cool weather), and their systems perform less efficiently. In Frank Shorter's gold-medal marathon at the 1972 Olympics in Munich, his average pace in five-mile segments was 5:03.6, 4:52.4, 4:56.6, 5:03.2, and 5:15.2, for a final time of 2:12:20. In the closing stages, Shorter was still pulling away from the field because everybody else was slowing more than he was.

Myers modified Henderson's tables for the Madison Marathon in Wisconsin in June 1979 and ran 3:19:58, slicing 23 minutes off his PR at the age of 48. After that, Myers decided to do some more fine-tuning. He began by dividing the 26.2-miles into segments. Then he decided how much time a runner should spend covering each segment, and stated it as a percentage.

We published Myers's tables in an article I wrote for *The Runner*, and after receiving feedback from additional runners, Myers modified the tables slightly. He encourages runners of all abilities to use his formula. He also emphasizes the following points:

• Choose a realistic goal.
• Carry your pacing schedule with you so you can figure out how close you are to pace at every point in the race.
• Believe in your pace chart: Check each mile, making no changes in the first 20 miles (no matter how "good" you feel).
• Be prepared to make the necessary adjustments if the course is especially hilly.
• Meet intermediate time goals. This gives you confidence and causes the miles to pass faster.
• At mile 20, if you feel good, go for it; if not, hang in there.

Myers usually writes down his pace carefully in large, clear numbers on a piece of paper, laminates the paper in plastic to protect it, then tapes it to his race number, upside down, so he can easily refer

MYERS PACE TABLE FOR 3:00 MARATHON		
Mile	Percentage	Per-Mile Pace
0–12	3.756	6:46
12–18	3.8086	6:51
18–23	3.8725	6:58
23–26	3.950	7:07

to it during the race. It's easy to flip the chart up each mile to see how close you are to predicted pace. More recently, Keith Stone, a computer specialist from Winston-Salem, North Carolina, has produced laminated wristbands for leaders of the *Runner's World* pacing teams. Another simple approach that I frequently take is to write my pace upside down on the front of my race number.

The marathon is divided into four segments, and you run each mile of the segment in a time that's a percentage of your desired finish time (see table above). Myers's formula allows for slower running as you progress: Your early miles are done in 3.756 percent of your finish time, and the final miles are run in 3.95 percent of the final time.

Sound complicated? It's easy. Figure your projected finish time in seconds. For example, four hours would be 14,400 seconds. To figure your pace for miles 0 to 12, multiply that 14,400 by .03756, which is 3.756 percent. The answer (540.9) gives you a per mile pace in seconds. Divide this by 60 to get your per mile pace in minutes (9:01).

One caveat concerning the Myers pace tables: They are designed under the assumption that the course is flat, with zero wind. If the course is hilly or windy, you may need to make adjustments. A tailwind will make you run faster, sometimes as much as several minutes. On a loop course where the wind may hit you from different directions at different times of the race, you may need to make mental adjustments at midrace to stay on pace.

Temperature can also affect your pace. When race temperatures rise or fall much above or below your comfort level, you may need to throw your pace table away.

Any pace table can be a trap, a series of numbers that can lure you into trying to keep up a faster pace than your capabilities on that day. The best pace-setting device becomes your own mind. Experienced runners eventually know when to slow down and when to speed up.

Chapter 15

Race-Day
LOGISTICS

After six months to a year of training—after the mileage buildup, the long runs, the taper, the carbo-loading—what can you expect once you arrive at the race site and head toward the starting line? Most veterans usually follow a well-rehearsed routine that makes their marathons easy. (Well, easier than they might otherwise be.)

Here are some suggestions that may make race day easier.

Your "final" preparation begins just before you leave home, when you pack your bag. In this case, you need to heed one doctor's advice: the late George Sheehan, M.D., who virtually never left home without his runner's suitcase—a bag in the trunk of his car packed with gear in case he stopped somewhere and wanted to run. Dr. Sheehan once wrote in his local New Jersey newspaper column about the bag—then forgot it the next time he left for a 10-mile race in New York's Van Cortlandt Park.

"I had to borrow shoes, shorts, and a shirt," Dr. Sheehan recalled. "I was completely outfitted by other runners, who fortunately hadn't forgotten their bags."

But running clothes and shoes are only the minimum essentials, whether you're heading for a workout or a race. Smart runners cram their bags with numerous other items.

A RUNNER'S SUITCASE

Before packing that bag consider the advice of Michigan's Doug Kurtis: "Break everything in before you race: socks, shorts, singlet, shoes." Kurtis recommends running one or two workouts in your racing gear to make certain everything fits and there are no problem areas, such as an imperfection inside a shoe that could cause a blister. That may not bother you in a 5-K, but it can draw blood and bring you to a halt in a marathon. "One good way to work out the bugs and test your equipment is to enter shorter races before the marathon," says Kurtis.

Here are some items you might want to include in your runner's suitcase, not only for the marathon, but for other long races.

The right shoes. The most essential item, obviously. Many runners (myself included) like to take training shoes for warming up, or riding the bus to the start, then shift to a lighter pair of racing flats. On rainy days, you'll want dry shoes for afterward. You may want to pack your racing shoes in your carry-on luggage. If the airline loses your bag, you can replace everything else, but not a well-broken-in pair of shoes. And make sure they're the right shoes before you pack them. One runner went to don his racing shoes the morning of the Boston Marathon and found that he had packed one left shoe of his and one right shoe of his wife's. (They wore identical racing shoes.)

Shorts and singlet. Also obvious. Some people wear the cotton race T-shirt they've been handed the day before, but I prefer to test everything. Do the shorts fit? Will the singlet or T-shirt chafe? (A snug shirt or a brand-new, unwashed one might. And, as for cotton, it's not a good choice for race wear since it will hold moisture and become heavy in rainy or humid conditions.) Also bring a warm-up shirt to shed before you go to the start. You'll be most comfortable standing at the starting line if you wait until after warming up to change into a dry racing singlet. Pin your number on the night before the race and check to make sure you haven't pinned the front of your singlet to the back.

Safety pins. Most races provide safety pins, but sometimes only two, and sometimes they run out. If you're like me, you'll want at least four to secure your number so it doesn't flap. A few races require two numbers. At Twin Cities, you wear a back number identifying your age group, a nice touch. If you're running in a marathon such as Chicago, which provides pacing teams, you'll need four pins to secure the back number identifying your team.

Pins also come in handy for other things, such as piercing blisters after the race (although podiatrists may not like my offering such advice, since you're supposed to use a sterilized pin). I usually take along four or more pins linked together and fastened to a snap on the outside of my bag or in my toilet kit.

Entry blank. If you should get lost en route, would you be able to find the starting line? At most major marathons this is hardly a problem, but it's good advice for the 5-K or 10-K you might race to get ready for the marathon. Are you certain what time the bus leaves for the start and when that start is? The race may start at 7:45 A.M. to accommodate TV coverage, not the more logical 8:00 you seem to remember because it's an even number. Use the time between the warmup and the start to read all the directions you picked up with your number. You may learn some vital detail that will help you in the race, such as the location of aid stations.

Gloves and a cap. If the day is cold, you'll want these extra items. Whether or not you wear them in the race, gloves and a cap can help you stay warm before and after. If you start a marathon in the morning cold, but you get too warm by midrace, you can always toss your gloves—or tuck them in the waistband of your shorts. A billed cap in summer will keep the sun off your face. As with other race gear, test each item for comfort during practice. I have a torn and battered cotton cap so formless and ugly that I wouldn't want to be seen in it anywhere else but the starting line of a marathon. Another old road-runner trick is to knot a white handkerchief at its four corners to wear on your head.

Varied-weight clothing. Don't assume the weather will be warm if the month is July or cold if it's January. If a freak cold wave or heat wave hits, can you cope with it? The Boston Marathon in April is notorious for unpredictable weather. I wear shorts and a regular race singlet if the temperature is going to be in the mid-40s. If it's much colder, I'll don Lycra tights and a long-sleeved shirt—a big improvement over the heavy, cotton turtleneck top I had to wear for warmth in the cold and rainy 1964 Boston Marathon when I set my PR. Don't forget gloves and a headband to cover your ears on really cold days. The 1995 Columbus Marathon featured temperatures in the 20s, but the sun was out and I was comfortable because I had brought the right clothes.

Throwaway clothing. In large races where you may need to stand on the starting line for a long time, it's important to stay warm. If you can't hand your discarded warmup gear to a friend at the starting line at the last minute, take throwaway clothes that you won't mind having donated to the Salvation Army when you leave them behind. Garbage bags with armholes cut in them do protect against the wind, but they don't hold much warmth. At most marathons there are trucks right at the starting line for you to throw your gear into just before the start, but don't count on it. Particularly in crowded fields, you may have to stand a long time on the starting grid. Fortunately, most marathons today are so well organized that they start precisely on time, although the first Rock 'n' Roll Marathon in 1998 had a 38-minute delay, because an unprepared San Diego Police Department decided at the last minute to stop everything until they could secure several street crossings and remove some illegally parked cars along the course.

Money. Of course, you'll need money the day of the race for your entry fee, if you haven't preregistered. Cash also comes in handy after the race if a vendor is selling ice cream—or to take the subway home if you locked your keys in the car. Put a few extra dollars and some change in the bag that gets transported to the finish line just in case you need it. Is there a chance you might drop out? Tuck a $20 bill in your shorts pocket so you can take a taxi.

Extra little essentials. Pack these in a smaller bag: chafing lubricants, adhesive bandages, tape, sunscreen, aspirin, medication. Sure you can *probably* buy some or all of these items at the race expo, but don't leave any essential items home based on that assumption.

Fluids and food. Need a final prerace drink, either water or your favorite sports drink? It's easier to sip from a bottle you brought along than to go searching for fluids. I like to go to the line with a 12-ounce can of pop and drink it a few minutes before the gun sounds. Gels are handy for midrace carbo-*re*loading, and, by the way, you'll be happy I told you to pack extra safety pins so you can attach the energy gel packets to your singlet. (On cold days, the packets fit nicely inside your gloves.) Although most marathons will have bananas, yogurt, and other food items waiting for you after you clear the chute, if you finish too far back you may find they've run out. Or—and this has happened to me more than once—you may stumble head down through the finish area and retrieve your bag before realizing you've missed the food tables and need to go back.

Combination lock. This comes in handy if there's a dressing room where you can stow your gear in a locker, although access to lockers is more common at track meets than at marathons. Many races today are so large that runners come dressed to run. A word to the wise: Don't take chances with expensive items. If your bag will be transported to the finish line for you, don't put expensive gear such as

RACE-DAY CHECKLIST

Before leaving home for your next marathon, use a checklist such as this one to make certain you haven't forgotten any essential items. This list was developed by Ron Gunn, athletic director at Southwestern Michigan College, when we used to lead groups of runners on tours to races such as the Honolulu Marathon.

Carry-on Luggage
- Racing shoes
- Airline tickets
- Passport and other documents
- Toothbrush and toothpaste
- Hotel and rental car
    confirmation
- Event schedule and information
- Travel itinerary
- Toiletries
- Credit cards
- Camera and film
- Wallet and money

Other Gear
- Dress clothes
- Dress shoes
- Socks
- Underwear

- Coat
- Gloves
- Rain gear
- Sunglasses
- Sunscreen
- Alarm clock
- Race uniform
- Race socks
- Throwaway cold-weather gear
- Warmup suit
- Swimsuit
- Gloves and hat
- Safety pins
- Body lubricant
- Tape and adhesive bandages
- Medicine
- Special race drink

Have I forgotten anything? Experience will teach you how to organize your own runner's suitcase.

your Gore-Tex all-weather suit inside unless you can afford to lose it.

Postrace clothing. Once you finish, you'll want to change into dry clothing, including socks. Make sure you pack a towel so you can dry off. You'll want to look and feel your best hanging around and chatting with other runners.

Plastic bag. Bags—the kind they gave you at the store when you bought your last pair of running shoes—come in handy after the race to isolate your wet and sweaty gear from the rest of your clothing. A separate plastic bag for grimy shoes is also useful. A garbage bag into which you can punch armholes may be useful for keeping you warm and dry on cold or rainy days.

Notebook and pen. You'll want to record your finishing time, or splits, before you forget them. Or the phone number of that good-looking guy or gal you ran with for the last half dozen miles.

Checklist. Have you forgotten anything? You won't know unless you also have a checklist of all the necessary items. Experience eventually will guide you. When you determine what items work best in your runner's bag, make a personalized checklist similar to the one in the "Race-Day Checklist" on the opposite page to make sure you don't leave home without them.

THE MORNING OF THE RACE

For 5-K or 10-K races, I don't mind rising early and driving an hour or two to a race, and most runners feel the same. Not only do I want to avoid the extra expense of a hotel and meals away from home, but an overnight stay converts the race into an expedition requiring planning and commitment. Sometimes I like to just go, run and go home (unless, of course, I've won an age-group award).

But a marathon does require commitment, and because I usually run only one or two a year, I prefer to stay overnight before the race. I've run the Sunburst Marathon in South Bend, Indiana, on several occasions. Even though South Bend is only 45 minutes from my home in Long Beach, I check into a hotel the night before the event to avoid having to drive even that far on race morning, and to allow myself an extra hour's sleep before the 6:00 A.M. start.

Even if it costs a little more, I prefer to stay as close as possible to the race's start and/or finish. Usually race directors select their headquarters hotel with this in mind. One reason for the recent popularity of the Chicago Marathon is that runners began to realize that they could wait until the last minute in their hotel room. Five minutes after finishing the race, they're back in their room for a cleansing shower. For point-to-point marathons, most runners stay near the finish line so they can head to their rooms quickly after finishing. But make your hotel reservations early, because the most desirable hotels at big-city marathon often fill up fast, sometimes a year in advance.

GETTING UP AND GETTING GOING

You don't want to sleep through the start, or oversleep and have to rush your final preparations. This is particularly true at marathons that begin very early in the morning, such as Honolulu with its 5:00 A.M. start. Usually my internal body alarm wakes me up a few minutes before the actual alarm sounds. (Maybe I don't want to hear its jarring noise.) Before important races, I'll set my wristwatch alarm, set the clock radio alarm, and even ask the front desk for a wake-up call. If you're really a heavy sleeper, have a friend at home call you on the phone and stay on the line until you've stumbled out of bed.

Your first assignment after rising is to complete your carbo-load either by going down to the hotel coffee shop or snacking on items brought with you for that purpose. My favorite prerace "meal" is usually a 12-ounce can of soda. Forget nutrition: what you need in the final countdown is something sweet, instant energy that will go straight to your muscles.

I often do a very short warmup early, at the hotel, for several reasons. First, going outside and testing the weather for yourself is more reliable than listening to weather reports on TV or radio. Second, a short run usually loosens my bowels; I'd rather use the toilet in my hotel room than stand in a long line for a porta-potty. A half mile or so jogging and walking usually accomplishes this.

Becoming toilet-trained is a necessity if you don't want to waste energy and time standing in long porta-potty lines. If I'm driving to the start, I sometimes arrive with a nearly empty gas tank so I'll have an excuse to stop at a gas station and use the rest room. I'm adept at locating toilets away from the start that I can visit during my warmup. Driving the final miles to the race, I keep my eyes open for a friendly fast-food restaurant close enough to jog to, but far enough away so most of the other runners won't want to. That's one advantage of being a high-mileage runner: You can outrun the competition for an uncrowded toilet.

For my early morning warmup, I don't usually wear my racing gear. After visiting the john and changing, I gather any extra gear I need—including my runner's bag, packed the night before—and head for the start.

REACHING THE STARTING AREA

Each race has its own protocol requiring careful attention (and some experience—yours or that of friends) if you don't want to get to the starting line too early or too late. At the Boston Marathon, runners board buses in downtown Boston by 8:00 A.M. (four hours before the noon start) for transportation to where the race begins. After arriving near the start, they spend the next hour or two milling around the high school in suburban Hopkinton before being shooed to the starting line 30 to 60 minutes before the start. Until the Boston Athletic Association began providing outdoor tents at the 100th Boston, runners would cram into the gym so tightly no one could move, much less find a spot to lie down when the weather was cold or rainy. Weather can turn a good prerace experience into a bad one, so you need to learn each race's logistics to spare yourself discomfort.

At Boston and most other large races, the elite runners are supplied transportation and a private dressing area near the start. It makes the final hour before the marathon much more comfortable, a necessity for runners seeking peak performance. Because race directors hope for fast times to please sponsors, they do what they can to make the prerace conditions comfortable for top competitors.

But most race directors do a good job for the rest of us as well. Particularly during the fall marathon season, there's a lot of competition among race directors to make runners entering each race comfortable so that runners will continue to return and provide the numbers the sponsors like. Fortunately, many race directors are marathoners (or former marathoners) themselves and remember the type of user-friendly practices that kept them comfortable and happy. During the fall of 1991, when I crammed six marathons into six weeks, I was struck by how well organized each race was, and how well race directors provided the back of the pack with a reasonable amount of comfort.

Runners without the privileges of the elite dressing room need to organize themselves as much as possible on race day to minimize the hassle caused by being part of a 25,000-runner happening. This requires preplanning. Often you only learn how to cope with one specific marathon by running it once and returning the following year better prepared. Or if you're lucky, you attend the race with friends who were there the year before, and who can tell you what to expect. It's called "networking," and it works in marathoning as well as in business.

ON THE STARTING LINE

Warming up is difficult at large races because at the time when you normally might be doing some final strides or a bit of jogging, you often need to stay in place to secure your position on the starting line. At the really big marathons, such as New York or Honolulu, runners are marched to the line well before the gun. It's the only way to handle the crowds of starters, but if you like to follow a particular warmup routine as I do, this arrangement can wreak havoc with your preparation. The fortunate thing about marathons is that unless you're an elite runner planning a 4:30 first mile, you probably don't need as much warmup as you might for a 5-K race, where you need to run fast from the gun. You may lose a minute or two with a slow start, but this may not be that important over the length of a marathon. If you're a first-timer, you probably won't warm up because you don't want to waste even the amount of energy it requires to jog in place standing on the line. Experienced runners, however, often have different agendas. The inconvenience of crowds is one reason that you may want to try a small, intimate marathon when you try for a new personal record.

At races where I plan to try for first in my age group, I position myself as close to the starting line as I can without blocking faster runners. I don't like being passed, and I don't like having to pass others. Increasingly, major marathons have begun to make use of the ChampionChip (a computer chip that is easily laced onto your racing shoe) to provide runners with an official time that recognizes when they cross the starting line, not when the gun sounds. Leading a pacing team at the 1998 Chicago Marathon, I held the 5:00 group back until the starting line was nearly clear of runners. This meant crossing the line eight minutes late. Since those "lost minutes" would be subtracted from everybody's official time, it didn't really matter when we started.

At Chicago in 1998, my team experienced no delays caused by runners around us, and actually ran the first two miles somewhat faster than our planned pace. Several months later at the 1999 Walt Disney World Marathon, where I led the 4:30 pacing team for *Runner's World*, it took only four minutes to cross the line but we lost a minute a mile for the first three miles because of a narrower course.

Each marathon is slightly different, so you need to approach each with a plan that is both flexible and well defined. Only by understanding race-day logistics can you both maximize your comfort and increase your chances of success.

Chapter 16

Liquid Refreshment to

SURVIVE
AND EXCEL

The Chicago lakefront stretches 18 miles from the former South Shore Country Club on the South Side to Bryn Mawr Avenue on the North Side, encompassing Jackson, Grant, and Lincoln Parks. There are museums, one of the largest convention centers in the world, the football stadium where the Chicago Bears play, an airport, high-rise apartments, a lift bridge, several yacht clubs and golf courses, and numerous sandy beaches that are jammed with swimmers each summer.

Most important, there are water fountains: a total of 32 according to a map in the Chicago Area Runners Association's office. There are few places along Chicago's lakefront where you can run more than a mile without encountering a water fountain, called "bubblers" in some circles, because of the way the water bubbles out of them. And each summer, as my training class does its long runs to prepare for the Chicago Marathon, we stop frequently to drink. And drink. It is our means of survival. Survival is merely one reason that runners need to drink a lot when they run far. The other reasons are to replace lost energy and to enhance performance.

A generation ago, runners ignored fluids while running marathons because of a combination of arrogance, ignorance, and a lack of aid stations. Emil Zatopek, the great Czech runner, won the 1952 Olympic marathon without taking a sip. He was a world record holder in track, running his first 26-miler, and probably didn't know how to drink on the run. He was his era's best distance runner and succeeded on talent, training, and toughness.

But Zatopek's time was 2:23:03, a performance so ordinary by today's standards that it would barely put him in the top 100 in many major races today—and wouldn't qualify him for the U.S. Olympic trials. The world record for women is now several minutes faster than Zatopek's best, which seems astounding to those of us who are old enough to remember how the gritty runner totally dominated his competition.

But today's runners know how to drink. They drink often—water as well as replacement fluids such as Gatorade, Exceed, and de-fizzed Coke. They drink from paper cups handed to them by volunteers, or from squeeze bottles with straws so they don't have to slow their pace. At the Comrades Marathon (which is actually an ultramarathon that is about 54 miles long) in South Africa, runners are handed plastic bags that have to be torn open to get to the water within. One of the secrets to success at Comrades is to tear the top off the bags without spilling all the water inside.

At a nutritional seminar at Ohio State University in Columbus before the 1992 Olympic trials, Edward F. Coyle, Ph.D., of the Department of Kinesiology at the University of Texas at Austin, suggested that for efficient thermal regulation on a hot day, a runner may need to drink 1,000 milliliters of fluid an hour. That's a full liter! *Nearly one quart!* If you're a four- or five-hour marathoner, that would mean drinking four or five quart bottles; you could *drown* in that much water. I've drunk at that rate under controlled conditions in an exercise laboratory, running on a treadmill with someone handing me a plastic bottle with a straw every five minutes for two hours, and it's not easy. It took all my willpower to keep drinking as my belly filled with fluids and my mind sent signals that I was no longer thirsty. Yet that's what Dr. Coyle claims you need to do if you expect the best possible performance.

LEARNING HOW TO DRINK

We encourage participants in our training class for the Chicago Marathon to drink, drink, drink. Not only does drinking fluids make their weekend long runs more comfortable, but it teaches them how to drink and how often to drink. It underscores the importance of proper fluid replacement.

No tennis player would start a match without practicing lobs; no golfer would think a game complete without learning how to pitch from a sand trap. And no runner should enter a marathon without figuring out how and when to drink.

Drinking while running definitely is not easy. Unless you grasp the cup carefully, you can spill half the contents on the ground. If you gulp too quickly, you can spend the next mile coughing and gasping. If you dawdle at aid stations, you can waste precious seconds. And if you gulp down a replacement drink you aren't used to, it might make you nauseous.

Drinking on the run is a science—and so we practice. Although there are ample fountains along the lakefront, our classes in the northern, southern, and western suburbs aren't equally blessed. Class leaders at the first two locations must tour the course before weekend workouts, and place jugs of water and Gatorade along with paper cups at strategic points along the way. On the Prairie Path, the Rails-to-Trails gravel path heading westward from the city limits, there are a few fountains, but most of the members of our class have been conditioned to run wearing water belts, carrying their own fluids with them. I never forget mine when I run with the class along the Prairie Path.

DRINKING FOR SURVIVAL

Drinking on the run is necessary for survival. When the weather is warm or humid, runners sweat. You sweat even during cool weather, particularly if you are overdressed. If you sweat too much, you dehydrate. If you become dehydrated, body temperature rises and your performance drops. Too high a body temperature can result in heat prostration, or—in extreme circumstances—death.

Most people sweat efficiently and adapt quite well to changes in temperature. It is only when you undertake extreme activities like marathons that you need to worry about taking in enough liquid to balance losses from sweat. The average sedentary person loses two quarts of water a day under normal temperature conditions, but a marathoner can sweat away that much in half an hour, according to Lawrence E. Armstrong, Ph.D., of the University of Connecticut.

Some people sweat more than others. Alberto Salazar, for example, lost 12 *pounds* and placed a subpar 15th in the 1984 Olympic marathon, which he ran in the warm conditions of Los Angeles. "Without doubt, running marathons results in tremendous dehydration," states Peter B. Raven, Ph.D., a physiology professor at the Texas School of Osteopathic Medicine.

Nevertheless, sweating is a natural effect of exercise. "Every muscle is a tiny furnace that produces heat," writes Gabe Mirkin, M.D., in *The Sportsmedicine Book*. Muscles convert fuel to energy very inefficiently, resulting in excess heat that must be eliminated to keep the body from overheating.

A part of your brain called the hypothalamus detects the rise in temperature of the blood as it circulates, raising the body's core temperature. "The brain says sweat, and the body sweats," explains William Fink, a researcher at Ball State University's Human Performance Laboratory in Muncie, Indiana.

Perspiration begins almost immediately when you start to run, emerging through glands so numerous that an area of skin the size of a quarter contains a hundred. (Our bodies have between two and four million sweat glands.) The rise in body temperature triggers the production and excretion of sweat. As sweat evaporates from the skin, you cool off. This process is called thermoregulation, and when it works right it's an effective heating and air-conditioning system.

Not everybody's system functions effectively, however. In a running class I taught in Dowagiac, Michigan, in the early 1980s, there was a woman named Joyce who essentially did not sweat. Some people might consider that an advantage, but it isn't if you're a runner. Joyce's inability to sweat normally caused her to overheat so quickly that even on a cool day she couldn't run farther than three miles. For Joyce to run a marathon would have been an impossibility. After I began writing my "Ask the Expert" column for *Runner's World Daily*, I discovered that Joyce's problem was not unique. A number of individuals wrote me to ask about their inability to perspire and cool their bodies as they exercised.

Alberto Salazar had another problem. He had tremendous willpower and could push himself past the point where lesser runners would quit. Tested in Dr. David Costill's lab at Ball State University, he kept running on the treadmill at the point of maximum oxygen uptake for much longer than any other runner. But that same drive got Salazar into trouble. On two occasions at the peak of his career—once at the Falmouth Road Race and another time at the Boston Marathon—he collapsed after winning fast races and had to receive fluids intravenously. I'm convinced that Salazar's career as an elite athlete was shortened considerably because of the impact of those two events on his system.

THE SCIENCE OF SWEAT

As Salazar discovered, what scientists refer to as effective thermoregulation occurs at the expense of body fluids. The hotter it is, the more you sweat. "If sweat loss is not replaced during exercise," says Robert Murray, Ph.D., a consultant for the Quaker Oats Company, "the resulting dehydration compromises cardiovascular and thermoregulatory function, increases the risk of heat illness, and impairs exercise performance."

Dehydration reduces central blood volume. This prompts the body to decrease both blood flow and sweating in an attempt to conserve body fluids. Under these circumstances, the body's ability to cool itself declines, and the body temperature can rise to dangerous levels unless you stop running—and it may not decrease even then if you fail to get out of the sun.

You can't adapt to dehydration, explains Dr. Murray, but living and training in hot environments can help you *avoid* dehydration. As you adapt to warmer climates, your blood volume expands and your sweat glands conserve sodium, he says. "This helps assure that cardiovascular and thermoregulatory function can be maintained during exercise in the heat," he says.

In other words, Dr. Murray is saying that we can train ourselves to utilize fluids more efficiently. Humans are *homeotherms* who need to maintain a constant temperature; we're warm-blooded rather than cold-blooded. An internal temperature of 98.6°F is considered normal. Your body temperature drops *below* normal (called hypothermia) if you stay out in the cold too long or wear insufficient clothes. Your temperature rises *above* normal (hyperthermia) when you start to exercise. It also rises if you get the flu or a similar infection, one reason why it's not a good idea to exercise to excess—or even at all—when you're ill.

Hypothermia normally is not a problem for marathoners—except occasionally on cold days when runners may feel less urge to drink and/or slow down drastically in the last miles. (Drinking helps keep you warm as well as keep you cool, as I've discovered from competing in cross-country ski races.)

Hyperthermia is more of a problem. There are two types of sweat glands: apocrine and eccrine. Apocrine glands don't concern marathoners. Those are the "nervous" or "sexual" glands that are located mostly in the armpits and around the genital organs. Scientists don't entirely understand their function, but suspect they serve some purpose related to sexual attraction.The eccrine gland, however, keeps us cool. Even though we begin sweating almost immediately as a response to exercise, it may be 10 minutes or more before our skin becomes moist enough to notice. On hot but dry days, you may not realize you are sweating, because the moisture evaporates quickly.

Normally, sweat is very diluted water, containing only about one-tenth of a percent of electrolytes—mostly sodium chloride and some potassium. There has been some suggestion that perspiration is one of the body's means of ridding the bloodstream of waste products, including lactic acid. This is not true. The prime function of the eccrine glands is keeping us cool.

Cooling occurs when sweat evaporates from the body surface. "Evaporation is important," explains Dr. Raven. "The blood flows to the surface and transfers its heat by conduction."

During exercise, the body usually produces more heat than you can get rid of by sweating. A marathoner's body temperature gradually rises 3 or 4 degrees to 102°F, an efficient level for energy utilization. At this point, your air-conditioning system is in sync with the environment and you perform well. If the weather is too hot or too humid, or you become dehydrated—resulting in a drop in sweat production—the body's temperature can soar to dangerous levels. Your muscles will not perform efficiently at temperatures that are too high (104°F and up), so that will slow you down. This is an important defense mechanism, because if you fail to sweat and your core temperature rises past 108°F, you may suffer heatstroke, a potentially serious problem that can cause headaches and dizziness, and in extreme cases convulsions, unconsciousness, and death.

The body's ability to safely regulate its internal temperature while exercising is influenced by four factors: the environment, exercise intensity, clothing, and the athlete's level of fitness and acclimatization. You can train yourself to resist both cold and hot weather, but extremes of either can cause problems.

EFFECTIVE SWEATING

Let's eliminate one myth. Although Joyce in my running class virtually did not sweat, in general, women sweat as much as men do. The suspicion that women's air-conditioning systems function less efficiently than men's was one excuse the International Olympic Committee offered for resisting adding the marathon or any other long-distance race for women to the Olympic Games. As has been proved since 1984, women Olympic marathoners run just as hard as men do; their somewhat slower times being more a matter of their genetic muscular efficiency than anything having to do with thermoregulation.

One person who helped disprove the myth about women's capacity to sweat has a particularly appropriate name: Barbara L. Drinkwater, Ph.D., of the Department of Medicine at Pacific Medical Center in Seattle, Washington. In 1977, Dr. Drinkwater asked a number of female runners, including one world record holder, to exercise for two hours in an environmental chamber at 118°F. "They came out looking like they had climbed out of a swimming pool," Dr. Drinkwater recalls.

Yes, women sweat, and, in fact, they have more sweat glands than men do. In some studies involving men and women, men did sweat more, but Dr. Drinkwater suspects that's because the men and women compared didn't have comparable weights and oxygen uptake levels.

Regardless of your sex, conditioning improves your ability to sweat. Carl Gisolfi, Ph.D., an exercise physiologist at the University of Iowa, believes that we can increase our heat tolerance 50 percent by conditioning. According to Dr. Gisolfi, you train your sweat glands to function more efficiently by using them.

Acclimatization also improves our ability to tolerate heat. That is why marathoners experience more problems when the weather turns hot at Boston in April than at New York in the fall. By New York, they've had an entire summer to become acclimatized.

One year at the Shamrock Shuffle, a popular 8-K race held in Chicago each March, a freak warm spell raised the temperature to an unseasonal 70°F. I was astounded to see runners starting the race in tights and jackets, even cotton sweat suits—clothing they had worn through the winter. Most finished the race sweaty and bedraggled, with jackets wrapped around their waists. Several overheated runners were taken to the hospital. A midsummer race with 70°F temperatures, however, would have caused few problems. Runners would have been conditioned both physically and psychologically to tolerate the heat.

Buddy Edelen, the only American marathoner ever to hold the world record for the 26.2-mile distance, sometimes wore three sweat suits while training for the 1964 Olympic marathon trials to simulate hot conditions. Sure enough, temperatures rose into the 90s during the May trials in Yonkers, New York, and Edelen soundly beat his rivals. Later Olympic marathoners Ron Daws of Minnesota and Benji Durden of Colorado, adopted Edelen's training strategy with success.

TIPS FOR STAYING COOL

Other than training in multiple sweat suits, what strategies can runners use to prevent heat problems? Let's talk first about practice. Here are some training tips for proper hydration.

Drink before running. Drink adequately and drink often. Dr. Murray recommends drinking 16 ounces of water an hour before training: "Excess body water will be passed as urine before practice begins," he says. Marathoner Doug Kurtis says that he never passes a water fountain at work without stopping for at least a quick drink.

Drink while you run. For years, an old-fashioned notion among coaches was that drinking was for sissies; today's more knowledgeable coaches realize their athletes practice and play better if allowed time to drink. That was the motivation behind the development of Gatorade, a replacement drink formulated for University of Florida football players. Runners need to drink frequently during practice, especially during warm weather. You'll run faster and recover faster. Most runners quickly become adept at locating available water in their neighborhood. I sometimes carry coins in my shorts if I know I'll be passing a soft drink machine.

I live on Lake Shore Drive in Long Beach, Indiana, the area's most popular route for joggers, bikers, and walkers. When I recently added an extra parking space in front of my house, I asked the landscaper to install a water fountain. My popularity in the neighborhood soared as those exercising stopped to cool off. After George Hirsch, the publisher of *Runner's World*, mentioned my water fountain in his "Publisher's Letter," at least one runner coming from Detroit to run the Chicago Marathon told me at the expo that he had detoured off I-95 to drink from "Hal Higdon's fountain." I guess he wanted to sip from the fountain of knowledge.

Walk to drink. In preparing for the marathon at the 1981 World Veterans Championships in Christchurch, New Zealand, I experimented with walking through aid stations at several shorter races and discovered I lost only seven seconds off my time if I walked to drink. That's inconsequential. In the race, I walked through every aid station (positioned at 5-K intervals) and figure I lost less than a minute en route to victory in the 45 to 49 age group with a time of 2:29:27. Many of the runners I beat that day had posted faster times coming into the race, but finished behind me on a warm day.

If you lose only seven seconds each time you walk through an aid station running at a 5:30 pace, you'll lose even less running time at a slower pace. When I lead 4:30 pacing groups at marathons, we average 10:18 per mile. Most fit runners can walk 15:00 per mile, or faster, so the drop-off between running pace and walking pace is little, but the gain is great.

Drink after running. Most runners don't need to be told this. Their natural instinct sends them immediately to the water fountain or refrigerator. But even after your initial thirst is quenched, you still may be dehydrated. One way of evaluating your intake is to check the color of your urine. If it's yellow, you probably need to keep drinking. Clear urine is a sign of good hydration. Another clue is body weight. If your weight is abnormally low following a long run on a hot day, don't congratulate yourself that you are losing weight;

you're most likely badly dehydrated. Particularly after long runs, it's a good idea to use sports drinks to help replenish glycogen burned during your run. You'll recover much more rapidly and help prevent injuries if you do so.

Run when it's cool. Because of my flexible schedule as a writer, I can choose my running times. During the winter, I usually train at midday, because it's warmer. During the summer, I switch to running at dawn, before it gets too hot. Running in the evening is slightly less satisfactory because it can still be hot and humid. And running in the dark has its own perils. You may need to do some hot-weather running to acclimatize yourself for races, but you don't want extreme temperatures to affect the quality of your training. I've run at 4.00 in the afternoon near my brother-in-law's house in Mesa, Arizona, when the temperature was 104°F. I didn't run far, and I didn't run fast, but I ran—partly to prove I could do it. But I was glad I didn't have to run in those conditions every day.

Shift your training. The message in my earlier book, *Run Fast*, was, "If you want to run fast, you have to run fast." Every coach will tell you that one secret to success—even in the marathon—is speedwork. The best time for speedwork is the summer, when the warm weather helps warm your muscles so you're less likely to suffer injuries. You can train on the track, never more than a short sprint from the water fountain. Short, intense workouts can get you just as hot as long, slow ones, but you'll be closer to home if you do overheat.

Beware of the sun. Wear a hat. Every runner should own a sloppy, floppy hat that can be used to douse yourself with water when you stop at water fountains. There are some excellent runner's hats on the market now made of lightweight, breathable materials. Purchase one of those rather than using the standard baseball caps that are popular today. Particularly in spring, you may want to use sunscreen (use a sun protection factor, SPF, of 15 or higher for best results) to protect vulnerable areas, such as your face, shoulders, and the front of your legs. Apply the sunscreen half an hour before you run to give it time to be absorbed, then apply more. Wash your hands thoroughly to avoid rubbing the lotion into your eyes if you wipe your forehead—it can sting badly. For the same reason, you may want to apply the lotion only below your eyes, trusting your cap to protect your forehead.

MARATHON MEALS

Unlike cyclists and skiers, most fast marathoners avoid solid foods when they run for a simple reason: It's difficult to eat while moving faster than a 7:00 per mile pace.

But Coach Bill Wenmark of Deephaven, Minnesota, recommends mid-marathon snacks for people who take longer than three hours to finish. "If you're on the road four or five hours, you're running the equivalent of an ultramarathon," says Wenmark. "You need more energy than you can get from the drinks race directors provide. Someone running an 8:00 pace or slower can take time to eat. Digestion is less of a problem than for elite runners." Wenmark recommends saltines and high-energy bars for his back-of-the-packers, and positions support crews along the course to provide this extra boost.

What do the scientists say? At Ohio State University, W. Michael Sherman, Ph.D., tested 10 cyclists who rode at 70 percent of their maximum capacity for 90 minutes, then did the equivalent of a 20-mile time trial. (Their total time approached 2½ hours.) In one trial they ate a specific amount of carbohydrates and in the other they got the carbo in liquid form. "We found no performance difference in their response," reports Dr. Sherman. He adds that in warm weather, liquids certainly would be preferable to solids, because the fluid would help combat dehydration.

Of course, Dr. Sherman admits that his study failed to explore the outer realm of endurance beyond four and five hours where ultramarathoners (and slow marathoners) tread. Conventional wisdom among this breed suggests that food may be as important as drink—if only for the psychological reason that you want something solid in your stomach. First-time marathoners seem to have a stronger desire to eat solid food than experienced marathoners, who have adapted to a liquids-only diet while racing. Liquids

I can't overestimate the importance of running covered when the sun is strong. I wish I had done a better job of protecting my skin while younger. I have a couple of scaly areas on my forehead that now make me nervous. My former coach Fred Wilt died of skin cancer. I could name another famous high-mileage runner recently diagnosed with that disease. Always—and I mean *always*—run with a hat when the sun is high overhead!

Don't overestimate your ability. Realize that you can't run as fast high in sugar can cause stomach distress—nausea and diarrhea—if you are not used to them.

Solid food for energy replacement was more common in Europe a quarter century ago. When I ran the 1963 Kosice Marathon in Czechoslovakia (an invitational race with only a few finishers slower than three hours), I was surprised to encounter fruit and vegetable soup at the refreshment tables. This was in an era when you were lucky to get water at a U.S. marathon. Running the (54-mile) 1998 Comrades Marathon in South Africa, I found boiled potatoes at some of the aid stations. Knowing this in advance, I had trained using potatoes as an energy supplement.

Inevitably, runners must determine their own regimen. I usually stick with liquids when running races, but I have eaten solid food in other endurance events. In triathlons lasting six hours, I've experimented successfully with fruit and candy bars. In a 60-K cross-country ski race, several chocolate chip cookies provided a boost near the end. But during a snowshoe marathon, a combination of soft drinks and candy bars so nauseated me that I failed to finish.

Until recently, few American marathons provided anything other than liquids. If you wanted food and were unwilling to carry what you wanted in a fanny pack, you needed to enlist a support crew. Lately, manufacturers have provided gelatin supplements (gels) that can be carried easily in a pocket, pinned to a singlet, or carried inside your running gloves. I usually pin them to my singlet, positioning them near the waistband so they can be tucked into my shorts to prevent flapping. They are best taken with water as a chaser.

Most important: If you plan to eat on the run, experiment often in practice before you race.

when it's warm. Don't expect to achieve a preplanned time, and don't be afraid to bail out early when you're starting to overheat.

I learned that lesson the hard way. During the prime of my running career, I set out one morning determined to run at a 5:30 pace on a long run of 23 miles without realizing that the temperature was climbing through the 80s. I finished the workout, but barely jogging. Two days later, I came down with a knee injury, which I attributed to my still-dehydrated state. I failed to make the Olympic team even though I had the second-fastest time of the year among Americans. I'm convinced my body lacked sufficient fluid to lubricate the joints. Whether or not that theory is true, it's certain that you can't ignore Mother Nature while running in the heat. Warm-weather training must of necessity be a compromise. But if you learn to live with the heat, you can survive and condition yourself for any type of weather.

Still, it's sometimes difficult to gauge the weather. My oldest son Kevin qualified for the 1984 Olympic Trials with a time of 2:18:51. He was not a threat to make the top three, but the level of his training suggested that he might be able to shave several minutes off that PR in the trials race that began in Buffalo and finished at Niagara Falls, Ontario. As his coach, I designed an even pace to achieve that goal. Carefully watching his splits, he cruised past 10 miles right on pace, but he had to drop out a half dozen miles later because that pace was too fast for that day's hot and humid conditions, which we had failed to recognize at the start. Meanwhile, the runners at the front of the pack ran against each other, not against their watches, and had many fewer problems—although their times were several minutes slower than might have been expected.

As a leader of pacing teams at various marathons, I warn runners on the danger of connecting with a team that is too fast, particularly on a hot or humid day. At the prerace clinics, I usually advise those who had planned to join the 4:00 team to move back to the 4:10 or 4:20 team. Those planning 4:10 finishes, move back to 4:20 or 4:30, and so forth. But runners often come to marathons preprogrammed to run specific times. It's sometimes difficult to realize that, despite all your hard training, you are not going to achieve your time goal because of the environment.

DRINKING DURING THE RACE

Drinking during a marathon is almost a separate subject, because in addition to your need to stay cool, you also need to adopt a strategy that permits you to refuel on the run. You need energy as well as fluid replacement.

Timing your prerace hydration can be tricky. I recommend that runners drink as often as possible until two hours before the race—

CHOOSING YOUR BEVERAGE

Early research in fluid replacement suggested that drinks high in sugar content emptied from the stomach more slowly than water did. Then scientists fine-tuned their experiments and determined that fluids with a 6 percent sugar solution emptied from the stomach almost as fast as water. Most replacement drinks now offered in major marathons are formulated at that level. So don't bypass the replacement drink at refreshment stations (unless the sugar in the drink makes you nauseous).

My approach is usually to grab the replacement drink first, then wash it down with water, although many marathons offer water first, replacement drink second. Temperature usually dictates how much of each I drink. In warmer weather, I shade the ratio more toward water. I've found that too much replacement drink causes me stomach problems, but everyone is different in this respect.

Edward F. Coyle, Ph.D., of the University of Texas at Austin, estimates that ingesting 30 to 60 grams of carbohydrates with each hour of exercise will generally help you maintain blood glucose oxidation late in exercise and delay fatigue.

You can reach this level by drinking between 625 and 1,250 milliliters (about ⅔ quart to 1¼ quarts) per hour of a beverage that contains between 4 and 8 percent carbohydrates. For races beyond the marathon distance, during which energy replacement becomes as important as thermoregulation, supersaturated sugar solutions higher than 8 percent may be necessary. (You can adjust the percentage by varying how much water you mix with powdered replacement drinks. Check the directions.)

then stop until just before the race. Otherwise they may need to urinate at midrace, an obvious inconvenience. In the last five minutes before the gun, I start drinking again, often downing a 12-ounce soft drink (usually a Coke or a Pepsi) while standing on the starting line, knowing it will be absorbed by the body before it reaches the kidneys. One advantage of using a soft drink is that they come nicely packaged and can usually be easily obtained in vending machines in most hotels. At international races, everything else about the experience might be different, but you can usually find a Coke or Pepsi. Sipping a soft drink on the starting line works for me, but every runner has to experiment and come up with a workable drinking routine before practice and before races.

"Know what types of replacement beverages will be available during your race," advises Clark Campbell, a coach and professional triathlete from Lawrence, Kansas. "Then practice with that drink by using it during quality workouts and long-distance runs."

You should begin drinking early in the race. If you wait until you get thirsty, you may already have passed several aid stations that could have helped you avoid dehydration. Because of the crowds in the early miles, it may be difficult to get near the aid station for your first drink. But that drink may be the most important one you take in a race; it's worth losing a few seconds to grab at least a cup of water. Remember Dr. Coyle's recommendation to drink a quart an hour. Keep that as your goal.

Dr. Coyle says the largest factor affecting gastric emptying is volume. In other words, the more fluids you can force into your stomach, the faster fluids will empty from the stomach to be absorbed by the body. Dr. Coyle suggests that you may need to take in between 1,300 and 1,700 milliliters to force 1,000 milliliters to be emptied from the stomach during a marathon.

There are certain trade-offs to consider when deciding how much of what liquid to drink. One question is, Are the physical benefits of drinking large volumes of fluids worth the discomfort of making yourself drink so often?

On the hottest days, *yes!*

But the important goal is staying cool. "Any dehydration causes problems," says Dr. Coyle. "None can be tolerated." This is true not only in terms of safety but also in terms of performance. For every liter of fluid lost, your heartbeat will increase eight beats and your core temperature will increase accordingly. As a result, you'll be unable to maintain your race pace. If your goal is safety and performance, there's no question that the closer you match your intake of fluids to your rate of dehydration, the better.

In the closing stages of the race, water splashed on the body may help you more than water taken into the body. This is because it normally takes 30 minutes for water to migrate through the system to be released as sweat to provide an air-conditioning effect. One way to shortcut that system is to pour water directly on your body, permitting the water to evaporate. In the last few miles of the race, you're drinking for recovery after the race as much as for performance during it. My motto for the last half hour of running is "water on" as much as "water in." Some scientists suggest that splashing water on your body will not cool you significantly. Maybe so, but it sure feels good—and the psychological boost is worth something.

If you're wearing a hat, pour water onto the hat, and let it drip onto your face. Rather than splashing yourself in front, pour water down your back, since it's less likely to flow downward into your shoes and cause blisters. If you pass someone standing beside the road with a water spray, stop to stand under the spray for at least a few seconds rather than running through or around the spray.

The more attention you give to staying cool, the better you'll run. Once you get across the finish line, you'll want to begin drinking immediately to speed your recovery, but that's a subject for another chapter.

Chapter 17

MIND GAMES

It was chilly one year at the Twin Cities Marathon: a day for tights, long-sleeved tops, hats and gloves. I brought a pair of gloves with me but somehow lost one on the way to the starting line. To keep both hands warm as I ran, I switched the glove from hand to hand every third mile. It became a game for me, something to think about, something to help chart my progress. I could look forward to the switch each third mile.

If you think in those terms, a marathon is merely eight glove changes long.

Psychologists have long insisted that the mind is as important as the body when it comes to success in sports, particularly in an event like the marathon where the mind must push the body to extremes. During the glory days of Eastern Bloc athletes, sports psychologists were as important as other coaches or trainers in preparing East German and Soviet athletes for competition. The U.S. Olympic Committee employs psychologists as consultants, as do many professional football and baseball teams. But anyone can use mind games to help get through long-distance events.

I use mind games for survival in the marathon, physically as well as mentally. I divide marathons into fourths and thirds. At 3 miles, I think: "Just done a 5-K. Piece of cake." At 6 miles, it's: "A fourth of the race done." And at 8 miles, "A third." At 10, I console myself: "Double digits." At 13: "Past the half. Fewer miles ahead of me than behind me." At 16: "Only single digits remain." At 20: "I've passed the wall," or, "Only a 10-K left now." By that time, you're close enough to count down like the liftoff of a rocket: "Six-five-four-three-two-one. I'm done."

When I was researching *Boston: A Century of Running*, I interviewed Dick Beardsley, who finished second to Alberto Salazar at the 1982 Boston Marathon. Coming off Heartbreak Hill in the lead, but with Salazar stalking him, Beardsley was toast. At 21 miles, he decided to adopt a strategy that ignored the fact that five grueling miles still remained. He decided he would run those miles one at a time, not caring whether there was another, not worrying whether or not there would be a tomorrow. "You can hold this pace for one more mile," Beardsley told himself. "One more mile! Only *one mile* to go!"

At 22 miles, Beardsley punched the reset button on his mental speedometer. "One mile to go!"

And at 23: "You're beating the world record holder. One more mile!"

Salazar eventually did outsprint Beardsley on the final straightaway, beating him 2:08:52 to 2:08:54. But it was Beardsley's mental strength that made their duel one of the closest in Boston Marathon history.

I've adopted that strategy in several races, most recently at the 1999 Walt Disney World Marathon, in which I lead the 4:30 pacing team for *Runner's World*. I arrived in Orlando undertrained, having failed to do any workouts beyond 13 miles in the months before the race. Though in respectable shape for a 5-K or a 10-K, I doubted my ability to keep the pace for a full 26. I told my coleader Leesa Weichert that I only planned to go 20, then she could take the group the rest of the way.

But at 20 I felt okay, so I tucked in behind Leesa, focused on the ears of the Mickey Mouse cap she was wearing, and told myself, "One mile to go. You can hold this pace *for one more mile!*" And, like Beardsley, I reset my mental speedometer for each of the next half dozen miles. Although Weichert did pull ahead by 40 seconds in those closing miles, I finished in 4:30:27. That gave me more satisfaction than many races in which my times were several hours faster.

POSITIVE THINKING PAYS OFF

Marathon mind games are more than strategies for coping with pain and boredom. According to Charles A. Garfield, author of *Peak*

Performance, 60 to 90 percent of success in sports can be attributed to mental factors and psychological mastery. Psychologist Thomas Tutko quotes retired baseball player Maury Wills as saying that success is *all* mental. "There is nothing mystical about the emotional side of sports," claims Dr. Tutko.

Unfortunately, your mind can also work *against* you. One individual commented to me about a top-ranked woman runner he formerly coached: "It's her thinking that keeps her from winning."

Confidence is an important factor in the mind games athletes play: The power of positive thinking relates to more than success in business. One study of skiers training for the Olympic team showed that those who didn't make the team had negative or tentative feelings about their abilities, and successful candidates were more positive. Does confidence breed success, or were the less successful skiers simply being realistic about their talents? A little bit of both, probably, but consider the cocky attitude of Alpine skier Bill Johnson before he won the 1984 Olympic downhill in Sarajevo: Did Johnson know he had a lock on the gold medal, or was he simply trying to psych himself up? The trash talk of NBA basketball players, as impolite as it seems, may serve some purpose.

If Johnson was only psyching himself up, he succeeded, as did British decathlete Daley Thompson, who also boasted of success before the 1984 games. Referring to his chief competitor, Thompson said, "The only way (Jurgen) Hingsen is going to get a gold medal here is to do another event—or steal mine." Thompson prevailed (defending his 1980 Olympic title), but Jamaica's Bert Cameron—who had claimed before the games that the 400-meter gold medal already had his name engraved on it—pulled a muscle in a semi-final heat and saw the medal go to another. There's a subtle line between confidence and overconfidence.

When we are confident, we can rationalize away any potential problems; without confidence, even slight threats become magnified.

Confident athletes can relax more easily than ones who feel threatened, but there are tricks to relaxing and eliminating fear. Robert M. Nideffer, Ph.D., a consultant for the U.S. Olympic Committee, recalled watching a diver about to execute a difficult $3\frac{1}{2}$ somersault in pike position off the 10-meter tower. The coach stood below counting down: "Five, four, three, two, one. Go!" The counting, Dr. Nideffer explained, helped the diver redirect his attention away from his anxiety and fear. He likened it to a hypnotic state. Marathoner Tony Sandoval used a similar five-to-zero countdown when he went to bed each night. "It relaxed me and helped me to fall asleep quickly," explains Sandoval.

VISUALIZING SUCCESS

As a steeplechaser, I had my own presleep technique. I would visualize myself hurdling over barriers. It was better, I thought, than the more traditional counting of sheep, but it served another purpose beyond self-hypnosis. I was perfecting my hurdling technique through a technique known as "imaging."

In their book *Sporting Body, Sporting Mind*, authors John Syer and Christopher Connolly refer to this same technique as instant *preplay*. They describe one horsewoman who would lock herself in the washroom—the only place she wouldn't be disturbed—immediately before competition to focus on her event. That might not work in a major marathon with 20,000 runners waiting outside the portapotties, but in *Golf My Way*, Jack Nicklaus describes visualizing each shot before he hits it. He first pictures the ball landing where he wants it, then he "sees" the ball going there, and finally he visualizes himself "making the kind of swing that will turn the previous images into reality." Jon Lugbill, world champion kayaker, pictures himself paddling down whitewater rivers and feels this helps his ability to choose the best path through the waves during competition. Similarly, runners who want to improve their form can picture themselves running like 1996 Olympic marathon champion Fatima Roba of Ethiopia. Has there ever been a more beautiful stride than hers? Tom Grogon, a coach from Cincinnati, suggests that runners mentally review the course before any distance race and think about how they will run it.

Another technique is instant replay, which Syer and Connolly describe as: "The reverse of instant preplay, it is a visualized review of an action you have just performed." This enables athletes to imprint a perfect action more deeply in their sensory memory. Members of the U.S. weightlifting team preparing for the Olympics used these techniques. Each weightlifter had a videotape of his lifts at various meets and in training. As additional meets were filmed, the athletes added new tapes to their collection. With their library of tapes, the athletes could compare their recent lift styles with previous lifts or those of other top lifters filmed during competition.

THE POWER OF CONCENTRATION

One way to succeed in sports is to eliminate outside distractions.That way, you can more easily relax. Bryant J. Cratty, author of *Psychological Preparation and Athletic Excellence*, believes that relaxation and concentration can be improved in competition if an athlete erects imaginary walls to block off distractions. He suggests that a basketball player visualize partitions in front of the other players and behind the backboard before attempting to shoot a free throw. Dr. Cratty recommends that a gymnast imagine not only that the gym is empty but that there is a tent over each apparatus. So, too, should a long-distance runner focus on a narrow corridor of the road ahead.

Dr. Garfield says concentration is important for weightlifters: "The trained lifter knows that during the few seconds before a lift, total attention must be focused on the bar, and the degree to which this is done is largely determined by how much he really wants to make the lift." He found that if the lifter's confidence was lacking, and his will was not intensely focused, he would not be able to muster the control of muscle power necessary for success. The same is true in running.

"The ability to concentrate," says William P. Morgan, Ed.D., "is the single element that separates the merely good athletes from the great ones. Concentration is the hallmark of the elite runner." Elite runners succeed, he says, because they are totally in tune with their bodies, monitoring all symptoms from the nerve endings.

In contrast, Dr. Morgan found that middle-of-the-pack marathoners more often thought of other activities (called dissociating) as a means of coping with pain. Dr. Morgan believes that in addition to possibly slowing them down, this tactic is dangerous: Runners could be ignoring important body signals and mindlessly run themselves into heatstroke or a stress fracture.

Owen Anderson, Ph.D., the editor of *Running Research News*, defines *dissociation* as "ignoring the sensory feedback you get from your body while focusing your mind on something outside yourself." He claims that although dissociation blocks negative messages, prevents boredom, and diverts the mind from the pain and fatigue you experience in the muscles during strenuous running, it can create some problems if it causes you to fail to take in enough fluid, relax, or exert efficient muscle control. "It's hard to sustain a coordinated, quality pace unless you concentrate," says Dr. Anderson.

Kazuo Takai of the University of Tsukuba split 60 runners into groups at a 20-K race in Tokyo. Half of the runners used what Takai described as "attention" techniques to stay on pace; the other half used "avoidance" techniques and followed the pace of the others. Takai found that the attentive runners outperformed the avoidance runners in achieving their predicted goals. *Attention* means that you tune in to your body's signals midrace and let how you feel dictate your pace. *Avoidance* means that you tune *out* your body's signals and go with the flow.

Takai's spin on the subject was to identify five attention strategies that contributed to good race times:

1. Body check. How does your whole body feel? Are you loose and relaxed? Any tight spots (such as a sore shoulder) might be a signal to slow down.
2. Tempo test. How's the rhythm of your running? Do you feel smo-o-o-oth? You should flow along the ground as though this is an easy practice run.
3. Leg rest. Can your legs continue to carry you at this pace? Any cramps? Discomfort? Maybe by speeding up you'll actually feel more comfortable.
4. Image replay. Remember your most successful races or practice run. Do you feel as well now as you did then? Recapture the glory by picturing past triumphs.
5. Motion study. Are you running well? Move out of your own body and see yourself as though through a video camera. Now improve that picture.

Takai asked each of his subjects to indicate on a seven-point rating scale (1 = never; 7 = very often) how often they used these strategies to recall pace in a race. He then compared how close the runners came to their "predicted" time compared to their ability to run a 5-K. This permitted Takai to rate them as "accurate" or "inaccurate" recallers. Results showed that the accurate recallers were better pacers, capable of running steady through the race. "Overall," says Takai, "the accurate recallers ran with a steady pace throughout the race, while the inaccurate recallers were likely to decrease the pace after the first 5-K."

When I ran marathons near the front of the pack, I always considered concentration to be as important an ability as a high max VO_2. I focused on every stride and was acutely aware of any signals my body was sending. I always liked the idea of running on scenic courses—except I almost never saw the scenery! Usually the better I ran, the less I recalled of the surroundings. I'd run the Boston Marathon a dozen times or more and knew that the course passed somewhere near Fenway Park, where the Boston Red Sox played, but I was unaware how near until one year in the 1970s when I first covered the race for *Runner's World* as a journalist. After the lead runners had finished the race and offered their postrace comments, I decided to wander backward over the course to watch the slower runners finishing. Less than a mile from the finish line, I came upon Fenway Park, home of the Boston Red Sox. I was startled. Intellectually, I had realized that Fenway Park was right on the course, but I had never seen it before. To have missed it while racing, my field of vision must have been very narrow.

WHAT TOP RUNNERS DO

Other runners agree on the value of concentration. Olympic marathoner Don Kardong states, "It's absolutely essential that you concentrate on your competition, monitor your body feedback, and not lose touch with what's happening around you. If you lose concentration in a good, competitive 10-K field, you immediately drop off the pace. There's never time to think those favorite thoughts you have on easy training runs."

Greg Meyer, who struggled to regain his form after winning Boston in 1983, ran several meets in Europe one summer. "I'd lose concentration for a lap or two," Meyer told me, "and that would get me out of the race. I'd drift off, get gapped and never make it up."

Meyer felt that a series of injuries contributed to his inability to concentrate. "You start focusing on the injuries instead of racing," he said. But it's possible that in winning Boston he had satisfied many of the inner demons that had driven him to success. He may have lost some of his will to win, and with it an ability to concentrate.

Dick Buerkle was top ranked in the 5000 meters on the track in 1974 and set an indoor mile record in 1978. He noticed that in both years his ability to concentrate was at its highest. "I'd go for an 18-miler every weekend and be totally focused," he recalls. "Other years, I'd find myself daydreaming."

Kardong notes that some distance runners have difficulty switching from roads to track or cross-country. He suspects that the biggest factor isn't training, but concentration: "When in an unfamiliar setting, you're distracted by it initially. Later, you adapt."

During a marathon Bill Rodgers would think of specific things to help him concentrate: splits, competition, the course, the wind. "If I have a chance to win," he thinks: "What's my best way to race certain individuals?"

Greg Meyer learned he could concentrate better if he ran fartlek rather than straight distance: "Rather than doing mindless 20-milers, you vary the pace, which forces you to pay attention." Sue King, while training for the New York City Marathon, found she could concentrate more by running long runs alone, so the conversation of friends didn't distract her.

Rodgers believes concentration must begin before a race. He would avoid warming up with others, preferring to think of the upcoming race. He also believes that the clinics, dinners, and social events he attended as part of sponsor commitments diminished his concentration. I agree. As a consultant to the Chicago Marathon, I have commitments the entire week leading up to the race. I need to visit all four of my training classes in four different areas of the city on four successive nights. There are press conferences and social events to attend. At the expo on Friday and Saturday, when I am not talking to individual runners at my booth, I'm usually standing on a stage talking to large groups. Race director Carey Pinkowski will usually ask me to say a few words at the pasta party—and lately Chicago has gotten so big there are two separate pasta parties, not including the one organized by the Leukemia Society of America.

It's fun, and I love it until that time on Sunday morning when I have to get up and run the race. I have rarely run well at Chicago. My mind wasn't in it. Recently, I've realized that I needed to either not run the race, or run it at a low throttle setting, leaving my serious racing for elsewhere. Leading pacing teams, which I now do at Chicago, and for *Runner's World* in other cities, also can be a draining experience, because you're focusing on the success of others rather than your own.

DEVELOPING YOUR POWERS OF CONCENTRATION

So how can you learn to concentrate? How do you focus your mind on the business at foot?

At least one study shows that the average runner can learn to think like the elite runner. Hein Helgo Schomer of the University of Cape Town in South Africa improved the concentration of a group of 10 non-elite runners over a period of five weeks. Before they were coached, the runners used association (being tuned into their bodies) only 45 percent of the time. By the fifth week under Schomer's instruction, they were associating 70 percent of the time while running, and their average training intensity also increased.

Dr. Anderson states that the average runner probably associates about 30 to 40 percent of the time while running. He considers 60 to 70 percent optimal, and 90 to 100 percent necessary for supreme efforts. "Association is clearly a strategy you can use to reach your true potential as a runner," he says. "Associative thinking can increase your ability to handle strenuous workouts and cope with tough races. While it boosts your aerobic fitness, association probably also minimizes your risk of overtraining by keeping you in tune with how your body is responding to your overall training intensity and volume."

But learning to concentrate takes time. Each spring, once the snow melts, I head for the track for weekly interval sessions to try to regain speed lost after a winter of slow running. When I begin running interval quarters, I know that to run my fastest, I have to concentrate. Yet invariably I'll get on the backstretch and my mind will wander and my pace will lag. Only after five or six weeks does my concentration improve to the point where I can keep my attention on running for a full quarter. My track times then start to drop, convincing me that the improvement results from both stronger muscles and a stronger mind.

To hone his ability to concentrate, Dick Buerkle would do long repeats, rather than short ones, running repeat miles between 4:14 and 4:20. "It requires more effort to concentrate for four minutes than for the 27 seconds it takes to run a 200," he says.

Like Buerkle, I've also found various forms of speedwork—intervals on the track, fartlek in the woods, strides on the grass—to be the most effective way of improving my concentration. Sometimes I'll head to the golf course several times a week to run a half dozen or more short sprints—not flat out, but close to the speed I reach in a track mile. I do these "strides" to loosen my muscles for other, longer and tougher workouts. Invariably I return from the golf course running much faster, my mind totally focused.

THE FINAL SIX MILES

Knowledgeable coaches often offer their runners mental strategies for the marathon, particularly for the final six miles, when the marathon gets toughest and when concentration often determines the difference between a good and a bad race.

Frank X. Mari of Toms River, New Jersey: Focus on positive thoughts. "Try to catch the next runner in front of you. Remember your hard training and that you are the greatest. Smile."

Tim Nicholls of Pembroke Pines, Florida: "Stick with someone in the race. Ask yourself how badly you want it."

Tom Grogon of Cincinnati: "Toward the end, concentrate on passing as many runners as possible. As soon as you pass one competitor, concentrate on reeling in the next. Think of the world as ending right after the race, thus there is no reason not to put everything into it."

David Cowein of Morrilton, Arkansas: "In the last six miles, think of how many times you've run a 10-K before. Focus on your achievements. You've trained hard. You deserve your best. You're nearly through. Tell yourself how tough you are."

As you run more marathons, you'll determine what mental strategies work best to get you through those final six miles.

I have difficulty concentrating during track workouts, and particularly on distance runs, but I usually manage to get my act together for important races: Competition tends to focus my mind. Maybe that's why I achieve speeds in competition that are beyond my reach in training.

BLOCKING OUT MIND DRIFT

How do you get mind and body in tune to run long distances faster? Here are several tips to help you block out mind drift.

Prepare yourself to run. Have a game plan for workouts and particularly for important races. Where are you going to run? How fast? How far? Against whom? Get yourself in a running frame of mind. Learn to relax. A regular warmup routine before running can get you into the mood to perform. Find a routine that works best for you—whether chanting a mantra or stretching—and stick with it.

Discover how your body works. While running fast, try to be aware of what the various parts of your body are doing. Can you discover what it feels like to run smoothly? If so, you may be able to duplicate that feeling on other occasions. Remember: Given equal physical skills, the ability to concentrate separates the merely good runners from the great ones.

Practice instant preplay and replay. If you can imagine before running how top runners run successfully—preplay—you're halfway to emulating them. Practice running mentally as well as physically. Try replay as well. When you run well, remember how you ran. Fix that image in your memory, adding it to your mental video library.

Head for the track. Running against the clock and attempting to match preset goals forces you to concentrate. Learning to adjust to the track's rhythm—running turns, for example—also helps, as do fartlek sessions and other forms of speedwork done elsewhere.

Plan days of maximum concentration. Not every workout need be fully focused, but select one or more days each week to practice concentration. Racing, particularly track or cross-country races, may help focus your mind.

Avoid race-day distractions. Friends, traffic, or dogs can distract you from the act and art of running. Run solo when you can to improve your concentration. If you want to succeed with your race plan, keep conversation to a minimum even if you're running with a friend.

Talk to yourself. Cardiologist Paul Thompson, M.D., believes runners need pep talks. "I talk to myself when I train," he says. "The year I ran best at Boston, I focused on what to tell myself during those last few miles when it hurts." Thompson placed 16th at Boston in 1976 by telling himself, "Keep going," and "I'm a tough dude."

Landmark the course. What are the key points on the course you plan to race? Where are the hills? Where are the flats? What sections of the course will drain you and what sections (such as Wellesley College, where the women come out to cheer Boston marathoners) will give you strength? Don't wait until the course tour the day before the race to learn what you will be running.

Focus hardest when it counts most. If you find it difficult to concentrate during the full 26 miles of a marathon, save your focus for the miles when you need it the most. Kardong used to dissociate the first half of the race, then associate the second half. "My mind wanders at times," admits marathoner Doug Kurtis. "I like to look around and check the scenery, but I particularly try to focus late in the race, especially when I know a sub-2:20 is on the line."

Concentration can't compensate for lack of training or basic ability, but it can help you maximize your potential.

Chapter 18

MILE 27

The most important mile of the marathon may be mile number 27, the one you walk to the hotel. Shortly after finishing the Boston Marathon one year, I sat huddled on a bench in Copley Square, wrapped in an aluminum blanket, with a soft drink in one hand and in the other a cup of frozen yogurt that I was too nauseated to eat. I cursed having stayed at a hotel whose distance from the finish line would require that I walk another mile—a 27th mile, so to speak—before I could end that day's marathon experience.

Yet 15 minutes later, halfway to the hotel, frozen yogurt consumed, sipping a second soft drink, I felt my energy returning. I knew I would recover and eventually run 26 miles again.

That 27th mile is particularly important when it comes to speeding postmarathon recovery, so that you can run and race again. Your actions during the first five seconds after crossing the line may be crucial to your recovery—as are the next five minutes, the next five hours, the next five days, and even the next five weeks. Postmarathon recovery is something many runners pay scant attention to. But by organizing your postrace plans as well as you organize your prerace plans, you can recover faster and more comfortably, and minimize future injuries.

MINIMIZING THE DAMAGE

"Runners need to take responsibility for the health of their muscles, not just how fast they go," warns Linda Jaros, a massage therapist from Dedham, Massachusetts, whose clients have included Bill Rodgers and Joan Benoit Samuelson. "Recovery has to become an integral part of their training."

Indeed, recovery may be the toughest skill for a marathon runner to master. How do you snap back after more than 26 hard miles on the road? Are fatigued and sore muscles inevitable, or are there strategies you can use to make marathon recovery not only faster but less painful? What secrets can we learn from both elite and ordinary marathoners that will allow a quick return to full training—and the next starting line? What do scientists suggest based on laboratory research, not only for the morning after but for the week after?

David L. Costill, Ph.D., of the Human Performance Laboratory at Ball State University in Muncie, Indiana, has researched the damage marathons do to the body, both in the lab and on the road. In numerous studies, Dr. Costill has reviewed the postrace drinking, eating, and training habits of marathoners. His suggestions for recovery: Drink plenty of fluids, carbo-load *after* the race (as well as before), and don't start running again too soon. "A lot of things happen to the body as a result of running the marathon," he says. "You become overheated, dehydrated, and muscle-depleted. Your hormonal milieu gets thrown out of whack, and you traumatize your muscles. You have to bide your time to get your body back in balance."

Since 1974, Jack H. Scaff Jr., M.D., has supervised the Honolulu Marathon Clinic, a group that meets Sundays in Kapiolani Park to train for that marathon. After watching his group's recuperative efforts after the race, Dr. Scaff commented, "The runners felt so good about their achievement, they would bounce back too soon. The rate of injuries was exponential. We finally canceled the clinic for three months following the marathon to try to get the runners to take it easy."

Benji Durden of Boulder, Colorado, has observed the effects of marathon running on the body as a runner and as a coach of others, including 2:26:40 marathoner Kim Jones. Durden recalls running a 2:15 at Boston in 1978—cutting four minutes off his best time—then spraining an ankle the following week. "My body had not fully recovered," he notes. While conceding that total rest may be the best postmarathon prescription, Durden contends that runners may have conflicting psychological needs. "As a coach I try to accept the best advice from the scientists and adapt it based on a combination of intuition and experience," he says.

KEEP MOVING

Want to recover as rapidly as possible following your next marathon? First, don't stop as soon as you cross the finish line. You may have no choice, particularly at major races where you will be prodded to jog and walk through the finish chute, after which you run a gauntlet that includes having various items pressed onto you: your medal, fluids and food, an aluminum blanket, and your gear brought from the starting line. Having accepted all this, you may need to walk what seems an unconscionably long distance to be greeted by friends and family.

At Chicago, race director Carey Pinkowski provides a special gathering tent for my marathon training class. The tent is near the starting line, but several blocks from the finish line. Being forced to walk those extra few blocks probably does all of us some good.

Whether prodded or not, you need to keep moving to allow your stressed system a chance to gradually attain a steady state and also to avoid what Dr. Scaff calls "the postrace collapse phenomenon." This, he says, is when "a runner looks good coming across the finish line, sits down too soon, then 20 minutes later must be taken to the first aid tent with heatstroke or cramps." Blood pressure can drop too quickly, sometimes with disastrous results. "Walking around a bit seems to prevent this from happening," says Dr. Scaff.

How much you walk depends on your condition at the end of the race. "If your body is telling you to collapse in a heap, walking around is not easy," says Dr. Costill. "But continuing to move for a while will maintain your circulation, keeping the blood pumping through the muscles. This should aid short-term recovery."

Warning: Don't take the advice to keep moving to excess. Many compulsive runners feel the need to "cool down" by jogging a mile or two, even after a marathon. Although this may make sense following a 10-K race, it is not wise after a 42.2-K race. No scientific studies have shown any benefits from postrace running. You simply increase your chance of injury by continuing to run.

DRINK UP

As long as you're walking, head in the direction of the tables with fluids. All the experts—scientists and experienced marathoners alike—advise that you make an immediate and continuing effort to replace the several liters of liquid your system has lost during 26 miles on the road. Grab the first cup of liquid thrust into your hand and start sipping at once, no matter how nauseated you feel.

Dr. Scaff recommends sipping at the rate of half an ounce a minute. And while going about other recuperative activities for the next several hours, keep a drink in your hand and continue drinking.

Like most experts, Dr. Costill emphasizes that human thirst is not an accurate gauge of dehydration. "Drink more than you desire," he advises.

If the first cup thrust into your hand is water, accept it thankfully and sip on it, but look for the table where they have drinks with at least some dilute form of sugar, whether in a so-called replacement drink (such as Gatorade or Exceed), a soft drink, or a fruit drink. Your primary need is to replace fluids, but you have also depleted your muscles of glycogen and need to replace that as well. "Try to get your blood sugar back to normal as quickly as possible," says Durden.

The best time for glycogen replacement, according to research by Edward F. Coyle, Ph.D., at the University of Texas at Austin, is during the first two hours after the race. "The muscles absorb glycogen like a sponge," he says. "Four and six hours after the race, the absorption rate starts to decline." Nutritionists may argue that, generally speaking, fruit drinks (because they contain vitamins and minerals) are superior to sugar drinks—and this certainly is true—but Dr. Costill claims that when it comes to glycogen replacement, the body doesn't know the difference between one sugar and another.

Doug Kurtis never minded having to undergo drug testing after winning a marathon. But in order to provide the necessary urine specimen, Kurtis found he had to drink steadily for two hours. "That forced me to ingest a lot of fluids," says Kurtis. "I feel that helped my recovery."

Two postmarathon drinks to avoid: diet soft drinks, because they provide no glucose boost (having just burned approximately 2,600 calories, your goal should *not* be weight loss), and alcoholic beverages, because they serve as a diuretic. That postrace beer may taste good, but it will eventually have a negative effect on fluid balance. If you drink a beer, do so only after you have already ingested twice the volume of other fluids.

GET OFF YOUR FEET

After spending the first 5 to 10 minutes walking around and obtaining something to drink, get off your feet. Listen to your body, "Do what it tells you to do," says Dr. Costill. "Get horizontal." Pick a comfortable spot, preferably in the shade, and elevate your feet, easing the flow of blood to the heart. Dr. Costill speculates that some of the muscle soreness and stiffness experienced immediately after a race may be related to edema, swelling caused by the intermuscular pressure of accumulated fluids in the lower legs. "Elevating the legs may speed recovery," he suggests.

You can assist your recovery with gentle self-massage. But don't knead, advises my massage therapist, Patty Longnecker of the Harbor Country Day Spa in New Buffalo, Michigan. Longnecker advises that you stroke your leg muscles gently toward the heart. Durden and New York City marathon winner Priscilla Welch recommend massaging with ice to reduce the swelling. Hosing your legs with cold water is another option.

Bill Rodgers, four-time winner of both the Boston and New York City marathons, likes to do some postrace stretching while lying down. If you choose to do the same, don't stretch excessively. Your muscles most likely are stiff and damaged; you don't want to traumatize them further.

Some experts even question the value of stretching. A study at the University of Texas at Tyler indicated that static stretching failed to prevent muscle soreness later. Researchers Katherine C. Buroker and James A. Schwane, Ph.D., concede that stretching helps maintain flexibility, but they say that stretching immediately after strenuous exercise is the wrong time for it. When Dr. Scaff surveyed members of his Honolulu Marathon Clinic, he discovered that those who stretched most also suffered the most injuries. Scientists remain divided on the value of stretching, so your best bet is to keep any stretching short and simple after a marathon.

While resting, continue to sip fluids—this is still your primary recovery strategy. Using a bent straw makes it easier to drink while horizontal. To guarantee a supply, place a bottle of your favorite postrace drink in your tote bag. If you don't have to use it, no problem. Better to have too much fluid available than too little.

BEGIN TO REFUEL

Your immediate concern after the race may be fluid replacement, but within an hour after the race you should begin shifting to more solid foods. This may be particularly important if sugar from replacement drinks makes you nauseous, as food can slow down sugar absorption to help prevent the nausea. Ken Young, a top trail runner from northern California and the former coach of 2:11 marathoner Don Janicki, likes to eat saltines to help settle his stomach. Fruit is a good start, particularly bananas, because they are easy to digest and are a good way to replace lost potassium. (Don't become obsessed with instant mineral replacement, however; eating several well-balanced meals within the next 24 hours will take care of electrolytes lost through sweating.)

"Food has real nutritional value, whereas sports drinks are just sugar," says Nancy Clark, R.D., author of *Nancy Clark's Sports Nutrition Guidebook* and a nutritionist with SportsMedicine Brookline in Boston. Clark recommends fruit or yogurt (frozen and otherwise) as a superior snack to cookies or candy bars. Research by Dr. Coyle indicates that 1 gram of carbohydrates per kilogram of body weight per hour is necessary for the most efficient glycogen replacement. That translates to 2 calories per pound, or 300 calories for a 150-pound runner. Clark suggests that a marathoner drink a glass of orange juice and eat one banana and a cup of yogurt the first hour, then repeat that the second hour.

As a practical matter, I'll grab anything handy, particularly those chocolate chip cookies at the end of the table. Immediately after a marathon, I'm like a shark feeding. Anything in close range of my mouth gets consumed.

CONSIDER MASSAGE

Many major marathons provide massage tents with teams of trained massage therapists ready to give a soothing rubdown. According to Jaros, massage helps push waste products from the muscles into the blood system for recirculation and elimination. Most runners find they feel better after a full-body massage.

Jaros cautions against getting a strenuous massage too soon after a marathon, however. Early finishers sometimes head straight to the massage tent to beat the crowd, but it's preferable to wait 45 minutes, so you can give yourself time to rehydrate and cool down. And don't allow therapists to poke and probe your muscles as vigorously as they might during a regular session. The best postmarathon massage, according to therapist Rich Phaigh of Eugene, Oregon, begins with the lower back and buttocks to relax those muscles and get intramuscular fluids flowing, then works gently on the legs with long, flowing motions toward the heart. If the massage hurts, ask the therapist to be more gentle; if it still hurts, thank the therapist graciously and get off the table.

For those athletes with a regular massage therapist, the best time for a massage may be 24 to 48 hours after the race, the time when muscle soreness usually peaks. In preparing for the Sunburst Marathon, I scheduled appointments with my regular massage therapist the afternoon before the race *and* two days after.

Avoid hot baths or showers that may increase inflammation and unnecessarily elevate your body temperature. That bubbling whirlpool back at the motel may look inviting, but leave it to the kids. Opt for a *cool* shower. "Getting your body temperature back down will help you recover faster," says Dr. Costill. Jaros suggests a cold bath followed by a warm (not hot) shower. Aspirin should be avoided, according to Tufts University research. Although it may reduce the pain of sore muscles, it also prolongs the time required to repair damage.

RECOVERY CONTINUES AT HOME

Most marathoners don't want to abandon the scene of battle too rapidly. Admittedly, part of the enjoyment of marathoning is hanging around to see old friends and rivals, cheering their finishes, and swapping stories about the miles just covered. Don't deny yourself the opportunity to wallow a while in the joy of your accomplishment.

But after you've gotten home and showered, jump into bed. Even if you have difficulty sleeping, at least rest for one to two hours. Then get up: It's time for more food. Three to four hours after finishing, sit down to a full meal. Dr. Costill claims that carbohydrates should still be the food of choice. "Nutritionally, your first meal after the marathon should resemble your last meal before," he says. Sound advice, although many marathoners rebel against having to look at one more plate of pasta and instead indulge a sudden craving for protein.

"I'm not afraid to eat a hamburger after a marathon," confesses Kurtis. "It almost feels like a reward." Bill Rodgers recalls going to a restaurant one year after placing third in the Boston Marathon and eating a hamburger followed by a hot fudge sundae. He also fondly recalls family victory celebrations at his store with picnic lunches of chicken sandwiches supplied by his mother.

But remember that spaghetti isn't the only source of carbohydrates. "Even high-carbohydrate diets have some protein," says Clark. "Your body needs to rebuild protein, so have your chicken or steak or fish, but start with some minestrone soup. Add some extra potatoes, rolls, and juice. The secret in anything you eat is moderation. Don't focus on the meat; focus on the carbohydrates that can accompany the meat."

TAKE A BREAK

Once home, too many marathoners make the mistake of resuming training too soon. They may fear getting out of shape or feel that some easy jogging will help speed their recovery. Kurtis always runs the next day, "even if only to limp through a mile" but most of us don't have his capabilities. The body of someone used to 105-mile training weeks and as many as a dozen marathons a year functions differently than that of an ordinary runner.

Research by Dr. Costill suggests that recovery is speeded and conditioning is not affected if you do nothing for 7 to 10 days after the race. Repeat: For the week after your marathon, *do nothing!*

Durden thinks it's all right to resume *easy* running by the fourth day. He wouldn't recommend the cross-training used by some recuperating marathoners. "When I say rest, I mean rest," he says. "Not Nautilus. Not exercycling. Not swimming. Not walking. You rest! I've worked with a few athletes who thought rest meant everything except run."

Moving in the pool is another matter. It may comfort the muscles if you immerse yourself in water and use gentle, nonaerobic movements to stretch and relax your arms and legs. But don't start paddling, because you will simply delay recovery by burning more glycogen.

EASE BACK INTO TRAINING

Once back with running, don't run too hard or too fast too soon. Dr. Scaff recommends the 10 percent rule: No more than 10 percent of your total mileage can be spent in racing or speedwork. "After you've run a marathon, you need 260 miles of training before you enter your next event or start doing speedwork," he says. "For someone running 30 to 40 miles a week, that means six to eight weeks of recovery running. Someone used to higher mileage probably recovers sooner."

Rodgers took his time coming back after marathons. "Slowly, over a period of weeks, I'd build back to regular mileage. I'd stick with once-a-day training for a while. No speed or long runs for at least two or three weeks."

Particularly after a good performance, runners need to resist the urge to come back too soon. It's tempting to increase training under the theory that more work may mean still better times. "You end up pushing yourself too hard," warns Durden. "You may get away with it for four to six weeks, then you collapse, get injured, get sick, or feel stale and overtrained. The period immediately after a good marathon is when you need to be especially cautious about your training."

Russell H. Pate, Ph.D., chairman of the Department of Exercise Science at the University of South Carolina, developed a two-week recovery method through trial and error. "I'd have very minimal activity for two to three days after the race, still modest running for the remainder of the first week, then over the second week gradually build to near my normal training loads. By the third week, I'd be ready to run hard again." But on one occasion when he felt good after three days and resumed heavy training too quickly, three weeks later he had a breakdown featuring minor injuries and fatigue. "I learned the hard way to put the brakes on," Dr. Pate recalls.

"Studies now show you do, indeed, damage the muscle, creating microtrauma in muscle fibers with activities like marathon running," he says. "No one knows what we do to the connective tissue and skeleton, but I suspect there's trauma there also. Since scientists do not yet know precisely how much time is needed for such trauma to be reversed, it's smart for runners to give themselves plenty of time with minimal running to let that healing process occur."

None of the experts, neither scientists, coaches, nor experienced road runners can offer an exact formula for marathon recovery. Too many factors are involved, from the condition of the runner going into the race to the conditions of the race itself. Hilly courses, particularly those with downhills near the end such as Boston, do more muscle damage than flat courses. Extremes of heat or cold slow the recovery process. And runners who start out too fast and crash usually have more difficulty recovering than do those who run an even pace.

"Nature takes care of us," says Dr. Costill. "Time heals most of the damage done in the marathon." Through careful attention to the 27th mile, most of us will be back on the road again, looking forward to our next trip to the starting line.

MARATHON TRAINING SCHEDULES

The training schedules that follow were designed for the marathon training class I teach in Chicago with Brian Piper and Bill Fitzgerald. As explained in chapter 4, these schedules evolved over a period of years. Each individual enrolling in our class, 18 weeks before the marathon, receives a booklet featuring day-by-day instructions similar to what follows. The same information is available on my Web site at www.halhigdon.com.

A few preliminary words of advice.

Novice. People differ greatly in ability, but we recommend that before starting a marathon program, you should have been running about a year, be able to comfortably run distances between three and six miles, and be training three to five days a week, averaging 15 to 25 miles a week. It helps if you've run a 5-K or 10-K race. It is possible to run a marathon with less base, but the higher your fitness level, the easier this 18-week program will be.

The key to the program is the long runs on weekends, which build from 6 to 20 miles. You can skip an occasional workout, or juggle the schedule depending on other commitments, but do not cheat on the long runs. As the weekend mileage builds, the weekday mileage also builds. Midweek workouts on Wednesdays build from 3 to 10 miles. Cross-training will help you relax the day after your long runs.

Expert. The training program for experienced marathoners follows a similar progressive buildup—except you start at 10 miles and peak with three 20-milers. There is also more training at marathon pace. Please note that I do not recommend doing your long runs at marathon pace. That adds too much stress, particularly when coupled with speed sessions, which consist of hill repeats, interval training and tempo runs in various combinations. Explanations of how to perform each workout follow in the text.

And now, lace up your running shoes. It is time to begin!

NOVICE MARATHON TRAINING SCHEDULE

Week	Mon.	Tue.	Wed.	Thu.	Fri.	Sat.	Sun.
18	rest	3 m run	3 m run	3 m run	rest	6	cross
17	rest	3 m run	3 m run	3 m run	rest	7	cross
16	rest	3 m run	4 m run	3 m run	rest	5	cross
15	rest	3 m run	4 m run	3 m run	rest	9	cross
14	rest	3 m run	5 m run	3 m run	rest	10	cross
13	rest	3 m run	5 m run	3 m run	rest	7	cross
12	rest	3 m run	6 m run	3 m run	rest	12	cross
11	rest	3 m run	6 m run	3 m run	rest	13	cross
10	rest	3 m run	7 m run	4 m run	rest	10	cross
9	rest	3 m run	7 m run	4 m run	rest	15	cross
8	rest	4 m run	8 m run	4 m run	rest	16	cross
7	rest	4 m run	8 m run	5 m run	rest	12	cross
6	rest	4 m run	9 m run	5 m run	rest	18	cross
5	rest	5 m run	9 m run	5 m run	rest	14	cross
4	rest	5 m run	10 m run	5 m run	rest	20	cross
3	rest	5 m run	8 m run	4 m run	rest	12	cross
2	rest	4 m run	6 m run	3 m run	rest	8	cross
1	rest	3 m run	4 m run	2 m run	rest	rest	**race**

EXPERT MARATHON TRAINING SCHEDULE

Week	Mon.	Tue.	Wed.	Thu.	Fri.	Sat.	Sun.
18	3 m run	3 × hill	3 m run	30 tempo	rest	5 m pace	10
17	3 m run	30 tempo	3 m run	3 m pace	rest	5 m run	11
16	3 m run	4 × 800	3 m run	30 tempo	rest	6 m pace	8
15	3 m run	4 × hill	3 m run	35 tempo	rest	6 m pace	13
14	3 m run	35 tempo	3 m run	3 m pace	rest	7 m run	14
13	3 m run	5 × 800	3 m run	35 tempo	rest	7 m pace	10
12	3 m run	5 × hill	4 m run	40 tempo	rest	8 m pace	16
11	3 m run	40 tempo	4 m run	3 m pace	rest	8 m run	17
10	3 m run	6 × 800	4 m run	40 tempo	rest	9 m pace	12
9	3 m run	6 × hill	4 m run	45 tempo	rest	9 m pace	19
8	4 m run	45 tempo	5 m run	4 m pace	rest	10 m run	20
7	4 m run	7 × 800	5 m run	45 tempo	rest	6 m pace	12
6	4 m run	7 × hill	5 m run	50 tempo	rest	10 m pace	20
5	5 m run	45 tempo	5 m run	5 m pace	rest	6 m run	12
4	5 m run	8 × 800	5 m run	40 tempo	rest	10 m pace	20
3	5 m run	6 × hill	5 m run	30 tempo	rest	4 m pace	12
2	4 m run	30 tempo	4 m run	4 m pace	rest	4 m run	8
1	3 m run	4 × 400	3 m run	rest	rest	2 m run	**race**

WEEK 18

Monday: Monday is a day of rest for novices to help your body recuperate from weekend workouts. (In the novice program, you will rest two days a week.) For expert runners, Monday is a day of *comparative* rest: 3 miles at an easy pace. What's an easy pace? You define that.

Tuesday: An easy day for novices: 3 miles at a comfortable pace. This is the speed day for experts, who alternate running hills, tempo runs and interval 800s. Warm up with a couple of miles. Find a hill 200–400 meters long. Run 3 uphill repeats on it, jogging back down between. Cool down with a mile or two.

Wednesday: Novice and experts run 3 miles, same as yesterday.

Thursday: Three miles for novices, comfortable pace. Experts do a tempo run of 30 minutes. Start slow. Push the pace 10 to 15 minutes into the run. Finish the last five minutes running easy. At peak, you should be running somewhere near your 10-K pace.

Friday: Novices and experts rest to get ready for the weekend.

Saturday: Experts run 5 miles at marathon pace, saving their long runs for Sunday in this schedule—although you can switch days if desired. The novice schedule has long runs on Saturday, starting at only 6 miles. Week by week, the distance will build to a peak of 20 just before the marathon. Don't worry about pace, just run easily.

Sunday: Novices use this second day of the weekend to recover from the weekly long run by doing some easy cross-training: an hour or so of walking, biking, swimming, or some other activity. Swimming is a particularly useful activity, because you can use it to loosen your muscles. If you run long Sundays, you can cross-train on Saturdays. Experts begin their long-run progression at 10 miles. By gradually lengthening your mileage 1 mile a week, you can reach 20 miles eight weeks before the marathon and have time for three 20-milers, instead of one. Run one or two minutes per mile slower than marathon pace.

WEEK 17

Monday: Rest for novices. Experts cruise an easy 3-miler. Don't run farther or harder thinking it will get you in better shape. More isn't always better.

Tuesday: Novices run 3 miles easy. Experts do a tempo run of 30 minutes, similar to that done last Thursday: Start slow. Push the pace 10 to15 minutes into the run. Finish the last 5 minutes running easy. At peak, you should be running near 10-K pace.

Wednesday: This is the "hard" day of the week for novices. If you want to run a bit faster than yesterday, do so. Experts run 3 miles easy.

Thursday: Another 3-miler for novices. Experts go the same distance, but at marathon pace.

Friday: Rest for all. Seemingly, you don't need this now, but wait until your weekend runs start getting longer in another few weeks.

Saturday: Novices run 7 miles. In your second week, you have now gone from 6 to 7 miles. This doesn't seem like much of a jump, but steady increases in distance will help prepare you for the stress of running 26 miles. Don't worry too much about how fast you run in these early weeks. Just run at a pace that will allow you to cover the 7-mile distance easily. Experts do a 5-miler at an easy pace.

Sunday: Experts do an 11-miler. For novices, this is the cross-training day, and it's here for two purposes. One, you want to train for about an hour to improve your aerobic base. Two, you want to exercise differently both to loosen your running muscles and to allow them to recover. Don't ignore this second weekend workout. It's important!

Week 16

Monday: This is an "easy" week in our training program. You will encounter these "step-back" weeks every third week in our program. Today is a day of rest for novices. Experts have the option or resting or running 3 miles.

Tuesday: Novices go 3 miles. Experts move to the track to run 4 × 800 meters. Jog or walk two to three minutes between each repetition. Run each rep at about the pace you might run in a 5-K race.

Wednesday: Novices run 4 miles, up from 3 the first two weeks. Your mileage on this midweek "hard" day will continue to build along with your weekend mileage. This is a rest day for experts: 3 miles.

Thursday: An easy 3-miler for novices. Experts do a 30-minute tempo run. Build in the middle so that you're running *near* 10-K pace. Notice I said "near." Don't run too hard.

Friday: Your day of rest. If the schedule of rest days doesn't always fit your schedule, feel free to adjust the days. It's consistency that counts, not slavishly following a schedule in a book.

Saturday: Since this is a step-back week, novices run only 5 miles. (Keep an invisible "8" in your mind, since we jump ahead to 9 miles next week.) Experts do 6 miles at marathon pace.

Sunday: Cross-training for novices. Aerobic activities work best: walking, cycling, swimming. Experts go 8 miles, the shortest you'll run during the 18 weeks of the program. Maintain an easy pace, slower than you would run in a marathon. If you're feeling strong, you can move the last few miles a little faster.

WEEK 15

Monday: Rest day for novices, 3 miles for experts. This is actually the first week of your second three-week cycle, after the step back.

Tuesday: Experts resume the mileage buildup that is integral to successful marathon training. Repeat the workout you did on this day during Week 18, only with one more hill. Warm up with a couple of miles. Go to the hill you ran three weeks ago. Run 4 up-hill repeats, jogging back down between. Cool down with a mile or two. One way to do this workout is to run to the hill, do the repeats, then run back. Novices do 3 miles easy.

Wednesday: Four miles for novices, who are invited to push the pace a bit if you're feeling good. Today's easy workout for experts remains at 3 miles.

Thursday: For experts, your tempo run increases to 35 minutes. Start slow. Begin to push the pace 10 to 15 minutes into the run, approaching your 10-K race pace for 10 to 15 minutes. Then gradually back off on your speed and finish the last 5 minutes running easy. Novices run 3 miles at a comfortable pace.

Friday: A day of rest to get ready for hard work on the weekend.

Saturday: Six miles at marathon pace for experts. Novices run 9 miles today. The pace should be comfortable, similar to the early miles of the marathon. Don't be afraid to walk occasionally to break the pace. (You may need to do so in the marathon.) Start teaching yourself to drink fluids before, during and after your runs.

Sunday: A cross-training day for novices. If you experience some fatigue after yesterday's 9-miler, that's natural. Use today's workout to relax and loosen your muscles. A lucky 13-miler today for experts. Your total mileage for the week should be about 35 miles, or about three times the length of your longest run. As the length of your long run increases, your total weekly mileage also will increase—but I don't want you to overtrain. This is not a mega-mileage training program!

WEEK 14

Monday: A day of rest. Nothing for novices; 3 miles easy for experts. Just a loosening-up workout after the weekend. Since running 3 miles won't take you that long, save some time for stretching.

Tuesday: Experts do a tempo run of 35 minutes. This is the same workout as last Thursday. Don't worry about how fast you're going as you push the pace in the middle of the run. Stopwatches don't count in tempo runs. Get used to reading body signals to dictate pace. You should finish this workout refreshed, not fatigued. Novices run 3 miles.

Wednesday: Novices go 5 miles, a jump of a mile from last week. Don't worry about the pace. Just cover the distance. Three easy miles for experts.

Thursday: Three easy miles for novices. Three at planned marathon pace for experts. Although this should seem "easy," you want to ingrain that pace in your mind.

Friday: Another day of rest.

Saturday: Novices run 10 miles. This is about the point in our training program that novices begin to decide—without my telling them—that maybe they need to head home early on Friday nights. Experts move up to 7 miles at an easy pace. You're gradually increasing your miles on this second run of the weekend. The Saturday/Sunday runs will work in combination to get you in shape.

Sunday: Cross-training for novices. Experts reach 14 miles on the long run. You're probably still feeling frisky, so don't make the too common mistake of doing your long runs at marathon race pace, thinking more is better. In the last 2 to 3 miles, if you're feeling strong, it's okay to pick up the pace slightly and finish fast—but you have more to lose than gain from overtraining at this point.

WEEK 13

Monday: Another week of comparative "rest," since the weekend mileage drops as part of our second step back. No running today for novices; 3 miles for experts—although feel free to take today off if you're tired from yesterday's 14-miler.

Tuesday: Novices go 3 miles at your normal pace. What is "normal"? You be the judge. Experts return to the track for more speed training. Today's track workout is 5 × 800 meters, jogging or walking two to three minutes between. Do the 800s at about 5-K race pace. You can run this same workout on the road or even on trails. If you don't have exact measurements, run for time instead of distance. For example, if you normally run a 6:00 mile pace in a 5-K, an equivalent workout would be $5 \times 3:00$.

Wednesday: Novices go 5 miles despite this being a step-back week, part of the steady mileage progression. Easy day for experts: 3 miles. Are you remembering to stretch?

Thursday: Another easy 3-miler for novices. Experts do a 35-minute tempo run. Build in the middle so that you're running near 10-K pace at peak. That sounds fast, but you don't need to be at this peak pace for more than a few hundred meters.

Friday: A day of rest for all. Consider doing some easy stretching on your rest days to loosen your muscles. Ten minutes or so will do. But don't stretch too hard. Stretching should never feel painful; otherwise you risk damaging the muscles you're trying to protect.

Saturday: Novice run 7 miles. In a logical arithmetic progression you would have done 11 miles today. Just because you're running fewer miles—and feeling good—don't make the mistake of turning this into a harder day than intended. Experts also go 7 miles.

Sunday: Novices cross-train for an hour. If you want to go out for a walk and feel the desire to shift back and forth from jogging to walking, that wouldn't be a bad idea. But feel free to do no jogging at all. Ten miles for experts: a no-pressure workout for you at this point of your training, so don't try to convert this into something else. Keep the pace easy, slower than marathon pace. If you *must* show how fit you are, finish at a faster pace, but don't overdo it.

Week 12

Monday: Nothing for novices; 3 miles for experts. You'll need these rest days as the mileage continues to build toward your marathon goal.

Tuesday: Experts head to the hills again: $5 \times$ hill. If you warm up well, you'll be able to run uphill with greater efficiency. To maintain good form, focus your eyes on the top of the hill. Pump your arms and lift your knees slightly to develop your quadricep muscles. You'll need strong quads in the closing miles of your upcoming marathon. Three miles for novices again today. Compared to the expert workouts, it may seem you're doing too little, but steady running will get you in shape.

Wednesday: Six miles for novices. As these midweek workouts continue to climb, you may need to budget more time out of your busy schedule. Experts run 4 miles easy, a slight jump in mileage from the previous six weeks.

Thursday: Three easy miles for novices. The tempo run today increases to 40 minutes. Lead into it with 10 to 15 minutes of comfortable running, then gradually accelerate to a peak about 30 minutes into your workout before coasting home. Continue to think 10-K race pace, but the entire middle part of the workout need not be that fast.

Friday: A day of rest to get ready for hard work on the weekend.

Saturday: Eight miles at marathon pace for experts. Novices go 12 miles. You have now doubled the distance of your longest run in the previous six weeks. Make certain you don't run this workout too fast. Don't be embarrassed to stop and walk briefly. You may need to do so in the marathon. The trick is to walk *before* being forced to.

Sunday: Cross-training today for novices. Don't overlook strength training as you build toward your marathon goal. You don't want to be doing full squats with maximum weights, but some lifting could fit into your routine. Keep the weights low and the repetitions high. Include some aerobic training and stretching as part of a total body workout. The long run today for experts is 16 miles. Consider that when you get this far in the marathon, you will have only 10 more miles to run. (Did we say "only"?) As with all the other long runs, train slower than your marathon race pace.

WEEK 11

Monday: Rest day for novices. You'll need it, because the mileage continues to climb this week—subtly, though inexorably. Experts go 3 miles, as usual, and run them easy. Stop in the middle of the workout to stretch for five minutes or so. Or save some time for stretching at the end.

Tuesday: Three miles for novices. The experts' tempo run today is 40 minutes, the same as last Thursday. For a variation, build to a peak speed about 25 minutes into the run, back off slightly for a few minutes and then build to another peak. Sort of like riding a rollercoaster. But this should not be a killer workout. We still want you to finish feeling better than when you started.

Wednesday: Experts go 4 miles, novices 6. For the latter: Did you handle this distance pretty well last week? If so, you might want to run a nudge faster this day. Don't push too hard at the start, but see if you can pick up the pace over the last mile or two.

Thursday: Another 3-miler for novices and experts, the latter running at marathon pace.

Friday: Preparing for the weekend's long run, claim a day of rest.

Saturday: Novices run 13 miles, a significant milestone, since it is half the distance you need to run in the marathon. You may finish this workout wondering how you'll ever be able to run twice as far, or twice as long. Trust me. You're not yet halfway through your training program. In another 10 weeks, you'll be standing on the starting line well-trained and ready to roll. Experts do 8 miles at an easy pace. The mileage continues to climb. Combining this with Sunday's run, you'll cover 25 miles for the weekend. That's just a mile short of marathon distance.

Sunday: Cross-training for novices. An hour of aerobic training. Don't push yourself too hard the day after your longest run so far. Experts reach 17 miles for the long run. Continue to do these workouts at a pace a minute or two slower than marathon pace. Depending on how you feel, it's okay to pick up the pace in the last 3- to 4 miles. Evaluate how you feel afterward: Are you handling the training well? Any nagging injuries? Are you tired? Next week is our step-back week, so you'll have time to recover before the next step upward.

WEEK 10

Monday: The beginning of our third step-back week featuring reduced weekend mileage. Today is a day of complete rest for novices, and experts may consider following their lead rather than doing the 3-miler planned for today.

Tuesday: The track workout for experts is 6 × 800 meters, jogging or walking for two to three minutes between each rep for recovery. Run the 800s at about your 5-K race pace. There's nothing magic about 800s, by the way. You might just as easily do 10 × 400, or

3×1600. The reason to go to the track is to run faster than race pace to help you in three areas: speed, efficiency, and mental focus. Novices do 3 miles today.

Wednesday: Though this is a step-back week, the midweek mileage progression continues for novices. Run 7 miles. These relatively long weekday workouts may be increasingly difficult for those of you with busy work schedules, not because of the extra training load but because of the extra time required. Plan ahead. Make sure you allow yourself ample time for this workout. But experts get to float through an easy 4-miler today. Hey, no sweat!

Thursday: Four miles for novices. Today, it's the experts' turn to sweat. A 40-minute tempo run. As with other tempo workouts, at peak speed you should be running near 10-K race pace. When I say "near" what do I mean: faster or slower? Actually, I mean either. Some days, you may feel fatigued for reasons unrelated to your running. Other days, you want to fly. Weather can be a factor too. You need to adjust your training pace from day to day according to signals received from your body. That takes experience—but, hey, you did say you were an "expert," didn't you?

Friday: Another day of rest.

Saturday: Novices run 10 miles. In a straight progression, you might have done 14 miles today (and you'll do 15 next week). Make this an easy run. Resist the temptation to run faster, because you're running shorter. You'll need the energy you save when we get back on schedule next week. Experts run 9 miles at marathon pace, not as "easy" a workout as when we first began.

Sunday: Cross-training for an hour for novices. Do some running if you're feeling strong, but walking, cycling, swimming and a mixture of strength training and stretching will keep us happy and you fit. In this step-back week, experts run 12 miles. Resist the urge to run fast to prove to yourself (or others) what great shape you're in. You'll get an opportunity to do that next week, as our upward progression continues.

WEEK 9

Monday: Halfway home. You have nine weeks of marathon training behind you and nine more to go. Rest day for novices; experts go 3 miles.

Tuesday: Novices run 3 miles. Experts do hill training. Add one more repetition from three weeks ago: 6 × hill. And maybe it's time to add some additional mileage before and/or after. If you've warmed up with 2 miles, it's time to go 2.5 or 3. Subtle changes in mileage distances work better than quick jumps, which can cause injuries or extra fatigue.

Wednesday: Four miles easy for experts. Novices do 7 for your midweek, mini-long run. Do you know what pace you plan to run in the marathon? This might be a good time to practice it—at least in the middle miles.

Thursday: Three easy miles for novices. For experts, the tempo run today increases to 15 minutes. Start with 10 to 15 minutes of easy running, then begin to accelerate to near 10-K race pace. The central (fast) part of your workout should now last about 20 minutes, so that's why I said "near." Hold the peak speed for several minutes, then gradually decelerate to a gentle jog.

Friday: Rest.

Saturday: Experts run 9 miles at marathon pace. Add this to tomorrow's long run, and it adds up to more miles than you'll run in the marathon. Novices run 15. That's three-fourths of the longest distance (20) I'll ask you to run in this marathon training program. By now, you should begin to adapt to the rhythm of these long runs. Don't run them too fast. Take walking breaks if necessary. Drink plenty of water. If you can't find water fountains along your route, consider purchasing a belt for carrying fluids. Yes, you will finish this 15-miler feeling tired, but you should not finish exhausted. Running steady pace is the secret to marathon success.

Sunday: Cross-training day for novices. By now you probably have determined the cross-training routine that works best for you. But don't be afraid to vary it. And the day after a long run is a good time to do some extra stretching. Even a 5-to-10-minute swim at the end of a cross-training workout will help loosen you up. Experts cover 19 miles as their long run. Continue to train well below marathon race pace. One of the reasons for these long runs is to get your body used to moving for a long period of time, as well as distance. If you cut the time length of your workouts short by running too fast, you don't get the full benefit. Marathon running is a psychological, as well as a physical, game.

Week 8

Monday: Rest day for novices. Experts go 4 miles, an increase of 1 mile and part of the subtle mileage build-up.

Tuesday: Novices now do 4 miles for your easy run, also an increase. Experts: Your tempo run today is 45 minutes, repeating your run from last Thursday. Can you stay near peak speed—your approximate 10-K race pace—for just a bit longer?

Wednesday: Eight miles for novices. The mileage of this midweek "mini-long" run will continue to build gradually over the next five weeks. This is an essential part of your training program. Be sure to take it seriously. For experts, this is still billed as an "easy" day, but your mileage climbs to 5 miles, an increase from previous weeks.

Thursday: Four miles for novices, done at an easy pace mainly to loosen up after yesterday's longer run. Experts run 4 miles at marathon pace.

Friday: This will come as a welcome day of rest.

Saturday: Novices run 16 miles, another landmark of sorts. When you pass this point in the marathon, you'll get a psychological lift in that only 10 miles remain, and you'll be facing single digits (9, 8, 7, and so on) as you cruise toward the finish line. Next week you'll run a shorter distance, so tough this out. Experts run 10 miles, but at an easy pace.

Sunday: The Big 20 for experts—and it comes at the end of a 45-mile week. I've emphasized on previous pages that I would rather have you do the long runs slow than fast. Here's one reason. Part of your training is to become used to being on your feet for the same length of time as in the marathon. So think "marathon time" today. If you're a 3:20 marathoner, take that much time to run the 20 miles. That's 10:00 mile pace, and it may seem too slow for you, but the purpose of today's workout is to train yourself psychologically as much as physically. You have to know how and when to hold back in the early miles. If this means doing more walking mid-workout while taking fluids, do it. Better to walk now than in the marathon. Novices cross-train, but don't overdo it, since your mileage also has been building. If you're out on a bike, for example, you don't want your head down and your legs pushing high gears. As for strength training, you probably need to begin to cut back on the heavy weights.

WEEK 7

Monday: This is our fourth step-back week featuring reduced weekend mileage. Today is a day of complete rest for novices. Experts go 4 miles as part of your recovery from yesterday's 20-miler.

Tuesday: Four miles for novices. Experts go to the track and run 7 × 800 meters, jogging or walking for two to three minutes between for recovery. Continue to run the 800s at about 5-K pace. One way to obtain maximum performance in marathon running is to learn how to concentrate. Doing interval training of this sort will help your concentration.

Wednesday: The midweek mini-long run remains at 8 miles for novices, same as last week. Whether you run this in the morning before work, or after, be sure to budget enough time so you don't have to cut the workout short. Experts do 5 miles at an easy pace.

Thursday: A 45-minute tempo run for experts. This is the third tempo run of 45 minutes you've done in the last three weeks. You should be getting the rhythm. For variation, pick a different course for each of these runs. Novices do 5 miles, an increase of a mile from last week.

Friday: This day of rest is well earned.

Saturday: Novices run 12 miles. This is in place of the 17-miler you might have expected in a straight progression. Today's pace run for experts is only 6 miles. We want this to be a true step-back week, because we are in the middle of the toughest part of your training. Remember: this should be at marathon pace. That may mean picking a course with measured miles so you can stay exactly on pace.

Sunday: An hour's cross-training for novices. Since you didn't run as far yesterday, you might even want to include some running today. Otherwise, do whatever appeals to you in the way of walking, cycling, swimming, or other exercises. Experts also have an "easy" workout: only 12 miles. The first of your three 20-milers was last Sunday. The second will be next Sunday. In order to get full benefit from running three 20-milers within a five-week period, you need to cut mileage between. So don't make the mistake of running this workout at a pace faster than usual.

WEEK 6

Monday: With another step-back week behind us, we continue our mileage buildup. But for today, novices do nothing; experts go 4 miles.

Tuesday: Four miles for novices. Hill training for experts. The workout today is: 7 × hill. This is a good time to remind yourself to focus on form. Don't let your chin drop toward your chest as you go up the hill. Keep your eyes forward. Pump your arms and lift your knees. (This isn't necessarily good form for running hills in a marathon, since floating up them will save more energy; but the purpose of today's workout is strengthening your legs, particularly your quadriceps muscles.)

Wednesday: Experts run 5 miles; novices go 9. For the latter, your most difficult task will not be to go the distance—since you can handle this many miles easily now—but rather to fit a run that may last 90 minutes into your workweek.

Thursday: Five easy miles for novices. The tempo run for experts today moves up to 50 minutes. This is the maximum length of time you will run this particular workout. I've been telling you to do these tempo runs near 10-K pace, and you'll have a hard time doing that today for 20 to 25 minutes, but keep a good pace going.

Friday: A day of rest preparatory to some tough training on the weekend. Get some extra sleep tonight, so you're ready to run long.

Saturday: Eighteen miles for novices. That's almost 30 kilometers, close to three-fourths of the full marathon distance (of 42 kilometers). Remember that when you sail past mile 18 in the race. But for now, it's the longest run so far in your training program. Do you need to walk a bit to finish this run comfortably? Do so while taking fluids. That's good practice for the race, since you can take more water if you walk through water stops. Experiment also with replacement gels for extra energy. When you finish today's workout, congratulate yourself for what may be a personal best in distance. Experts run 10 miles at marathon pace. Depending on how much ground you covered Tuesday and Thursday, this workout will help you to a 50-mile training week. You'll benefit from the hard work in the marathon.

Sunday: This is the second of three 20-milers for experts. You might want to run a slightly faster time than what you ran two weeks ago. Do that not by running at a faster pace for all 20 miles, but by picking up the pace in the last 4 to 5 miles. But don't overdo it. Novices cross-train today. An hour-long spin on a bike might do. Don't train too hard, regardless of which cross-training discipline you select.

WEEK 5

Monday: This is a step-back week—even though only one week has passed since the last one. With mileage building to a peak, it's important to gather your forces for the final training push. Novices rest; experts go 5 miles, up a mile from previous Monday workouts.

Tuesday: Novices do 5 miles at an easy pace, a subtle increase. Experts do a tempo run of 45 minutes, actually a slight reduction from the last time you ran this workout.

Wednesday: Nine miles today for novices. Depending on how you feel, you might want to pick up the pace slightly for a few of the middle miles. Try picking up the pace a bit between miles 5 and 7, then come in at a gentler pace. Experts do 5 miles easy.

Thursday: Five miles for novices. Experts also go 5, but at marathon race pace. It's important to do some running at race pace to train your muscles to accept that pace. I'd rather you not run race pace during the long runs, so I offer you the opportunity for race-pace workouts at other times.

Friday: Total rest.

Saturday: Experts run 6 miles. Novices run 14 miles. Did you believe when you started this program that there would come a day when we would tell you to go that distance, and you'd think, "Oh, an easy day." It all depends on your point of view. You're now looking down on 14, rather than up at it. Next Saturday's run will *not* be easy. That's a promise.

Sunday: An hour of cross-training for novices today. Don't overlook this important part of your training. Since yesterday's workout was so "easy," you might consider doing some jogging today. If so, keep the pace at a very, very low stress level—and walk more than usual. Experts run 12 easy miles. If you want to do a final "test" race to give you an idea of your fitness level and help you plan race pace, this would be a good weekend to do so. Substitute a 10-K race for today's workout. If the race is on Saturday, switch days and run 6 to 12 miles for your other workout. Let how you feel dictate the distance.

WEEK 4

Monday: This is the peak week of your training. Rather than fear it, you should greet it with nearly the same enthusiasm you will greet the marathon one month from now. But for the time being, novices take a day of rest. Experts go 5 easy miles.

Tuesday: Novices do 5 miles at your normal pace. Experts run at the track: 8 × 800 meters, jogging or walking for two to three minutes between. Stick with 5-K pace. Add up all the 800s, and you'll actually be running farther than 5-K (6,400 meters). Resting between each repetition allows you to maintain this difficult pace. Be sure to warm up adequately and cool down afterward with some light jogging.

Wednesday: Experts go 5 miles. Novices run 10 miles, peak distance for the midweek mini-long run.

Thursday: Five miles for novices. You are entitled to feel a bit tired today. It's normal. That's what training is all about. A 40-minute tempo run for experts. Although the mileage buildup continues, we've already begun to cut back on your tempo runs. Don't overdo today's workout. Save something for a very tough weekend.

Friday: No running today. Get to bed early tonight.

Saturday: Ten miles at race pace for experts. Although novices may have been doing your long runs on Saturdays, I suggest you switch days and do the climactic long run on Sunday. Today, do an hour of cross-training. And it should be an *easy* hour, because you don't want to start tomorrow's run fatigued. An hour of walking sounds about right. Tonight, skip the lamb chops and go for spaghetti. In fact, eat a similar meal to that planned for the night before the marathon: pasta with a marinara sauce, bread, salad and a non-caffeine, high-carbohydrate beverage.

Sunday: For novices: The Big Twenty! Next to the actual marathon itself, you will find finishing today's workout to be the most important achievement of the 18-week training program. Not merely will you run 20 miles, but you will do it at the climax of a 40-mile training week! Experts run the third of your three 20-milers. Climaxing your training program with this long run should give you a feeling of confidence as you begin your marathon taper. Caution: Don't turn this final long run into a race.

WEEK 3

Monday: Everyone deserves a day of rest after the weekend 20-miler. Today begins the taper for the actual marathon. Start cutting back on miles. Experts have the option of going 5 miles, or taking an extra day of rest.

Tuesday: Five miles easy for novices. Experts run 6 × hill instead of the 7 × hill you did last week. Maintain the same intensity. The secret in tapering is to maintain the quality of your workouts while lessening the quantity.

Wednesday: Eight miles for novices, the first midweek decrease in distance. You had reached a peak of 10 miles last Tuesday. The drop in mileage will be subtle at first, then more pronounced. The serious training is done. You will now focus on getting to the starting line well rested. Five miles today for experts.

Thursday: Four easy miles for novices. (You did 5 miles last Thursday.) Experts do 30 minutes for the tempo run. That's the same as the first week of your training. Build a little faster to your peak near 10-K race pace, but hold that pace for less time. A good pattern might be 10 to 15 minutes at the start, then 10 to 15 fast in the middle, with 5 minutes for cooling down. But listen to what your body tells you to do. You've done this workout enough in the last three months to know how it works.

Friday: Rest day.

Saturday: Today's novice run is 12 miles, long by the standards of three months ago, but I hope an easy stroll in the park following all the training we've done. Maintain the same pace as your usual weekend runs. The only difference is that you get to quit early. Experts do 4 miles at marathon pace. Just enough to remember what it feels like.

Sunday: With the 20-milers past, the focus for experts shifts to maintaining your endurance peak. Run 12 miles today, and resist the urge to pick up the pace in this "easy" run. It's okay to run the last miles somewhat faster, but not the entire workout. For novices, don't do anything in the area of cross-training that will push you too hard. Keep the bike ride gentle. Swim more to loosen your muscles, not to strengthen them. And if you've been doing strength training, you might want to stop, or do very little, with the marathon almost in sight. Walking always remains a good off-day exercise for runners.

WEEK 2

Monday: You're into your final taper now. This rest day takes on more significance as you try to store energy. Nothing for novices; experts do 4 miles, but make sure the pace is easy.

Tuesday: Four easy miles for today's novice run. The tempo run for experts today is 30 minutes. In contrast to last week, don't push the middle miles as fast or as far.

Wednesday: Six miles today for novices. The decreased mileage on this key, midweek workout should make it easier for you to manage your busy schedule. Experts go 4 miles today. Easy! Easy!

Thursday: Three miles for novices. Four miles at marathon race pace for experts. This is the last time you get to run this pace before the marathon itself. Focus on the amount of effort (or lack of effort) it requires to run at exactly this pace, mile after mile. You're going to have to add 22 to this 4 in another week.

Friday: Total rest. Don't stay out too late tonight. You want to catch up on any sleep you might have lost during the hard weeks of our training. Sleep loss is cumulative, and it's time to catch up.

Saturday: Novices run 8 miles; experts do only 4. This would be a good day for a final test run on your equipment: the shoes you plan to wear, your "race" uniform (conceding that you can't always predict next weekend's weather). You want to avoid, as much as possible, any blisters or chafing that might make next weekend's run uncomfortable.

Sunday: Eight miles for experts. Run your miles at the same pace you've been doing your long runs each of the previous 16 weekends. In other words, a minute or two slower than race pace. Save your speed for next Sunday. An hour of cross-training today for novices. Keeping with the spirit of this second tapering week, whatever you do today should not be done with high intensity. Stay away from pick-up basketball games. Don't throw away the work of the last three months by doing something foolish.

WEEK 1

Monday: For novices and experts, your whole final week leading up to the marathon should be devoted to rest. The schedule for experts says 3 miles. If you feel like using this as an extra day of rest, take it.

Tuesday: Novices run 3 miles at your normal pace. Experts run a final track workout: 4 × 400 meters, jogging or walking for two to three minutes between. Stick with 5-K pace. You barely want to break a sweat doing this workout. The purpose is merely to loosen you up. Maintain the same quality of the workout, but drop the quantity. We want you to walk away from the workout knowing you could have done much more.

Wednesday: Four miles for novices; 3 miles for experts.

Thursday: Experts take a day of complete rest. Two miles of gentle jogging for novices—barely enough to work up a sweat. Carbo-loading begins in earnest today. Pasta, rice, potatoes, cereals, fruits. Don't make radical changes in your regular diet, but now is not the time for filet mignon. Cut back slightly on your intake of calories, since you will be burning fewer calories in this final week of tapering.

Friday: Get a good night's sleep tonight. You may have more difficulty sleeping tomorrow night because of nervous anticipation. Also, you may need to get up early to get to the start on time. For this reason, your Friday night's sleep is even more important than your Saturday night's sleep.

Saturday: Schedule this day as a day of rest, although experts may want to do some light jogging the day before the marathon, particularly to loosen up after traveling to the race. If so, you might want to switch with Thursday's workout, using that as an extra rest day. Do a couple miles of running to loosen your muscles, including a few strides of 100 meters, run at marathon pace, walking or jogging between. My approach to the last three days before the marathon is to run on no more than one of those days—and it could be on any one of those days. Usually, however, I like a final shake-down workout the day before.

Sunday: There's not much more I can say, other than this is the day and the moment for which you all have spent 18 weeks training. Remember everything you learned over those weeks. And have a good day!

INDEX

Underscored page references indicate boxed text.
Italic references indicate tables.